third edition

Spain

since 1812

third edition
Spain
since 1812

Christopher J. Ross

Routledge
Taylor & Francis Group

LONDON AND NEW YORK

First published 2004 by Hodder Arnold
Third edition published 2009 by
Hodder Education, a member of the Hodder Headline Group

Published 2014 by Routledge
2 Park Square, Milton Park, Abingdon, Oxon OX14 4RN
711 Third Avenue, New York, NY, 10017, USA

Routledge is an imprint of the Taylor & Francis Group, an informa business

The advice and information in this book are believed to be true and accurate at the
date of going to press, but neither the authors nor the publisher can accept any legal
responsibility or liability for any errors or omissions.

British Library Cataloguing in Publication Data
A catalogue record for this book is available from the British Library

Library of Congress Cataloging-in-Publication Data
A catalog record for this book is available from the Library of Congress

ISBN 13: 978-0-340-98174-0 (pbk)

Cover © Ian Dagnall/Alamy

Typeset in 9.5 on 13pt Lucida by Phoenix Photosetting, Chatham, Kent

Contents

Preface to First Edition

It is perhaps easiest, and best, to begin by saying what this book is not. It is neither a detailed, chronological account of events in Spain, nor an attempt to provide new insights into their historical significance. The latter, in particular, it could not be, because I am not a trained historian. Nor is the book aimed primarily at students of history. Instead, its intention is to help students, in the widest sense, of contemporary Spain to recognise and understand the historical references that come up so frequently in contacts with the country and in reading about it. It is also intended to be accessible to them, regardless of whether they are currently studying other aspects of modern history, or have done so in the past.

One obvious prerequisite for understanding is information. However, I have taken the view that the provision of facts – stating dates, describing events, naming names – should not be the book's main concern. I have tried to concentrate instead on giving an overview of developments and the relationships between them. In doing so, I am well aware of laying myself open to charges of superficiality and over-simplification. All the more so as the book's focus is almost entirely on politics and on one of its major components, economics; social and cultural aspects are touched on only in passing. I can but hope that the generalisations involved are on balance more enlightening than misleading and, above all, that the book might encourage and allow readers to go more deeply into subjects which, inevitably, are covered only briefly here.

Any history book of finite length faces the problem of limits – of where to begin and where to end. Many courses on modern Spanish history, I know, concentrate mainly or wholly on the twentieth century. However, I felt that the best way of grasping the country's political development in the modern era was to consider the last two centuries as a unit, bound together by a single theme: the arduous but ultimately successful struggle to establish democratic institutions and practices. In that sense, the year 1812 provides an obvious starting point, with the appearance of Spain's first constitution. As the endpoint I have chosen 1996, because the general election held in that year completed a full cycle of alternation in power from Right to Left and back again, under free democratic conditions, for the first time in the country's history.

The book begins with a prologue which gives an outline picture of what Spain was like in 1812, and why. The main text consists of ten chapters, arranged chronologically, with the level of detail increasing significantly as time progresses. Internally, the chapters are divided into thematic sections. Each begins with a paragraph outlining the main contemporary developments in the wider world which impinged on those in Spain, for the benefit of readers who have not previously studied modern western history. Each is followed by one or more 'exhibits', contemporary Spanish texts relating to the themes covered in the chapter, and accompanied by a number of questions designed to raise discussion on them. Following the last chapter, an 'afterword' attempts to draw out some themes of relevance to current events.

The overview approach notwithstanding, some concepts and institutions either crop up recurrently or are particularly important during a particular period. A brief summary of their main features and complete evolution, not restricted to the period of the particular chapter in which they are included, have been highlighted in special 'inserts'. They are given in their Spanish form, with an English equivalent. Throughout I have tried to use natural English terminology; where reference is made to specifically Spanish concepts I have tried to render them in a way which transmits the meaning rather than the appearance of the words (e.g. 'clans' rather than 'families' for the groups that jostled for influence under the Franco regime, and were known in Spanish as *familias*). Where words appear in single inverted commas they are a direct literal translation of the Spanish (e.g. 'social concertation' for *concertación social*). Bracketed Spanish terms are intended to give an indication of usage in context; there is no suggestion that they are the sole Spanish equivalent to the preceding English word or phrase.

I have included relatively frequent cross-references, of the form '(pxxx)', since otherwise the thematic structure would require an unreasonable amount of repetition. No direct references to other works are included in the text, however, as I believe they serve little purpose in a book of this sort. I make no claims of originality, and any given statement could be checked or followed up in a number of the sources cited in the 'Further Reading' section. Here, again, I have only attempted to scratch the surface, and to indicate works that should be reasonably accessible to non-historians. Anyone who subsequently takes a serious academic interest in some aspect of the period discussed will find them a useful starting point for further bibliographic searching.

I owe a number of debts of gratitude to the various authors whose works I have consulted. I should also like to thank Elena Seymenliyska for coming up with the original idea for the book, and for her advice during its gestation, and to thank Mag. Rafael de la Dueña, of the Instituto Cervantes in Vienna, for his help in locating appropriate exhibits. I am deeply grateful to my parents and brother, who in their various ways planted and nurtured an interest in history that has given me enormous pleasure, and ultimately allowed me to undertake the task of writing this book. Most of all, though, I am indebted to my wife Ulli for her encouragement and support, and for putting up with the emotional ups and downs of the book's production while living through an altogether more fundamental and demanding type of gestation period.

Christopher J. Ross, Vienna, December 1999

Preface to Second Edition

In addition to those expressed previously, I should like to offer my thanks to Eva Martínez of Arnold for her advice and support, and to Ann McFall for pointing out a number of errors in the First Edition; the responsibility for those that remain and for any new ones is, of course, entirely my own. The translations of the various Exhibits now included are my own; since the purpose of them is to make the texts more accessible. I have opted for fairly free renderings in places, although hopefully without altogether destroying the 'flavour' of the originals. Finally, while it cannot be anything but an inadequate gesture, I would wish to place on record my sorrow for the victims of the terrorist attack in Madrid on 11 March 2004, and my respect for the way in which the Spanish people and their new leaders have responded to the atrocity.

Christopher J. Ross, Vienna, April 2004

Preface to Third Edition

The question of where a book of this nature, aimed specifically at non-historians, should start is a tricky one indeed. A number of people have urged me to omit the material on the nineteenth century from this edition, on the grounds that the period is no longer studied on many relevant courses. Others seem to feel, like me, that it is still of importance both in understanding subsequent developments and because of the surprising frequency with which Spanish accounts of contemporary events still make reference to names and concepts from the nineteenth century. (One reader even suggested that more space should be devoted to it.) I eventually decided on a compromise, retaining coverage of the period but contracting it from two chapters into one. Apart from that, a minor re-arrangement relating to the years 1917–1923, and (I hope) the correction and clarification of certain points, the only novelty is the addition of a chapter on the period since 2004. Finally, I would like to add to previous thanks the names of Tamsin Smith and Bianca Knights at Hodder Education and to repeat the usual statement of sole responsibility for any errors.

Christopher J. Ross, Vienna, 2008

Chronology of main events

1812	Constitution of Cadiz issued
1814	Ferdinand VII restores absolute rule
1820–23	Constitutional interlude
1833	Outbreak of First Carlist War; moderate liberals called to government
1840	Carlist War ends; Progressives stage revolution
1843	Beginning of Moderates' authoritarian rule
1854	Progressives stage revolution but hold power for only two years
1868	'Glorious Revolution' deposes Isabella II
1873	First Republic declared
1874	Monarchy restored in the person of Alfonso XII
1895	Formation of Basque Nationalist Party (PNV)
1898	Defeat in war with US leads to loss of Cuba and most other colonies
1906	Jurisdictions Act confirms *de facto* Army supremacy over civilian politicians
1909	Unrest in Barcelona culminates in the 'Tragic Week'
1914	Catalan regional government established
1917	Protests by various groups lead to severe crisis
1918	Formation and collapse of national government
1923	General Primo de Rivera seizes power
1930	Primo de Rivera resigns
1931	King Alfonso XIII flees the country; Second Republic declared
1933	Right-wing government elected
1934	Attempted left-wing revolution fails disastrously
1936	Popular Front government elected; attempted right-wing coup leads to outbreak of civil war
1939	General Franco wins civil war, establishes dictatorship
1946	UN recommends international boycott of Spain
1953	Agreements signed with Vatican and US; end of Spain's isolation
1959	Stabilisation Plan marks change of economic strategy
1962	Spain refused admission to European Economic Community
1968	ETA begins campaign of violence
1973	ETA assassinates Admiral Carrero Blanco
1975	Franco dies, Juan Carlos I pronounced king
1977	Democratic general election is held, won by centrist UCD
1978	Adoption of new constitution
1979	Devolution granted to Catalonia and the Basque Country
1980	Regionalist/nationalist parties take power in both regions (CiU in Catalonia, the PNV in the Basque Country)
1981	Military extremists attempt coup
1982	Socialist government elected
1983	Initial devolution process completed, with creation of 17 regions

1986	Spain enters European Community; Socialist government re-elected; PNV-PSOE coalition in the Basque Country
1988	Main trade unions stage general strike
1989	Socialist government re-elected for third term
1992	Government adopts convergence plan to meet Maastricht criteria
1993	Socialists re-elected again, but lose absolute majority and forced to rely on CiU's support
1994	Further round of devolution completed
1995	GAL affair results in arrest of former Interior Minister
1996	People's Party wins election, forms government with CiU's support
1997	Spain achieves conditions to join EMU
1998	Basque nationalists sign Lizarra Pact, ETA announces ceasefire; Socialists abandon Basque regional government
1999	ETA ceasefire ends
2000	PP re-elected with overall majority
2001	Further round of devolution; Basque government launches 'Ibarretxe Plan'
2003	Spain takes part in invasion of Iraq; Socialists take over Catalan government with support of nationalist ERC
2004	Terrorist attack on Madrid; PP government voted out; Socialists return to office, pull troops out of Iraq and begin programme of social reforms
2005	ETA announces ceasefire
2006	Controversial new Catalan Statute of Autonomy approved; ETA ends ceasefire
2008	Socialists re-elected; Spain severely hit by world financial crisis

Prologue

To an astonishing degree, the course of Spain's modern history was determined by one, brief period. In little over 50 years, the country was transformed from a collection of rather insignificant statelets into Europe's leading power and the centre of a transcontinental empire. The gross mismatch between this new status and Spain's limited resources meant that her imperial glory was short-lived and followed by a rapid decline – relative to her European neighbours – that was not reversed until the recent past. Hence the crucial importance of that fateful half-century and of its key moment, the most famous date in Spanish history.

The first significance of 1492 is that it marks the end of the Reconquest (*Reconquista*), the almost eight-centuries-long process of expelling the Moors from the Iberian Peninsula. For much of that time large tracts of what is now Spain were under Muslim rule, especially in the south. Yet the lasting impact of Arab occupation was relatively slight. More important were the effects of the Reconquest itself on the various kingdoms of the gradually expanding Christian north: Portugal, Castile, Navarre and Aragon.

One enduring effect of occupation was the high value accorded in Spain, as in other societies frequently at war, to military activities and prowess; another was the tendency to grant extensive rights over newly recovered territory to local communities or powerful nobles. Perhaps most important of all, as it progressed the Reconquest became less a matter of regaining land and more a religious affair, a Crusade comparable – and explicitly compared – to the attempts to recover the Holy Land from Muslim rule. As a result, the inhabitants and rulers of Christian Spain came to see themselves as having a particularly close relationship with the Catholic Church.

These features were most marked in Castile, which by the fifteenth century was the only Christian kingdom with a Moorish frontier. Already the strongest Iberian power, Castile's influence was further extended when Ferdinand, husband of its reigning Queen Isabella I, succeeded to the throne of Aragon, thus uniting the two kingdoms under Castilian leadership. From this strengthened base the 'Catholic Monarchs' launched the campaign that enabled them, in January 1492, to capture the last Moorish stronghold of Granada. With the exception of Navarre, which was not incorporated until 1515, a united Spain had been established within its modern boundaries.

Before the momentous year was out, the young kingdom was presented with a dazzling challenge and opportunity. In December, Columbus returned from his first voyage under Isabella's sponsorship to announce the discovery of the 'Indies', which as it transpired were, in fact, the Americas. Over the next half century, he and his successors were to establish a vast Spanish Empire, whose mineral riches – above all, silver – were shipped in vast quantities to the motherland.

Spain's imperial power was by no means limited to the New World. In 1519, Ferdinand's grandson and successor as King of Spain, Charles I, inherited from his other grandfather a collection of territories sprawling from the Netherlands to Italy – the family possessions of the Hapsburgs. While these made him the most powerful man in Christian Europe, they also brought him numerous and powerful enemies. Charles was engaged in almost constant struggle throughout his reign: as defender of Christendom against the Turks, of Catholicism against the newly emerged threat of Protestantism, and of the Hapsburg lands against the rising power of France.

On Charles' death the Hapsburg inheritance was divided. Yet Spain's position as Europe's leading power, and her sense of a special link with the Church, meant that there was no reduction in the commitments faced by Philip II, his son and successor on its throne. The effects on what was essentially a poor country, with few natural resources, were devastating. The costs of constant war soaked up the flow of American treasure, saddling Spain with debts that were to burden it for centuries and leaving nothing over for the country's development.

The primacy of foreign affairs also prevented much-needed reform at home, where the former kingdoms of Castile, Aragon and Navarre, like the colonies and the European possessions, were governed as distinct entities. Moreover, the various Aragonese territories – Catalonia, Valencia and Aragon itself – and also the Basque provinces, including Navarre, were effectively exempted from taxation and military service, so that the burden of these fell almost entirely on Castile. Conversely, the merchants of Barcelona and Valencia were excluded from trade with the Americas, which remained the preserve of Castile. Yet, since it was lacking in commercial expertise, the main beneficiaries of the American treasure were actually Italian and German bankers.

These conditions precipitated a rapid decline in Spanish fortunes during the seventeenth century, a process paralleled by the degeneration of the Hapsburg line, whose last representative – Charles II – died childless in 1700. His death triggered off the War of Succession, in which Spain was reduced to the status of battleground and booty for the European powers. It was ended in 1713 by the Treaty of Utrecht, under which Gibraltar was ceded to Britain. The Treaty's main effect, however, was to place a representative of the French Bourbon dynasty on the vacant Spanish throne, in the person of Philip V.

Although Spain was permitted to retain her American Empire, she was stripped of all her European possessions. By removing the temptation to play the role of European power that had so overstretched its limited resources, these provisions contributed to a modest revival in the country's fortunes. This process was helped along by Philip's reforms, brought together in the New Structure (*Nueva Planta*) decrees, which abolished the privileges of the former Aragonese territories, and of Catalonia in particular. Henceforth the whole of Spain was to be run on the King's behalf by a single council of ministers: the 'Council of Castile'.

These measures were a foretaste of the Spanish Bourbons' intention to install the system of absolute monarchy (*absolutismo*) already established by their French cousins. This differed from earlier, feudal forms of rule in that the King's authority was untrammelled by the rights of particular social groups, institutions or regions. However, the Bourbons enjoyed limited success in Spain. This was partly due to the country's terrain, which made it much harder to centralise administration. But their plans also met stubborn resistance from those who stood to lose power and influence, especially the nobles and the Church. Above all, the royal authorities' chronic poverty severely limited the Bourbons' capacity to impose their rule.

Later in the century Spain was touched by another form of French influence, the intellectual revolution known as the Enlightenment (*Ilustración*). Its main impact was felt after 1759, when Charles III came to the throne. Able and energetic, he was strongly influenced by the enlightened despotism (*absolutismo ilustrado*) then in vogue among Europe's monarchs, the lessons of which he attempted to apply in Spain. He encouraged agricultural improvement, through irrigation programmes and the settlement of sparsely populated areas. Crafts and primitive industry were promoted by government funding and the relaxation of restrictions on trade, such as internal customs duties.

Yet, once again, a lack of resources restricted the impact of Charles' measures. He was not helped by the fact that the new thinking was associated with a country against which Spain had spent the better part of two centuries at war; its adherents were widely despised as 'Frenchified' (*afrancesados*). Moreover, despite taking steps to restrict the power of the Catholic Church – most controversially, by expelling the Jesuits from Spain and her colonies in 1767 – he could not break its hold over much of the population. Controlling most of what passed for an education system, the

antiguo régimen

old order

The name *ancien régime*, associated above all with France, was given in retrospect to the structures characteristic of late eighteenth-century Europe. Its main features were: politically, the system of absolute monarchy, under which individuals were subjects without rights of their own; socially, a strict hierarchy dominated by the court and aristocracy; and, economically, extensive intervention by the royal authorities into the workings of an embryonic market. In Spain it also encompassed a number of features left over from earlier periods, including the nobles' rights of jurisdiction over their tenants (*señoríos*), the system of entail, which meant that much land could not be bought or sold, and the traditional privileges (p3) still retained by a number of areas.

Church was well placed to resist tooth and nail the new philosophical and scientific ideas with which Europe was abuzz.

Thus, as the eighteenth century drew to a close, the 'old order' that was about to be shaken by the French Revolution was far from fully developed in Spain. Not only the Church but most of the landowning aristocracy and the mass of the people were deeply conservative, tied firmly to traditional ideas and practices. The state apparatus was weak and there were few signs of the modern economic development that was starting to take place elsewhere in western Europe. Militarily insignificant, Spain became more and more of a backwater, cut off from events to the north.

Spain's isolation was abruptly interrupted by the 1789 Revolution and the subsequent wars between France's new rulers and their enemies. Too weak to resist her neighbour, she was drawn into a series of costly campaigns on France's side; in 1805 almost her entire fleet was destroyed at Trafalgar. Three years later Napoleon Bonaparte, by now Emperor of France, decided he needed direct control over Spain in order to invade Britain's ally, Portugal. His troops occupied much of northern Spain, and in May 1808 he forced King Charles IV and his son Ferdinand to renounce their claims to the Spanish throne, which he awarded to his brother Joseph, thereby triggering the 'War of Independence' (known to English-speakers as the Peninsular War).

The War lasted until 1813, when the last French troops were driven out of Spain. During the intervening years they controlled much of the country, or at least the larger towns, the main routes and the surrounding districts. In the occupied areas they imposed the changes of their own Revolution, removing restrictions on the use of land and property, and the privileges enjoyed by Church and aristocracy. Such reforms earned the French a degree of support, especially from government officials influenced by Enlightenment ideas. But only a tiny minority were 'Frenchified' in that way; the vast majority of Spaniards bitterly opposed French occupation. To a considerable extent, the War was the first genuinely national experience in Spanish history.

The mass of the people saw the War in very traditional terms, as a struggle to place their rightful King, Ferdinand – 'Our Heart's Desire' (*El Deseado*), as he became known – on his father's throne. As well as monarchism, however, the War also served to reinforce support for the Church, whose clergy often played a leading role in organising and sustaining resistance. At the same time, there was a redoubled hatred of all things French – a not unnatural response to the occupiers' sometimes gruesome methods, which were often repaid in kind. These three factors – Church, King and visceral anti-French feeling – came to form the basis of a primitive and deeply conservative patriotism.

Another important aspect of the War was the nature of the fighting. After their regular army had suffered several crushing defeats, the Spaniards wisely left conventional warfare to the British forces that had landed in Portugal. They concentrated instead on guerrilla warfare (*guerra de guerrillas*), with irregular, locally based bands using their knowledge of the terrain to harry the superior French forces, one effect of which was to establish a tradition and experience of such techniques among the civilian population.

Another was to reconfirm the strong local loyalties to individual regions, districts and even villages, which Spain's geography and history had always encouraged and which received a further boost from a second feature of the War. For, with their master gone, most local representatives of the old royal authorities held back from organising resistance to the French. The task fell instead to *ad hoc* local committees (*juntas*), which, with the French in control of most main roads, operated more or less autonomously, under the leadership of prominent figures in local society.

To the extent that this role fell to the landowning nobility, the emergence of the committees also served to reinforce the status of traditional institutions. In some cases, however, precisely the opposite occurred. In many towns in the south and south-east, where the French presence was weakest, direction of the committees was seized by merchants and early manufacturers, representatives of the new commercial forces in society. As such they were especially susceptible to the revolutionary ideas brought by the French, including the notion that a country should be governed, not by the whim of a hereditary monarch but by the will of its people, of the nation as a whole (or at least of its propertied classes).

Among a populace that had been left largely to fight for its own liberation, this idea of national sovereignty had a broader appeal and came to suffuse much of the anti-French resistance. In 1810, it inspired local committees around the country to send representatives to an impromptu Parliament. The assembly met in Cadiz, which, protected by a British fleet, had become the effective capital of unoccupied Spain. Two years later it completed drawing up a blueprint for the country's future government. Spain had acquired its first Constitution.

Summary of main points

- After dominating Europe for a century, from about 1660 Spain fell into sharp decline and became increasingly isolated from its neighbours.
- The Peninsular War had a profound impact on Spain, strengthening traditional and local loyalties but also allowing revolutionary ideas of national sovereignty to find expression.

CHAPTER 1

A liberal century? (1812–1898)

In western Europe the nineteenth century was the golden age of liberal ideas. Broadly speaking, liberalism wished to remove the widespread restrictions on economic and political freedoms typical of absolute monarchy, while its rise went hand in hand with industrialisation and the emergence of a commercially-minded middle class. In Britain, these processes advanced relatively quickly. On the continent, however, they were initially held back by the restoration of absolute monarchies at the end of the Napoleonic Wars and by the defeat of the Europe-wide revolutionary outbreaks of 1830 and 1848. By the 1870s, however, most western European states, including newly-united Italy, had adopted parliamentary constitutions with fairly broad (male) franchises. Liberal influence was also apparent in the establishment of a legal framework for capitalist economic activity and in state promotion of economic development. The results were a second, more sophisticated wave of industrialisation and a significant rise in general living standards, assisted in some countries by the exploitation of colonies. A further feature of the century's last decades was a massive expansion of education provision, with universal primary schooling becoming the norm.

The approval of the 1812 Constitution placed Spain in the vanguard of European liberalism; in fact, its architects were the first men to be dubbed 'liberals'. However, they and their successors proved unable to implement the massive reforms the country needed, or even maintain a minimal state of order. These failings allowed the Spanish Army, already unusually predisposed to political intervention, to play a major role in the country's affairs, a role that became increasingly conservative as the century wore on. During its last quarter a regime was finally implanted that appeared to combine stability with liberal principles. But appearances were deceptive.

Liberals before their time

The Spanish liberal movement (*liberalismo*) was weak from the outset, lacking a strong social basis and confronted with powerful enemies. It was also divided into two main strands with widely differing views of what liberalism meant in practice. While both were able to secure some significant advances, these were undermined by the fact that neither was ultimately prepared to practise the constitutionalist principles it preached. As a result, more than forty years after the Cadiz Constitution was passed Spain

Carlistas
....
Carlists

The original Carlists were so
named because they supported
the claim of 'Charles V', as they
called him, to the throne of his
dead brother, Ferdinand VII.
Extreme conservatives, they
advocated a return to the **old
order** (pxvi), in which cause they
staged three armed rebellions
during the nineteenth century
(1833–40, 1846–49 and
1872–76). Their main support
came from the Church and rural
areas in Aragon, Catalonia and,
above all, Navarre and the Basque
Country, where the retention of
traditional local privileges was
a major issue. After its third defeat,
the Carlist movement (*carlismo*)
split, the most reactionary
elements (*integristas*) abandoning
the claim of Charles's heirs to the
throne in favour of demands in
other areas, especially regarding
the Church's status. The
movement was later reunited as
Traditionalism (p66) and played
a significant role during the Civil
War of the 1930s (p73) and
under the Franco regime (p85).
When democracy returned after
1975 the official Carlist pretender
bizarrely adopted extreme left-
wing ideas, splitting his followers
again and confirming the end of
Carlism as a serious political player
even in its Navarrese heartland.
See also: *monarquistas* (p56)

continued to be governed by principles very different from those set out in it.

The changes this envisaged represented a truly radical break with the old order (pxvi) and covered a wide range of political, social and economic aspects. While the monarch was to remain head of state, effective power would pass to a single-chamber Parliament (*Cortes*) elected mainly by universal (male) suffrage. Previous restrictions on the right to buy and sell land were abolished along with various barriers to trade within Spain, such as internal customs barriers. Also struck down were the special privileges enjoyed by the aristocracy, the Catholic Church and particular towns or districts. Finally, the Constitution established a range of freedoms, in particular that of expression, previously denied, one result being the emergence of a lively – and highly partisan – press.

At the time, such measures would have been seen as extremely advanced almost anywhere: in Spain they were frankly utopian. Having fallen steadily behind its neighbours, the country had generated very little commerce or industry, elsewhere the breeding ground of liberal ideas. The vast bulk of the population continued to eke an uncertain living from the land – famines and epidemics were to remain common almost to the century's end – in a state of ignorance and illiteracy. Repeated wars (pp3,8) imposed the further burdens of taxation and conscription.

The result was a constant mood of popular discontent, even anger, that left little room for inevitably disruptive reforms. Moreover, powerful influences remained resolutely opposed to liberalism *per se*, never mind the maximalist version whose 1812 triumph was possible only thanks to the exceptional circumstances of the Peninsular War (pxvii). As soon as the French were driven out of Spain, the wind changed dramatically.

Thus, when Ferdinand VII (pxvi) set aside the Constitution and re-assumed absolute powers in 1814, he was virtually unopposed. But merely restoring absolutism was insufficient to satisfy many conservatives. When financial reality forced the royal authorities into a mild rationalisation of the country's administration and economy, they triggered off a series of minor uprisings. Significantly, these often enjoyed clerical backing, as did the French invasion that – again with negligible resistance – put an end to the next, three-year constitutional interlude (*trienio constitucional*) in 1823. And, indeed, it was the Spanish Church that would prove liberals' most implacable opponent, threatened as it was not just by the spread of their ideas, but also by concrete measures such as the abolition of tithes, expulsion or restriction of the monastic orders and the loss of its lands.

Matters came to a head in 1833 when Ferdinand died leaving the crown to his infant daughter, who now became Queen Isabella II. His brother Charles promptly claimed the throne for himself and led his reactionary supporters in armed revolt. The battle cry of these **Carlists** – 'God, King and the **old laws**' – invoked the three main pillars of the old order in Spain. Backed by the Pope, they enjoyed considerable support among the deeply Catholic northern peasantry, where liberal attacks on local privileges were also resented, above all in Navarre and the Basque Country. Elsewhere, though, their extremist message found little resonance and after a bloody seven-year war the Carlists were forced to concede defeat.

> ### *fueros*
>
> traditional local privileges; old laws
>
> Under the **old order** (pxvi), many towns and districts in Spain enjoyed traditional privileges, such as exemption from taxes or military service. By the 1830s, most had been abolished, as much in the interests of administrative efficiency as from liberal principles. However, the three Basque provinces (Alava, Guipúzcoa, Vizcaya) and Navarre retained a number of special features. In particular, Spanish tariffs on imports and exports did not apply to goods entering these areas from outside, while the provincial authorities were entitled to levy customs duties on goods coming and going from the rest of Spain; in effect, the four provinces constituted a duty-free zone. This and some other privileges – or 'old laws', as they were known in Basque – were suppressed following the defeat of the **Carlists'** first uprising and the remainder abolished after the movement's final defeat in 1876. See also: *concierto económico* (p9)

Ironically, their revolt forced the royal authorities to turn to the liberals, or more precisely a group of the least radically-minded, to form a government. These Moderates (*Moderados*), as they became known, wished essentially to implement the provisions of the Cadiz Constitution removing the innumerable restrictions then constraining business activity. Above all, they were anxious to permit, or even require, the sale of common lands, aristocratic estates and Church properties. From this process of disentailment (*desamortización*) many Moderates profited handsomely.

Having done so, their interest was less in promoting further, political reform than in avoiding social unrest. Yet for that very reason they appreciated the need for some change. Over the next two decades Moderate governments therefore introduced substantial reforms to the administration of justice and government. Most importantly, they overhauled the tax system to place it on a sounder and more rational footing, thus at last providing Spain's rulers with an assured income, albeit a meagre one.

Meanwhile, liberalism's political aims, in particular the extension of voting rights, were kept alive by the movement's more radical wing, the Progressives (*Progresistas*). However, on the brief occasions when their leaders managed to reach power they tended to forget these commitments. Instead, the Progressives' greatest achievement was to provide Spain with a legal framework for modern business activity during the period 1854–1856 (*bienio progresista*). At the same time, they pushed through a further major tranche of disentailment, as they had in 1837. In neither case, though, did they even attempt to ensure a more equitable distribution of disentailed land, something else they had always preached.

Worse, the Progressives – like the Moderates – consistently made nonsense of the constitutionalist principles they purported to uphold. In power, both liberal factions adopted partisan constitutions tailored to their own interests. In the 44 years after 1812, Spain was blessed with a further four, none as radical as the original, at least in their political aspects. Even under those drawn up by the Progressives, the monarch retained significant powers and the franchise was severely restricted. Similarly, both factions routinely resorted to election-rigging (*fraude electoral*), an absurdly easy practice since votes were cast in public but counted in secret.

Anomalies were especially widespread under the Moderate governments of 1843–1852, a regime that verged on dictatorship (p6). These conditions further strengthened the notion espoused by Progressives and more radical elements of lawful revolution (*revolución legal*) and local uprisings continued to be frequent. All were rapidly crushed, however, their main effect being to create a dread of radicalism among the better-off and also the Church, whose personnel and property were often the subject of verbal and physical attack.

Such anticlerical violence widened the breach between Catholics and the liberal Left opened by the provisions of the 1837 Progressive Constitution, which asserted the state's authority over the Church in all temporal matters. On the other hand, the Moderates became ever more conscious that the stability they craved would hardly be served by the Church's destruction as a social institution. As well as declaring Catholicism Spain's sole religion, their 1845 Constitution restored tithes, halted disentailment and confirmed the Church in the possession of its remaining lands. The rapprochement was taken a step further in 1851, when the Moderate government signed a Concordat with the Vatican that, in practice, proved highly beneficial to the Spanish Church (e.g. by providing for state payment of clerical salaries).

Meanwhile, Queen Isabella moved steadily back to the Church fold. In fact, her court became a stronghold of the most reactionary of Catholic thinking; there was talk of reuniting, by marriage, her Bourbon line with their Carlist cousins, in order to present a united front against liberalism. Even the Moderates were too radical for Isabella's taste. In 1852 she arbitrarily removed them from office and appointed a series of Catholic ultraconservatives to head her government – something she was quite entitled to do under the 1845 Constitution. By her actions, she united almost all liberals against her. Yet, hamstrung by their own timidity and still lacking mass popular support, these were powerless to call the Queen to heel without the help of what had become the true arbiter of Spanish politics: the Army.

The changing role of the Army

The Spanish Army, previously a pillar of the old order (pxvi), emerged from the Peninsular War much changed in both composition and attitudes. Combined with the failure of civilian politicians to establish lasting order, this led to a marked willingness on the Army's part to intervene in politics. Initially, it tended to do so in support of the more radical liberals. As the century wore on, however, the officer class acquired an increasing interest in the status quo, and its views moved correspondingly to the Right.

The Army's first forays into politics had come in the confused build-up to the Peninsular War (pxvi) but it was wartime developments that turned them into regular events. The old, aristocratic officer corps now incorporated successful guerrilla leaders, who, even more than the regulars, were accustomed to operating with no royal, and little other authority. Many felt themselves to be the country's true representatives, with a duty to act in its defence as they saw fit. And, in some cases, this feeling was linked to the idea that ultimate authority lay with the people rather than any monarch.

Despite that, the first post-war coup, in 1814, was instrumental in the re-imposition of absolutist rule (p2). It understandably fanned fears that the Army would always be an agent of reaction and led radical liberals to espouse the idea of a militia (p68). However, the various wars waged to defend Spain's American possessions were a constant cause of discontent among officers and rankers alike, at least until the mainland colonies were finally lost in 1828. Partly as a result, most military insurrections were to remain radical in tenor for some time ahead.

Whatever their political colour, such revolts soon adopted the peculiarly Spanish format of the **military declaration**. Initially, declarations tended to be led by junior officers – such as Major Riego in 1820 – or even by non-commissioned ones, as in

pronunciamiento

(military) declaration

A characteristically Spanish form of military revolt, declarations typically began with the reading of a statement of grievances by officers to their troops (hence the name) as an appeal for support. If successful, this would be followed by risings at other barracks, and by a march on Madrid to force a change of government. Such risings tended to be linked to attempted popular 'revolutions' (p4); the vast majority failed. In their heyday, the period 1812–68, declarations were seen within the Army as a legitimate form of protest, with their own etiquette; for instance, that those involved in an unsuccessful revolt should be dealt with leniently. Thereafter, these peculiarities disappeared and risings in general became much less frequent. But the tradition of military insubordination lived on, as was to be seen in the right-wing coups of 1923 (p38) and 1936 (p67). As recently as 1981 military officers attempted to overthrow an elected civilian government, but the danger of such intervention now seems finally to have been banished.
See also: ***23-F*** (p124)

the sergeants' mutiny of 1836. By this time, however, new factors were entering the equation, largely owing to the civil war that raged for much of the 1830s (p3).

Although it brought liberals back to power (p3), the conflict also placed their survival in the hands of the Army and, in particular, its leaders. They in turn were reinforced in their self-esteem and sense of mission, and confirmed in a certain ingrained contempt for civilian politicians. At the same time, the government's failure to pay its troops regularly further aggravated discontent in the lower ranks, while both of the constantly squabbling liberal factions began to actively seek military backing against each other.

These various influences were to be seen in the Revolution of 1840, which began as a typical Progressive 'revolution', with a small 'r' (p4). But it became something more when General Baldomero Espartero, popularly viewed as the hero of the Carlist War, disobeyed orders to crush it. Instead, he placed himself at the insurrection's head and forced the royal authorities to appoint him regent – effectively, the country's ruler. This was a new development; previous military interventions had merely aimed at replacing one civilian government with another. Possible only because of Espartero's rank and prestige, it was to establish a trend: from now on, declarations were to be a matter for generals.

Politically inept, Espartero rapidly antagonised not only his civilian supporters but also, and crucially, the Army, whose pay and conditions he did little to improve. After only three years in power he was ousted by the 'sword', or military backer, of the Moderates (p3), General Ramón Narváez. Learning from his predecessor's error, he went to great lengths to avoid any military rumblings, a danger that had been increased by the agreement that had allowed former Carlist officers to join the regular Army without loss of rank.

Thus, in order to assure the many superfluous officers of posts, Narváez maintained the Army's complement and budget at inflated levels, brooking no interference in these matters by civilian politicians. He also returned powers over local administration and justice removed in 1812 to the Army, entrenching its already powerful position in the state. All these measures served to further inflate officers' growing sense of themselves as a caste apart from, and superior to, civil society.

For that, Narváez showed little respect. He subjected radicals to a range of repressive legislation, imposed martial law at the least sign of unrest and crushed any uprisings ruthlessly; in liberalism's homeland the emblematic year of 1848 passed virtually without incident. Yet he considered himself a Liberal and, indeed, his governments undertook significant reforms (pp3–4) and resisted mounting pressure to restore the influence of liberalism's chief enemy, the Church, not least from the court.

Narváez did, though, accept his eventual dismissal by the Queen (p4), an action that ultimately led to a further full-scale Revolution in 1854. As in 1840, its success hinged on army support, again with Espartero as figurehead. This time he managed only two years in power, admittedly long enough to allow some significant reforms (p4), before being replaced by yet another military strongman.

General Leopoldo O'Donnell, a former Moderate, had managed to establish himself as the Queen's most trusted adviser despite having been a prime mover in the recent Revolution. He began by following in Narváez's footsteps, crushing opposition to his takeover and abolishing the Progressive militia. Thereafter, though, he showed some tolerance of dissent and also some new ideas, encouraging leading liberals of all varieties to come together in a 'Liberal Union' and keeping the Army busy by undertaking military expeditions to Mexico and Morocco, Spain's first since 1828.

O'Donnell also extended the practice of having generals appointed to the upper house of parliament. Furthermore, during the economic upswing – based on a railway boom and the recent Progressive reforms – that marked his first years in power, many senior officers became involved in business and so even more closely bound into the country's establishment. Meanwhile, lower down the ranks, the army's considerable administrative role ensured civilian careers for many. When Queen Isabella, still determined to be done with liberals of all stripes, sent O'Donnell the way of Narváez, she unwittingly threatened what, for many, was becoming a comfortable and privileged existence – and so provoked another Army intervention.

Military discontent was not the only factor behind the 'Glorious' or 'September', Revolution' of 1868. Isabella's behaviour had alienated virtually the entire political elite. The economic upswing had petered out, having done little other than to widen the already yawning social divide; its end brought a general drop in living standards that threatened the very existence of the poorest – of which there were all too many. Yet, once again, the Revolution's success would have been impossible without military support. This time it was led by General Juan Prim, who made his declaration on 19 September, perhaps symbolically at Cadiz. Within a month he and his supporters had defeated all opposition and – a truly radical departure this – forced the Queen into exile.

The Constitution – yet another – drawn up in 1869, incorporated various long-cherished Progressive aims known as the 'liberal conquests' (universal male suffrage, religious freedom, trial by jury, and freedom of association and the press). However, it also stipulated that Spain should remain a monarchy. This infuriated the most radical revolutionaries, by now firmly republican in their sympathies, who set about agitating against the new government. It also meant that a suitable monarch had to be found.

As the Crown was to retain substantive powers, including the right to appoint Prime Ministers, the choice inevitably became a point of contention among liberals of different tendencies. Eventually, in 1870, Prim imposed his own candidate, Amadeus of Savoy, son of the first king of newly-united Italy under its strongly liberal constitution. That made him a red rag to Prim's more conservative allies, who now began to consider a return to the old regime. However, it was not conservatives but radicals who, on the very day Amadeus landed in Spain, assassinated his mentor.

Prim died without fulfilling his promises to abolish the hated system of conscription (*quinta*) and reduce taxation. The reason was the anti-colonial revolt that had broken out on Cuba, where the poorly trained and equipped Spanish forces suffered severe casualties. The Cuban War thus provided ample cause for popular

Republicanos

Republicans; the Republican Party

The Republican Party was founded in 1869 by dissidents from the Democratic Party, itself a breakaway by left-wing Progressives (p4). These first Republicans believed strongly in federalism, i.e. the decentralisation of power to Spain's regions (or even smaller units) as the necessary accompaniment to abolition of the monarchy. Their support came mainly from the lower middle classes in the country's provincial capitals and other towns, and they governed briefly during the first phase of the First Republic. Thereafter, the memory of this disastrous experiment (p8) kept the Republican movement (*Republicanismo*) in the political doldrums, until in 1908 it split into two factions: the **Radical Republicans** (p27) and the **Reformists** (p19). Both of these influenced – in very different ways – Spain's Second Republic (pp50,55), proclaimed in 1931. During the Civil War of 1936–39, the term 'Republican' was extended to cover all those fighting in support of the elected government, whether or not their origins lay in the Republican movement (p68). In the narrow sense, Republicanism still exists in Spain today but has been utterly marginalised by the popularity of King Juan Carlos I.
See also: *Pacto de San Sebastián* (p44)

discontent. It was also a further source of tension among the country's new rulers; while Progressives sympathised with the rebel cause, the liberal Right regarded Cuba as Spain's last imperial jewel, to be retained at all cost. With Prim gone, there was no one capable of keeping the situation under control. Exasperated by the squabbles of his supposed supporters, Amadeus abdicated on 11 February 1873.

That same day, Parliament proclaimed Spain a republic and, with other parties abstaining, the **Republicans** voted themselves into power. From that point the downward spiral accelerated. For one thing, the country's new leaders enjoyed very little popular support and were in no position to impose their authority. For another, the relatively moderate Republican leadership was constantly at odds with its provincial activists, many of whom wanted very extensive decentralisation of power.

Later in 1873 the most extreme of these federalists, the so-called 'cantonalists', actually rose in revolt. Their uprising was soon crushed but another, by the reanimated Carlists (p2), proved harder to deal with. Inevitably these renewed conflicts increased dissatisfaction still further, as well as bringing the Army back to centre stage. In January 1874 its patience broke. General Pavía forcibly dissolved Parliament and a unitary – i.e. centralist – republic was established, with another general, Serrano, as President.

Ruling mainly by decree, its governments made a mockery of the 'liberal conquests', indeed of liberalism in any form. The end came as the Carlist War drifted into a second winter. On 29 December 1874, at Sagunto, Brigadier-General Martínez Campos staged a declaration in favour of ex-Queen Isabella's son, Alfonso. Within days Spain's First Republic had collapsed, its longterm legacy being to identify the pre-existing fear of unrest with republicanism, and to extend it well beyond the rich.

Meanwhile, the Army gradually withdrew to the wings. In 1876, it finally managed to defeat the Carlists, eliminating them as an effective threat; two years later, hostilities in Cuba were ended by agreement. No officer of any significance showed any desire to reverse the verdict of Sagunto. Yet military quiescence did not mean that the Army had retired from politics. Rather, it reflected the fact that civilian politicians were careful not to interfere with the privileges officers had accumulated since the 1840s, thereby ensuring that these became ever more opposed to change. Spain had not seen its last military revolt, merely the last from the Left.

The Restoration period

From 1875 on universal exhaustion, the ending of the Carlist and Cuban Wars, and improved economic conditions all helped to bring to bring peace and order to Spain at last. A further factor was the establishment of a new set of apparently democratic political rules – and their acceptance by the main political players. Unfortunately, though, these arrangements were not only a sham, they also made it impossible to address the country's deepening economic and social problems. What seemed like stability was, in fact, stagnation.

The Restoration, as the period from 1875 is known, began in a climate more favourable than for many years. Peace in itself significantly eased the burdens on ordinary Spaniards, and virtually nobody wanted to risk disturbing it again. The Carlists' defeat also led to the abolition of the customs border around the Basque County and Navarre (p3), the regions being granted a **special fiscal accord** in partial compensation. Their integration into the Spanish market, along with the free trade and other liberalising legislation passed after the 1868 Revolution (p7), encouraged a wave of foreign investment in mining, which in turn led to a general improvement in economic conditions.

Thereafter a number of factors combined to sustain the upturn: a phylloxera epidemic decimated the French wine sector; the Bessemer process was discovered, making Basque iron ore commercially viable; the railways experienced a second boom. These various developments relieved, at least to some extent, the conditions of the poor and gave the small but growing middle class a

> ### *concierto económico*
>
> special (Basque and Navarrese) fiscal accord
>
> In partial compensation for the suppression of their **traditional local privileges** (p3) in 1876, special accords were concluded with the Basque provinces and Navarre, under which the provincial authorities collected taxes in their area and paid the central government a lump sum for the services it provided. Franco suppressed some of these arrangements in 1937 (p80) but, under the devolution arrangements introduced after his death (p122), all were re-instated. Subsequently, the desire felt in some other regions (notably Catalonia) for similar arrangements has been a recurrent theme in the ongoing debate about these arrangements (pp176–7).

strong stake, symbolised by the aristocratic titles granted to a number of industrialists, in the Restoration regime.

In political terms, this was essentially the creation of Antonio Cánovas del Castillo, a right-wing liberal who had assiduously prepared influential opinion for the monarchy's return and now became Prime Minister. His Restoration settlement, as it is generally known, took Britain as its model and rested less on the new Constitution approved in 1876 than on the way its provisions were interpreted by leading players, in the first instance the new King.

Constitutionally, Alfonso XII retained the power to appoint and dismiss prime ministers, his mother's abuse of which had triggered off the recent chaos (p7). However, under Cánovas's instruction Alfonso scrupulously refrained from using it. When he died unexpectedly in 1885, leaving an unborn child as heir, Cánovas feared the worst. However, Alfonso's widow, acting as regent for her infant son, proved an equally adept pupil and also held back from political meddling.

The settlement's second pillar was formed by two new political groupings. These 'dynastic parties' – so called for their allegiance to the Bourbon line – were both of Cánovas's making; bizarrely, he not only founded his own Conservative Party (*Partido Conservador*) but also helped to set up its sparring-partner, the confusingly-named 'Liberal Party'. In fact, both parties belonged in Spain's liberal tradition, the Conservatives on the right, the Liberals (with a capital 'l') on the left. Respectively they were the heirs of the mid-century Moderates and Progressives (pp3–4), but as a pair they differed from their forerunners in two key respects.

First, they agreed to peaceful alternation in power (*turno pacífico*), that is, each consented to cede power voluntarily to the other after a certain period in office, so that neither would need to call on Army support. And second, both were relatively disciplined, partly by the personal authority and political skills of Cánovas and his Liberal counterpart, Práxedes Sagasta, and partly by the prospect of returning to office within a reasonable period. This second factor also meant that the parties were no longer afflicted by constant breakaways at the edges. Quite the opposite, in fact: it promoted the assimilation of potentially disruptive elements into their ranks (*atraccionismo*), examples being ex-Republicans on the Left and all but the Church's most extreme protagonists on the Right.

Key to this last development were a number of compromises on the religious issue. Although the 1876 Constitution made Catholicism the official state religion, it explicitly permitted the private practice of other faiths. Certainly, Cánovas maintained the Church's virtual monopoly over school education (not by legislation but simply by omitting to raise the tax income necessary to provide the state schooling required by law). However, his Conservatives made no attempt to block the establishment of private lay schools, while refusing to accept the Church's demands to set up its own universities. Equally importantly, the Liberal Party was prepared to accept this package of measures, just as the Conservatives accepted its reintroduction of universal (male) suffrage – suppressed in 1876 – once it came to power.

Indeed, Cánovas's settlement generally encouraged a more relaxed and tolerant climate, probably its greatest achievement in fact. Sadly, though, it was rotten at its core, the arrangements for peaceful alternation in power. For these relied, not on free elections, but on a corrupt system of **political clientilism,** tightly controlled through the government's power to appoint local mayors, provincial governors and even magistrates. This ensured a respectable majority for whichever dynastic party whose turn had come over the other – and the virtual exclusion of all other parties.

In the absence of a significant industrial lobby or even much pressure for agricultural reform, the dynastic parties never got round to drawing up, far less implementing coherent programmes. Instead, they remained little more than self-serving cliques, using power merely to distribute favours – jobs, contracts, honours – to their supporters. Virtually the only real resemblance to the British model lay in the names Cánovas had selected for them.

Ironically, it was among his own Conservatives that the first crack in his edifice appeared, when a 'puritan' faction, led by Francisco Silvela, proposed loosening central control by allowing un-rigged elections to local councils. The proposal was rejected outright by the Liberal Party and also by Cánovas himself, who thereby split his party. In the event, his political arrangements survived this upset, as they did his own murder (p27) and Sagasta's retirement. Nonetheless, the cosy immobilism that characterised them and the Restoration regime as a whole was steadily aggravating a number of Spain's problems.

Thus the religious compromise may have led many better-off Spaniards to return to the Catholic fold. Simultaneously, though, the Church's failure to denounce the appalling conditions in the southern countryside and the embryonic industrial areas meant that the poorer classes, apart from the peasant farmers of Old Castile, abandoned it in droves. Both social division and popular anticlericalism were greatly strengthened as a result. At the same time, those unable to afford a private lay education – the vast majority – were condemned to attend Church-run establishments hopelessly antiquated in both equipment and ideas.

---

caciquismo

political clientilism

After 1875, various factors – introduction of the secret ballot; increase in the electorate; growth of urban areas – made election-rigging (p4) much more difficult. At the same time, the Restoration settlement (p10) depended crucially on the major parties continuing to control the results of elections. In order to do that they created a much more sophisticated system of clientilism. Its agents were local party bosses (*caciques*), drawn from the influential members of local society, such as landowners, mayors and even priests, who dispensed favours and official jobs on orders from their masters in Madrid, as well as resorting to straightforward bribery and intimidation. Clientilism thus became a byword for corruption in general, and so a major focus of attempts to reform Spanish politics and society (p19). However, in some backward areas – notably Galicia – it survived into the Second Republic and, some would say, even into the post-1975 democratic era.

Apart from any other considerations, the lack of a proper education system was a severe drag on the economy. So, too, were the sclerotic arrangements for local government administration and, above all, a tax system that, despite the reform of the 1850s, remained totally unfit for purpose. Taxes were absurdly low and their application little better than arbitrary. However, as reform would have meant taking on powerful vested interests, no government dared attempt to raise the funds urgently needed to improve the country's infrastructure. So poor were transport links, for example, that Castile's wheat-growers could not compete outside their home region with the American imports now flooding in.

Added to the advance of phylloxera over the Pyrenees in 1885, that halted the rural economic revival in its tracks. Its end was all the more devastating since industrial development remained essentially confined to two sectors; Catalan textiles and Basque iron and steel. Moreover, both of these used outdated technology and were thus also liable to be undercut by imports. Along with the wheat farmers their leaders therefore pushed for an end to free trade, with such success that, in 1891, prohibitive import tariffs were imposed.

Yet not only did protection raise prices and so further aggravate the living conditions of the poor; it also proved disastrous for the three sectors themselves by removing any incentive to invest in newer technology. Meanwhile, successive governments did little or nothing to encourage other types of industry. Spain was missing out on the economic advances being made elsewhere, just as it had failed to progress on the political and social fronts. As the century drew to a close, it was given a rude indication of what this implied.

The shock came, again, from Cuba. Spain's prized colony was itself a good example of how the country had failed to move with the times and exploit its assets. For successive governments had stood back and allowed the island's economy to fall largely into US hands. When a fresh rebellion broke out there in 1895, American commercial interests sniffed an opportunity and pressured their government into declaring war.

Starved of public funds and adequate materials, the Spanish fleet was hopelessly outmatched and suffered a catastrophic defeat. Cuba, nominally independent, became a *de facto* American dependency, Puerto Rico and the Philippines *de jure* US colonies. At home, reactions among the Restoration elite ranged from shock to cynicism; of meaningful reforms there was no sign. Yet, even so, 'the disaster' marked a turning point, in that it gave fresh impetus to those currents within Spanish opinion convinced of the urgent need for real change.

Summary of main points

Liberals

- Although liberal ideas gained a foothold in Spain relatively early, the Spanish liberal movement lacked a solid social basis in the form of a commercially-minded middle class and was divided between conservative and radical wings.

- Moreover, the changes it proposed met with determined resistance, above all from Spain's reactionary Catholic Church, but also from Carlists and the Court; indeed. political reform was effectively opposed by the movement's own conservative wing and largely ignored by leaders of its more radical one when these obtained power.
- As a result, little progress was made in modernising Spain either politically or economically up to 1868. Liberals' most significant reform was to disentail and sell large quantities of Church land, a measure that served to slow down other changes.

The Army

- The Peninsular War encouraged a tendency for the Spanish army to intervene in politics. Initially it did so mainly in support of civilian politicians, particularly the more radical liberals, but from 1840 on generals repeatedly took effective power themselves.
- Meanwhile the Army, especially its senior officers, became integrated into Spain's establishment, and its sympathies became correspondingly more conservative. Even so, in 1868 it was still prepared to defend liberalism against the reactionary Queen.
- The disastrous aftermath of the 1868 Revolution, including the chaotic First Republic, led the Army to intervene again in 1874, this time to restore the monarchy. It also deepened and extended fear of insurrection and disorder in Spanish society.

Restoration period

- The period began with a general desire for order as well as signs of economic progress, while political conflict was regulated by the so-called Restoration settlement. This was based on the monarchy refraining from use of its constitutional powers and, above all, on the creation of two relatively cohesive political parties prepared to share power on an alternating basis.
- This 'peaceful alternation', however, was a sham, depending as it did on a corrupt system of political clientilism, while the 'dynastic parties' were mere vehicles for the selfish interests of their leaders and members, incapable of significant reform.
- As a result, the education and taxation systems remained utterly inadequate, hampering attempts to maintain economic progress once the initial upturn ended. Imposition of protectionist policies in response to pressure from cereal farmers and the few and poorly developed industries also held Spain back relative to other Western countries.

Exhibit 1.1: General O'Donnell's Manifiesto de Manzanares (1854)

One of the most famous military declarations

Españoles: La entusiasta acogida que va encontrando en los pueblos el Ejército liberal; el esfuerzo de los soldados que le componen, tan heróicamente mostrado en los campos de Vicálvaro; el aplauso con que en todas partes ha sido recibida la noticia de nuestro patriótico alzamiento, aseguran desde ahora el triunfo de la libertad y de las leyes que hemos jurado defender. Dentro de pocos días, la mayor parte de las provincias habrán sacudido el yugo de los tiranos; el Ejército entero habrá venido a ponerse bajo nuestras banderas, que son las leales; la nación disfrutará los beneficios del régimen representativo, por el cual ha derramado hasta ahora tanta sangre inútil y ha soportado tan costosos sacrificios. Día es, pues, de decir lo que estamos resueltos a hacer en el día de la victoria. Nosotros queremos la conservación del trono, pero sin camarilla que lo deshonre; queremos la práctica rigurosa de las leyes fundamentales, mejorándolas, sobre todo la electoral y la de imprenta; queremos la rebaja de los impuestos, fundada en una estricta economía; queremos que se respeten en los empleos militares y civiles la antigüedad y los merecimientos; queremos arrancar los pueblos a la centralización que los devora, dándoles la independencia local necesaria para que conserven y aumenten sus intereses propios, y como garantía de todo esto queremos y plantearemos, bajo sólidas bases, la Milicia Nacional. Tales son nuestros intentos, que expresamos francamente, sin imponerlos por eso a la nación. Las Juntas de gobierno que deben irse constituyendo en las provincias libres; las Cortes generales que luego se reúnan; la misma nación, en fin, fijará las bases definitivas de la regeneración liberal a que aspiramos. Nosotros tenemos consagradas a la voluntad nacional nuestras espadas, y no las envainaremos hasta que ella esté cumplida.

Spaniards: the enthusiastic reception which the liberal army has been receiving throughout the country; the commitment of its soldiers, demonstrated so heroically on the field of Vicálvaro; and the applause which, on every side, has greeted the news of our patriotic rising; all these things ensure the triumph, from this day on, of freedom and of the laws we have sworn to defend. Within the next few days, most of Spain's provinces will have thrown off the yoke of tyranny, the entire Army will have come over to ours, the one true cause, and the nation will enjoy the benefits of representative government, for which it has spilt so much blood in vain and made so many costly sacrifices. The time has come, then, to state what we intend to do once victory is ours. We wish to see the monarchy preserved, but without a clique of courtiers to dishonour it; we wish to see basic laws enforced rigorously but also improved, especially those relating to elections and publishing; we wish to see taxes reduced, based on the practice of strict economy; we wish to see proper respect paid, in both civilian and military professions, to seniority and merit; we wish to see our communities freed from the centralism which is destroying them, by giving them the local autonomy they need to protect and promote their own interests; and, in order to guarantee this, we wish to see the National Militia re-established on a proper basis. These are our aims, which we state openly, but without any intention of imposing them on the nation. The liberal regeneration to which we aspire will be given its definitive form by the governing Committees to be set up as each province is liberated, and by the national Parliament which will meet thereafter – in other words, by the nation itself. We have dedicated our swords to the will of the nation, and we shall not sheathe them until it has been asserted.

Source: Artola, M. (1991) *Partidos y programas políticos 1808–1936: Tomo II.* Madrid: Alianza.

Exhibit 1.2: Cánovas on the monarchy (1886)

Extracts from a speech to Parliament

La idea de todos los monárquicos y en todas partes, es que la monarquía, que para eso es hereditaria, porque de otra suerte sería una irrisión que hereditaria se llamase, es, por su naturaleza, perpetua. [...]

No hay que pensar, pues, que con esta convicción nosotros podamos aceptar ni poco ni mucho, ni de cerca ni de lejos, el principio de una evolución pacífica y falsamente apellidada legal, detrás de la cual pudiera estar la supresión de la monarquía. Nosotros concebimos una monarquía que puede errar, que puede caer; pero nosotros no podemos admitir que eso se prevea por las leyes de un país; no podemos admitir que, en las circunstancias normales de la nación, se tenga por sobreentendida en las leyes y en el régimen político, que el rey pueda ser a cada instante separado por un funcionario cualquiera, sin los beneficios siquiera de la inamovilidad, ni de los reglamentos. [...]

Para nosotros jamás, por ningún camino se puede llegar, por medio de la legalidad, a la supresión de la monarquía, a causa de que no hay legalidad sin la monarquía, a causa de que sin la monarquía puede haber hechos, puede haber fuerza, puede haber batallas, pero no hay, ni puede haber, legalidad. [...]

For monarchists everywhere, the monarchy – and this is why it is hereditary, since otherwise it would be ludicrous to call it so – is, by its very nature, eternal. […]

So nobody should think that, believing this as we do, we could ever accept, to any extent or in any form, the idea of a peaceful process of evolution, allegedly legal but in reality not so, at the end of which might lie the monarchy's abolition. We can conceive of a monarchy that is fallible, or overthrown. But we cannot allow that the law of the land provide for such an eventuality. We cannot allow that, under the country's normal circumstances, it is somehow assumed in legislation and political practice that the King could be deposed by a mere public servant, lacking even the protection of his irremovable status or the disciplinary code. […]

In our view, there can be no way that leads, within the ambit of legality, to the monarchy's abolition, since without the monarchy there can be deeds, there can be power, there can be battles, but there is not, and there never can be, any such thing as legality.

Source: Diario de Sesiones (3 July 1886).

Topics for discussion

- What social and political interests are reflected in the demands set out in O'Donnell's declaration (Exhibit 1.1)? How compatible are they with each other? How do they relate to O'Donnell's later career?
- How does Cánovas (Exhibit 1.2) see the role of the monarchy in Spain? How does his stance differ from that implied in Exhibit 1.1?
- What was 'politics' in Spain during the nineteenth century? Who did it involve? With what issues was it concerned?
- In a sense, the Restoration period was the 'golden age' of the Spanish liberal movement. How did political and economic conditions during it match up to the aspirations embodied in the Cadiz Constitution?

CHAPTER 2

Change frustrated (1898–1917)

As the new century began and industrialisation continued in Europe, the workers' movement formed in the old one gathered strength. It was divided into various branches. The largest, Marxist socialism, held that economic advance would lead inevitably to the fall of capitalism and social revolution, a process some socialists sought to accelerate by working for political reform. Anarchists thought such activity pointless, believing that revolution must come spontaneously; their main strength was in Russia, the great power where industrialisation had made least headway. Common to all these groups, however, was the belief that workers' loyalties were to their class, rather than to their country. A major factor in holding them in check was thus the rise of nationalism, which in 1914 culminated in the outbreak of the First World War. In most countries, ideas of international class solidarity were forgotten as workers flocked to join up. Russia took a different path, however, and the Communist revolution of 1917 gave renewed heart to militant workers across the world.

Although its direct impact was limited – the framework of the Restoration settlement remained in place for a further quarter-century – the 'disaster' of 1898 had a profound effect on Spain. By setting off a process of national self-examination, it stimulated various forces which sought to bring about far-reaching change in the way the country was run, including a vague but widely-felt urge to 'regenerate' it. Another was the feeling of distinctiveness in certain regions which led to demands for some form of self-government. Yet a third was the workers' movement, which believed in a quite different form of salvation, through social revolution. The three were very different, mutually hostile and internally divided into often antagonistic strands. The result was their common frustration.

The 'Regenerationists'

Some Spaniards had long been aware of their country's failure to keep pace with its neighbours, politically, socially and above all economically. But the events of 1898 brought that failure into sharp relief for many, and crystallised a belief that drastic action was needed. Such 'regenerationist' thinking emanated from all the better-informed sections of society, from both within and without the elite, which had

regeneracionismo

'regenerationist'
ideas/thinking

Although the term had already
been in use before (see Exhibit
1.1), the events of 1898 brought
the notion of regeneration to the
forefront of public debate in Spain.
Indeed, the literary and
philosophical strand of
regenerationist thinking is
associated with the group known
as the '1898 generation'
(*generación del 98*), whose most
significant members were Miguel
de Unamuno, José Ortega y
Gasset and Ramón Maeztu. The
group's ideas were diverse and
varied over time, so that it is
impossible to speak of a coherent
'movement'. The same is even
more true of the wide range of
regenerationist proposals
emanating from various sources,
for changes in political, economic
and social structures. However,
they all had two things in
common; a concern about Spain's
general backwardness (*atraso*)
and the desire to eliminate it.

access to power under the Restoration settlement.

'Regenerationists' were not just a diverse crew; they were sometimes each other's enemies. They included Republicans, for whom regeneration meant abolishing the monarchy, but also the young King, Alfonso XIII, who came of age in 1902, with his keen interest in new technology and plans for Army reform. In fact, the closest thing to a coherent statement of **regenerationist ideas** was to be found in the life and works of one man: Joaquín Costa.

At the core of Costa's work were extensive proposals for agricultural reform through technical improvements, and especially for more and better irrigation, which he attempted with some success to implement in his native Aragon. To complement them he advocated drastic land reform (p53). He also argued that the large estates of the south, notoriously underused and thus unable to provide adequate employment, should be broken up and sold off to create the class of small farmers of which some early liberals had dreamt.

These changes would, Costa felt, release the 'live forces' in Spanish society that were excluded from influence by the practice of political clientilism (p11). To try and break its hold, in 1899 he set up a party-cum-business association, the 'National League of Producers'. This soon received support from the Chambers of Commerce, who were the representatives of small business in Spain's provincial towns. However, larger industrialists showed no desire to break their alliance with the large landowners (p12), and without their help the League made no headway. Its main achievement was to organise a non-payment campaign against what the government of the day understood by regeneration, tax reform, which was also the prerequisite for implementation of Costa's own plans.

In the face of such contradictions, and its powerful opponents, the League soon collapsed. This failure convinced Costa that clientilism could not be defeated under the existing system. To achieve that, he felt that Spain needed an 'iron surgeon' (*cirujano de hierro*), a charismatic leader who would enjoy virtually unlimited powers for a brief period, before returning the country to parliamentary rule.

An early candidate for this role was General Polavieja, who had commanded Spanish forces in the Philippines in the run-up to the 1898 'disaster'. On his return he took up Costa's attacks on the political system, quickly attracting such a substantial following that the government was forced to appoint him Minister of War. But his plans to modernise the Army – for him the key to regeneration – were also blocked by the government's budget reform plans. Polavieja resigned in protest and his support faded away.

Costa's other hope lay with the **Reformist Republicans**, who agreed with his emphasis on concrete, viable proposals rather than dogma. Thus, instead of just railing against Church control over the school system, as Republicans had tended to do in the past, the Reformists drew up detailed plans to change the content of education, and in particular to introduce an element of vocational training. However, they too ran up against clientilism, and remained a small minority, albeit one with a degree of influence (p35).

> ### *Partido Republicano Reformista*
>
> Reformist Republican Party
>
> The Reformists were one of the two factions into which the **Republican Party** (p8) divided in 1908. They subsequently abandoned their almost exclusive concern with constitutional reform (abolition of the monarchy, federalism) in favour of formulating practical proposals for change in specific fields, particularly education. The party enjoyed little electoral success, and disappeared under the Primo dictatorship, but from it emerged many of the **Left Republicans** (p50) responsible for major reforms during the Second Republic.

Given the workings of the Restoration settlement (pp10–11), the only feasible vehicles for regenerationist ideas at this time were the two 'dynastic parties'. Ironically, it was among the Conservatives that their influence was more evident, as had already been shown in Francisco Silvela's unsuccessful attempt to reform local government (p11). Now leader of his party, Silvela became Prime Minister in the wake of the 1898 'disaster'. Once confronted with the appalling state of public finances which had made that inevitable (p12), their reform became his top priority.

The plans of his Finance Minister, Villaverde, met widespread opposition, not least from Costa's League, because they included an element of tax reform. In fact, though, taxation remained very low. Villaverde's principal aim was actually to bring spending under control, which he achieved by the cuts that provoked Polavieja's departure. His changes set the tone of Spanish budget policy for the next 70 years, making it even harder for governments to stimulate economic development.

Economics were a minor concern for Silvela's protégé and successor, the greatest and most controversial of Conservative regenerationists. Like his mentor, Antonio Maura was a 'puritan' (p11); he believed that Spain's problems were essentially moral, and that he could solve them by 'dignifying' politics. He talked of a 'revolution from above', by which he meant that the steps necessary to eliminate corruption should be taken by the existing elite, to which he belonged. What he could not, or would not see was that its position depended on the very corruption he sought to eliminate.

In 1902 Maura received an early warning of the contradictions inherent in his ideas. As Interior Minister, he insisted on reducing the government's use of clientilist tactics in that year's election, which resulted in significant Republican gains in the larger cities. He was undeterred. Three years later, on becoming Prime Minister, he renewed his efforts to clean up politics with a fresh attempt at local government reform. However, like Silvela, he did not intend that free local elections should break the hold of the better-off on local politics, and therefore repeated his mentor's proposal for a form of corporate suffrage (by granting business owners additional votes). Once again the plans were frustrated by the Liberals, who could see more clearly than Maura the danger they posed to the two parties' common interests.

Not that Maura was blind to the threat of the new forces emerging in society. Indeed, he made no secret of the fact that his 'revolution from above' was intended primarily to pre-empt one 'from below', by the workers' movement. In 1908 his fears of such an outcome led him to introduce a number of repressive measures, including restrictions on the right of free association. The Liberals saw their chance and joined the Republicans in a 'Bloc of the Left' to run a campaign against the new measures, under the slogan 'Maura, No!'

To Maura, the Liberals' abandonment of the tacit alliance between the 'dynastic parties' was tantamount to treason. He offered his resignation to the King, demanding the chance to manufacture a vote of confidence in fresh elections. But Alfonso, worried by the re-entry of Republicanism into mainstream politics, now saw Maura as the biggest threat to stability. He accordingly accepted the resignation offer and handed power over to the Liberals. Many of Maura's Conservative colleagues backed the King's action, leaving their former leader an embittered and isolated figure (p35).

Up to this time the Liberal Party, which now returned to power, had shown little interest in regeneration. As the heir of the liberal movement's radical wing, its theoretical priority had been the restoration of the liberal conquests (p7), achieved during the 1880s – although by that time the arrangements which allowed the party to do that had rendered them meaningless! Since then, preserving those arrangements intact had been the Liberals' over-riding concern. Their differences with the Conservatives had been reduced to hysterical attacks on the revival of Church influence – partly because the Church posed a minor threat to the relative tolerance of Restoration society, but mainly because anticlericalism was an easy means of attracting popular support (p11).

This situation only began to change under the leadership of José Canalejas. After he was appointed Prime Minister in 1910, Canalejas sidelined the religious issue by introducing the Padlock Act (*Ley del Candado*). While seeming to place restrictions on the monastic orders that were the main focus of popular concern, the law effectively left their situation unchanged. This compromise opened the way for him to push through a second, more progressive tax reform, which for the first time hit rental incomes, and so acted as an incentive to more productive investments.

He also overhauled local government finance and abolished the right of the rich to buy themselves out of military service. His further plans included a scheme for rural land reform that would have allowed underused estates to be expropriated from their owners. However, before much of his programme could be implemented, Canalejas fell victim to an assassin in 1912 (p28). Thereafter, the only concerted attempt at regenerating Spain lasted for just a few months in 1918 (p35). Meanwhile, as the country continued to stagnate, the backwardness against which the regenerationists railed was increasing all the time.

Regionalists and nationalists

The extent of economic backwardness was far from uniform across Spain. By the 1890s Catalonia and the Basque Country, in particular, had undergone a considerable degree of industrialisation. In both regions, each of which was already distinctive in its own way, the experience gave rise to demands for self-government. But, just as the industrialisation processes and the historical backgrounds were very different, so too were Basque and Catalan regionalists – or, as many would see themselves, nationalists.

Regionalism first made its appearance in Catalonia. There, feelings of distinctive identity had deep roots, since for two centuries after the creation of a united Spain the region had enjoyed extensive self-government. Even after the loss of autonomy in 1713 (pxv), when Catalan ceased to be used officially, the language remained strong in daily use and literature. In the latter part of the nineteenth century it experienced a renaissance (Catalan: *renaixença*) whose leading figure, Valentí Almirall, was also the first man to give Catalan regionalism (*catalanismo*) a political dimension.

In 1892 Almirall's ideas were set out by his disciple, Enric Prat de la Riba, in what effectively became the movement's programme. These Manresa Principles (*Bases de Manresa*) were steeped in Catalan history and showed the influence of federal republicanism (p8) in the region. As well as calls for Catalan to become the region's official language there were demands for devolution within a federal Spain. Yet the Principles also reflected a newer concern: that Catalonia's development had been delayed by the backwardness of Spain as a whole, and by having to provide a disproportionate share of taxes from which it saw little return. The appearance of this grievance indicated how regionalism and economic development were closely connected.

In and around Barcelona, industrialisation was a gradual process, a natural extension of the city's tradition as a major port and commercial centre. It was founded on the textile industry, whose leaders' great concern in the later nineteenth century was to mount a successful campaign for import protection (p12). Although Catalan culture was important to the textile magnates, it did not spur them to political action. However, the events of 1898 persuaded them that their longer-term interests could only be protected by a fundamental change in the way Spain was run.

The industrialists turned first to General Polavieja (pp18–19), who had expressed sympathy for their views. When this hope proved vain, they decided to take up Almirall's strategy of a separate Catalan party and sponsored the foundation of the **Regionalist League**. Their financial and political clout enabled them to break

Lliga Regionalista

(Catalan) Regionalist League

Formed in 1901 with the support of local business interests, the League demanded home rule for Catalonia, while also seeking to influence the policies pursued by central governments through lobbying. Françesc Cambó, a leading industrialist, was responsible for fostering the necessary contacts in Madrid; the League's other main figure, Enric Prat de la Riba, was its head within Catalonia. Until the 1920s it was by far the largest Catalan regionalist party, but thereafter it was overtaken by other, more radical groupings (p36), and ceased to be a significant force after 1923. Nevertheless, the idea of a business-oriented Catalan party did not die and would eventually be revived in the 1980s by **Convergence and Union** (p145).

the shackles of clientilism (p11). Within a few months the party had made sweeping gains at the 1901 general election. Five years later, the League brought together a broad alliance of political forces, known as 'Catalan Solidarity', which in 1907 won an even more dramatic victory.

These electoral successes further increased the magnates' leverage over Madrid, and helped them to persuade the government to impose yet higher import tariffs. In 1914 they obtained another concession when a Catalan regional government, known in Catalan as the *Mancomunitat*, was established. Its powers were strictly limited. Run by the League and with Prat as its first head, however, it enabled the industrialists to implement what amounted to a form of conservative economic regeneration in Catalonia, with considerable success.

To a large extent that was exactly what the League had been seeking. Its aspirations for self-government went no further than devolution, partly for historical reasons but above all because it responded to the industrialists' present needs. They wanted to control their own affairs, but they knew that their businesses depended on the Spanish market. They also realised that the home market would grow only if the country as a whole prospered. Hence their desire for devolution rather than independence, and for influence over the development of Spain as a whole.

Such moderation and rationality sat oddly with another aspect of the Manresa Principles, which Prat in particular tended to play up during election campaigns: their stress on a fundamental clash of interests between the 'artificial' Spanish state and the Catalan fatherland (*patria*). Yet the indirectly elected *Mancomunitat* scarcely looked like a national assembly, while its existence also served to accentuate the contradiction between the League's policies in power and its claim to represent the people of Catalonia as a whole.

For it became clear that, as in Barcelona, whose city council the League had controlled for some time, its first priority was to protect the textile magnates' commercial interests. Little attention was paid to social policy or the conditions of the poor, and the result, especially in Barcelona, was an increase in the already high level of social tension. When this tension erupted in unrest, the League's leaders saw only a threat to their own property, and consistently backed a policy of outright repression. As a result, they alienated much of the mass support for regionalism which their early successes had first tapped, then further encouraged, leaving it for others to inherit.

The lack of popular backing for regionalism in the Basque Country was one difference between the situations in the two regions. A more fundamental one was that, while Catalan regionalism represented an attempt to seize the benefits of economic advance for Catalonia – or for some Catalans – its Basque counterpart was essentially a rejection of such development. It was also a reaction to a very different experience, since in the Basque Country – or more precisely, in and around Bilbao – industrialisation was anything but gradual. Instead it was a rapid and traumatic process, which transformed what was essentially an administrative and market town, together with its immediate hinterland, into a centre of large-scale heavy industry – and that in little over 20 years.

The historical and cultural background to these changes was also quite different from the Catalan case. By the 1890s the Basque language (*euskera*), whose literary tradition was minimal, was virtually extinct in much of the region, notably in the Bilbao area. Nor had the Basque Country ever formed an administrative unit. It is true that many Basques had a strong sense of local loyalty, as they had shown in their support for the Carlist movement (p2). However, their feelings focused mainly on the area's constituent provinces, with which its traditional privileges were associated (p3).

These factors strongly influenced early Basque nationalists, who shared the fiercely conservative Catholicism typical of the Carlists and regarded cultural issues as strictly secondary. As members of Bilbao's traditional social elite, they resented the tide of industrial development that had undermined their status and dreamed of turning it back. Their bitterness found expression in a political philosophy that often seemed more like a religious creed.

In a real sense, its father was Sabino Arana, to whom the very concept of a **Basque Country** can be attributed. For, under the influence of Catalan ideas, he moved away from an exclusive concern with his native province of Vizcaya and conceived the idea of a Basque nation which, in Arana's view, was defined not by cultural but by racial distinctiveness. Around these dubious notions Arana wove a complex web of nationalist mythology. Its main themes were

Euskadi

(the) Basque Country

This Basque word was coined by Sabino Arana (who spelled it Euzkadi) as the name for the Basques' supposed national homeland, to replace the earlier, less political notion of *Euskalherria*, meaning the 'territory occupied by Basque speakers'. In Arana's view, the Basque Country encompassed the Spanish provinces of Alava, Guipúzcoa, Vizcaya and Navarre, as well as three smaller territories in South-West France. Today the term is standardly applied to the Basque Autonomous Region established under the 1978 Constitution (p122), which comprises Alava, Guipúzcoa and Vizcaya only. For that reason, the radical nationalist supporters of ETA (p103) have re-adopted the older term *Euskalherria*.

Partido Nacionalista Vasco (PNV)

Basque Nationalist Party

The PNV was founded in 1895 by Sabino Arana. Its aim has always been Basque self-government, although it has usually been ambiguous as to whether by that it means complete independence. Heavily influenced by traditional Catholicism, for a long time the party's programme was socially conservative, with a strong egalitarian streak; in fact the PNV early acquired a sister trade union, Basque Workers' Solidarity (STV), with which it is still linked. By the 1920s it had established deep roots throughout Basque society, symbolised by the network of local PNV clubs (*batzokis*). This enabled it to survive attempts by Primo de Rivera and, above all, Franco to stamp out Basque national feeling (pp39,80); indeed, it emerged from the Franco period greatly strengthened. Since the restoration of democracy it has been the Basque Country's largest party, running the regional government set up in 1980, first on its own, later as the dominant partner in coalitions. After suffering a grave crisis and split in 1986 (p143), the PNV went through a moderate phase during which it retreated from talk of independence. More recently, however, it has taken a more radical turn and its differences with the Spanish government and parties have become a major feature of the country's politics. See also: **Frente Popular** (p59); **Euskadi ta Askatasuna** (p103); **Pacto de Lizarra** (p155)

Basques' unique relationship to the Church and their tradition of primitive democracy, embodied in the provincial privileges abolished in 1876 (p9).

Restoration of these 'old laws' was the platform of another of Arana's creations, the Basque Nationalist Party (PNV). As a national goal it sounded modest. However, on Arana's interpretation, it would have made Spanish rule over the Basque Country dependent on Basques' acquiescence, as well as separating the area from Spain economically (p3). It was therefore quite unacceptable to any Madrid administration; indeed, Arana and others were imprisoned for propagating the idea. Meanwhile, the PNV talked openly to its own followers of 'independence', an aim much more in tune with its diatribes against the despised Spanish immigrants (*maketos*) who flocked to the industries it hated.

Up to 1923 the PNV had minimal impact on Spanish politics. Its ideas held scant attraction for most Basque industrialists and financiers, the most powerful of whom had close links with politicians in Madrid and controlled the provincial councils which, under the 1876 settlement, enjoyed considerable financial autonomy (p9). More broadly, the party's quasi-racist rhetoric alienated industrial workers, including most indigenous ones, and the region's intellectuals. Outside Bilbao, nationalists remained a small and isolated minority.

Yet, arguably, isolation – from immigrants, from the modern world in general – was precisely what they sought. It allowed them to create a 'community', bound together by a dense network of associations, some social, others designed to provide mutual support for particular groups, especially the small farmers who became the PNV's bedrock. At the heart of this society-within-a-society was the PNV, giving it deeper roots across a wider social spectrum than any other party in Spain. That, together with the backing of some industrialists who wished to break the grip of the existing economic 'oligarchy', gave Basque nationalism its deceptive strength.

Like its Catalan cousin, it was helped considerably by the fact that Spain had missed out on developments which in other European states served to fuel a sense of nationhood, especially universal education and mass participation in the political system. Instead of engaging in the race for new colonies, it lost the remnants of Empire. Neutrality in the First World War, though it spared Spain the appalling bloodshed suffered by the belligerent nations, also meant that it never experienced the surge of social solidarity felt by these; indeed the conflict actually opened up a further split in what was already a deeply divided country, this time between partisans of France and Germany. For these, and other reasons, Spaniards largely lacked a strong sense of common identity to counter the competing claims, not just of regionalism but also of class loyalty.

The workers' movement

If Spain's economic backwardness was partly responsible for regionalism, it also meant that the country's industrial working class was small and its workers' movement correspondingly weak. Particularly affected was the Marxist branch. As in Russia, socialism was surpassed in both support and activity by anarchism, whose ideas were better suited to a country where poverty, often extreme, was concentrated on the land, but which also established a strong presence in Spain's premier industrial centre.

Marxism was represented in Spain by the **Spanish Socialist Party** (PSOE) and its sister trade union, the UGT (p140). Both were founded by Pablo Iglesias, who dominated

---

Partido Socialista Obrero Español (PSOE)

Spanish Socialist Party

Founded in 1879, the PSOE was long typified by a cautious approach to its declared aim of social revolution – which it held could only come after Spain had experienced industrialisation and genuine political reform – and by the belief that socialism was a matter purely for the working class (*obrerismo*). Prior to 1923 the party enjoyed very little electoral success; its main achievement was to build up, in its strongholds of Madrid, Asturias and the Basque Country, a party organisation based on the local socialist clubs (*casas del pueblo*). Under the Second Republic, however, despite being plagued by disputes between advocates of continuing moderation and supporters of immediate revolution (pp57–8), the PSOE became Spain's largest party. Banned by the Franco regime, the PSOE took little part in opposing it. Even so, on the restoration of democracy in 1975 it re-emerged as the largest party of the Left, winning power at the general election of 1982 and dominating Spanish politics for the rest of the 1980s and the early 1990s. During that time the party's policies continued the trend begun in opposition towards the political centre, while latterly it was involved a succession of financial and other scandals (p162). It was finally ousted from office in 1996 but returned to power in 2004 (p174).
See also: **Frente Popular** (p59); **Partido Comunista de España** (p70); **felipismo** (p139)

the Spanish socialist movement (*socialismo español*) until his death in 1925. He also embodied its strengths and weaknesses. A tireless organiser, he was renowned for a strict rectitude very different from the morally relaxed attitudes of most politicians. But he was no original thinker and his party. though disciplined and cohesive, lacked the intellectual wing common in other countries.

As a result, the PSOE's ideas remained a mere rehash of basic Marxist theory, taken almost entirely from the work of French socialists without due allowance for the massive differences between the two countries. In line with that, Iglesias defined his party's task as building up class loyalty among industrial workers in preparation for a revolution that would come only once Spain had properly modernised. Along with trade union work, that meant contesting elections, which offered a focus for mobilisation – but no realistic hopes of success under the prevailing conditions (pp10–11). Understandably, the appeal of this gradualist approach was limited, effectively to the small group of workers who already enjoyed some status and security in their jobs: Madrid printers like Iglesias himself, as well as workers in the mines and factories of Asturias and the Basque Country.

Elsewhere, the PSOE made little headway, most importantly in Catalonia, where its Madrid-centred leadership was resented. The potential for rural or middle-class support was ignored almost entirely, even if some intellectuals, including Unamuno (p18), did join the party in the wake of 1898. Moreover, Iglesias insisted on the view that all other parties were equally antagonistic to Socialist aspirations (*indiferencia*) and so refused to contemplate the sort of co-operation that might have given the PSOE the chance of a modest electoral advance.

That was not a concern for those who followed the principles of **anarchism**. They had greatest impact in the impoverished rural south, where day-labourers scraped a precarious existence on vast estates (*latifundios*), as well as in Aragon and the east. The dominant concern of this rural anarchism

---

anarquismo

anarchism; (Spanish) anarchist movement

Based on the idea that humans' natural habitat is an economically self-sufficient community modelled on a traditional rural village, pure anarchism – or primitive communism – holds that all decisions should be taken by direct and equal participation. All forms of imposed authority, internal or external to the commune, are anathema to anarchists, who reject any idea of political organisation, such as parties. The revolution that ushers in the anarchist utopia will, they believe, occur spontaneously. The only form of preparation countenanced by some followers is 'propaganda by deed', that is, acts of terrorism against established institutions and the rich. In Spain, such ideas were particularly associated with the landless rural labourers of Andalusia, and with the workers of Barcelona, among whom they tended to take the form of anarcho-syndicalism, which holds that workers should organise in trade unions (*sindicatos*) and engage in industrial agitation as the means of bringing about social revolution, in the form of a general strike.
See also: **CNT** (p36); **colectivización** (p69); **milicia** (p68)

was that the land should be handed over to, and divided up among those who worked it (*reparto de la tierra*), and the early 1880s saw regular incidents of estates being violently seized from their owners. The authorities' brutal response dampened down that expression of anarchist unrest. When it resurfaced in the 1890s it took the form of isolated terrorist actions, whose victims included Prime Minister Cánovas (p10). But, without an organised structure, that was as far as its capabilities stretched.

Where anarchism acquired greater significance was in and around Spain's largest and most dynamic city, Barcelona. As a great port, it was the entry point for new ideas, including more sophisticated versions of the anarchist creed. At the same time, its industrial growth attracted a steady stream of workers from rural areas where that had already established a hold. Furthermore, the region's textile firms were often small enough to make their operation as communes seem feasible, while the confrontational attitudes of Catalan employers meant that workers desperately needed some means of defending their interests. Under these circumstances, anarchist ideas flourished, particularly in the variant known as anarcho-syndicalism with its belief in a general strike as the catalyst for immediate revolution.

In 1907 anarcho-syndicalists established a trade union under the name of Workers' Solidarity (*Solidaridad Obrera*) to pursue this strategy. Two years later the simmering tensions in Barcelona, which the city government run by the Regionalist League had done nothing to relieve (p22), boiled over. By now they had been further exacerbated by working-class opposition to the colonial campaign being waged in Morocco (p39). In 1909 that prompted the Socialists to drop their refusal to cooperate with other parties and form a loose alliance (*conjunción*) with the Reformist Republicans (p19) in order to oppose the war. When reservists from Barcelona were called up, the new alliance began preparations for a massive protest. However, the plans were pre-empted by Workers' Solidarity, which on 26 July declared a general strike in Barcelona.

Thus began the notorious 'Tragic Week'. For days the city was in chaos, effectively cut off. Inflamed by the anticlerical rhetoric of the anarchists and of Alejandro Lerroux, populist leader of the **Radical Republican Party** and a formidable rabble-rouser, mobs sacked Church buildings and attacked both

Partido Republicano Radical

Radical Republican Party

The Radicals (not to be confused with a liberal splinter group of the 1870s) were one of the two factions into which the **Republican Party** (p8) divided in 1908. Offering no programme as such, it concentrated on vague references to revolution and virulent attacks against Catalan regionalism, the rich and existing institutions – the Church even more than the monarchy. Its main asset was the following for party leader Alejandro Lerroux in Barcelona. The party ran the city council several times, demonstrating a capacity for corruption to match that of the dominant dynastic parties (p10). During the Second Republic it emerged as a national political force, heading a number of governments before it suddenly collapsed in 1935 (pp55–6).
See also: **Pacto de San Sebastián** (p44)

priests and nuns. After initial hesitation – the country's leaders were still recovering from the political dramas in Madrid (p20) – the authorities restored order by force.

Many of the rioters received long prison sentences but Lerroux escaped in time to avoid punishment. Five men were executed for their part in the events, including – quite without justification – Francisco Ferrer, the organiser of the 'Modern Schools', which provided free education heavily influenced by anarchist and other libertarian ideas. His death provoked widespread protests at home and abroad and became a potent symbol of government repression.

This disastrous outcome had important effects on the workers' movement. The Socialists were confirmed in their view of anarchists as dangerous dreamers whose activities only served to hold back Spain's development – and thus its revolution too. The Republican alliance had at least brought them a parliamentary seat for Iglesias at the 1909 election and, for the moment, they turned away from radical agitation to concentrate on the less dramatic task of bettering the workers' lot through negotiation with employers.

For anarchists, by contrast, every industrial dispute was a potential revolution; the task was to foment such opportunities and then to exploit them. To that end, in 1911 they set up a new trade union federation to replace the now illegal Workers' Solidarity, the National Labour Confederation or CNT (p36), which quickly became by far the largest labour organisation in Spain. However, it was plagued by internal conflicts, and not just because of the inherent suspicion many anarchists felt for any sort of organisation. Thus, many of its rural supporters disliked the CNT's tendency to focus on industrial issues rather then land redistribution. Others, both urban and rural, placed less faith in trade union activity than in direct action; in 1912 they assassinated a second Prime Minister, Canalejas (pp20–1).

The First World War, in which Spain remained neutral, served to exacerbate the country's already massive inequalities. By exporting to the combatant countries, a small group of industrialists was able to make massive profits. The economy as a whole became badly distorted; prices soared and, outside the boom sectors, wages failed hopelessly to keep pace. Under these dire circumstances, Socialists and CNT again found common cause. During the general upheaval of 1917 they even joined in supporting a broader campaign for political reform (p34).

When this faltered, however, the frustration of their grassroots supporters forced the unwilling leaders of the workers' movement into another general strike. It was an even more violent affair than the one staged during the 'Tragic Week' eight years before, with strikers fighting pitched battles against the police. But the outcome was the same; once again the strike was crushed, leaving its supporters cowed and disillusioned.

Then, four months later, came the Revolution in Russia. Its success, in a country every bit as economically backward as Spain, seemed to contradict the PSOE's gradualist theories (if the effects of world war were left out of the equation). Conversely, it gave a significant boost to those anarchists for whom even a general strike was too weak a weapon and who instead advocated the use of violence. Over the next few years their intensified activities, directed against politicians and the better-off classes, would prove fundamental in finally bringing about change, although its nature would be very different from that which they envisaged.

Summary of main points

The 'regenerationists'

- The desire to 'regenerate' Spain came in many forms; common to all was their failure.
- The archetypical 'regenerationist' was Costa, a political outsider who advocated technological advance and an end to clientilism, the workings of which prevented him from exercising real influence.
- The leading regenerationists within the establishment were Maura (Conservative) and Canalejas (Liberal); while the former focused on the need to clean up politics, the latter's ideas centred on social reform. Neither achieved more than minor successes and Maura's policies split his own party.

Regionalists and nationalists

- In Catalonia, regionalism had deep historical and cultural roots and was moderate in its political demands. From 1898 the Regionalist League was backed by the region's industrialists and became an important factor in Spanish politics, but after 1918 it lost support to more radical groupings.
- In the Basque Country, regionalism was a more immediate product of rapid industrialisation. The Basque Nationalist Party (PNV) was traditionalist, inward-looking, unwilling to compromise and relatively weak, but its supporters formed a tightly knit and resilient 'community'.
- National feeling in Spain as a whole was much weaker than in neighbouring countries and was relatively powerless to counterbalance either regionalism or the workers' movement.

Workers' movement

- The Spanish workers' movement was small and divided between Socialists and anarchists. In 1909 and again in 1917, however, the two wings united to stage general strikes, both of which were violently crushed.
- Spanish socialism, represented by the Socialist Party (PSOE) and the trade union UGT, was the movement's weaker wing. Other than in 1909 and 1917 it took a markedly gradualist approach that attracted little support other than in Madrid, Asturias and the Basque Country.
- Anarchism attracted considerable support in the countryside, especially in Andalusia, and – in the form of anarcho-syndicalism – in and around Barcelona. Its trade union, the CNT, became Spain's largest worker organisation, but its supporters were split between advocates of a general strike and those who supported terrorist violence.

Exhibit 2.1: Maura's political philosophy (1917)

Extract from the Conservative politician's memoirs

Como es menester despertar a la opinión dormida, a la opinión desviada, a la opinión descreída y recelosa, hay un error que está muy en boga y que acaso sea lo más íntimo y transcendental del pensamiento del señor Cánovas del Castillo: el error de que las reformas que lastiman intereses colectivos, clases respetables, fuerzas del Estado se han de mirar con mucha circunspección y que no se puede tocar a las cosas. Si no se da con obras a la opinión algo de lo que pide, si no se ve que se la lleva por buen camino, no es fácil que se la despierte, ni se la atraiga por los organismos políticos que engendran los partidos. Por esto yo creo que algo de violencia necesitan las reformas: se trata de una operación de cirugía, y cuando de operar se trata el cirujano no va quitando el miembro muerto o corrompido parte por parte, sino que de una vez lo corta por donde es necesario. [...]

[...M]ás que nunca es ahora necesario restablecer aquella ya casi olvidada [...] confianza entre gobernantes y gobernados; y ya no hay más que un camino, que es la revolución audaz, la revolución temeraria desde el Gobierno, porque la temeridad es, no obra de nuestro albedrío, sino imposición histórica de los ajenos desaciertos. Nunca habría sido fácil la revolución desde el Gobierno, nunca habría sido recomendable, si hubiera podido dividirse la facultad y esparcirse la obra en el curso del tiempo; pero cada día que pasa, desde 1898, es mucho más escabrosa, mucho más difícil, y el éxito feliz mucho más incierto; y no está lejano el día en que ya no quede ni ese remedio.

We must stir up a public opinion that is sleeping, disorientated, sceptical and suspicious. We must alert it to a fashionable misconception, perhaps the most fundamental and significant error in Canovas's thinking: the idea that changes which threaten the interests of certain groups, or the better-off classes or the institutions of the state, must be approached with the utmost circumspection, and that it is best to let sleeping dogs lie. But if nothing concrete is done to meet the public's demands, if it does not believe that things are moving generally in the right direction, then it cannot easily be stirred or attracted by the organisations set up by political parties. That is why I believe that reform must include an element of violence. It is essentially a surgical operation, and when a surgeon operates he does not remove the lifeless or infected organ gradually, a piece at a time: he cuts out, once and for all, as much of it as is necessary.

[…N]ow, more than ever, we must re-establish that mutual confidence between rulers and ruled that has been almost forgotten. The only way to do that is by means of an audacious revolution, a bold revolution initiated by the government. For daring is no longer a matter of choice but has been forced on us by the failures of others. Such a government-led revolution would never have been easy. It would never have been advisable if the task could have been spread out over time and the responsibility for carrying it out divided up. But with every day that has passed since 1898 it has become ever trickier, ever more difficult, and its happy and successful conclusion ever more uncertain. Now the day is not far off when even this solution will have become impossible.

Source: Maura, A. (1917) *Treinta y cinco años de vida pública, 1902–1913*. Madrid: Biblioteca Nueva.

Exhibit 2.2: The Tragic Week (1909)

Statement approved at a public meeting organised by the anarcho-syndicalist Workers' Solidarity (*Solidaridad Obrera*) immediately before the events in Barcelona

Considerando que la guerra es una consecuencia fatal del régimen de producción capitalista;

Considerando, además, que, dado el sistema español de reclutamiento del ejército, sólo los obreros hacen la guerra que los burgueses declaran.

La asamblea protesta enérgicamente:

1. *Contra la acción del gobierno español en Marruecos;*
2. *Contra los procedimientos de ciertas damas de la aristocracia, que insultaron el dolor de los reservistas, de sus mujeres y de sus hijos, dándoles medallas y escapularios, en vez de proporcionarles los medios de subsistencia que les arrebatan con la marcha del jefe de familia;*
3. *Contra el envío a la guerra de ciudadanos útiles a la producción y, en general, indiferentes al triunfo de la cruz sobre la media luna, cuando se podrían formar regimientos de curas y de frailes que, además de estar directamente interesados en el éxito de la religión católica, no tienen familia, ni hogar, ni son de utilidad alguna al país; y*
4. *Contra la actitud de los diputados republicanos que ostentando un mandato del pueblo no han aprovechado su inmunidad parlamentaria para ponerse al frente de las masas en su protesta contra la guerra.*

Y compromete a la clase obrera a concentrar todas sus fuerzas, por si se hubiera de declarar la huelga general para obligar al gobierno a respetar los derechos que tienen los marroquíes a conservar intacta la independencia de su país.

Considering that the war [in Morocco] is a fatal consequence of the capitalist mode of production:

Considering also that, given the Spanish system of army recruitment, it is the workers who must fight a war declared by the middle classes.

This meeting expresses its vehement protest:

1. Against the government's actions in Morocco;
2. Against the behaviour of certain aristocratic ladies who have insulted the suffering of the reservists, their wives and children, by presenting them with religious medallions and scapulars,[1] rather than with the means of subsistence of which they have been deprived by the absence of the family's head;
3. Against the dispatch to the front of productive citizens to whom the triumph of Christianity over Islam is a matter of indifference, when it would be possible to form whole regiments of priests and monks who, as well as having a direct interest in the Catholic Church's fate, have no home or family, and are of no material use to the country; and
4. Against the attitude of Republican MPs who, although elected by the people, have failed to take advantage of their parliamentary immunity to place themselves at the head of the masses in their protest against the war.

The meeting also calls on the working class to unite should a general strike be called to force the government to respect the rights of Moroccans to defend their country's independence.

[1] The distinctive strip of cloth worn by monks over their habits.

Source: Ullman, J. (1972) *La semana trágica*. Barcelona.

Topics for discussion

■ What typical 'regenerationist' themes are identifiable in Exhibit 2.1? Which of them were to reappear in Spain's history, and in which periods?

■ What are the main grievances expressed in Exhibit 2.2? Other than Spanish workers, with whom do its authors appear to feel solidarity?

■ Are there any points of similarity between Exhibits 2.1 and 2.2?

■ What did the various forces working for change in Spain – 'regenerationists', regionalists, the workers' movement – have in common, in terms of their following and their aims? What role did Spain play in the thinking of each?

■ Why was it so hard to achieve meaningful change in Spain at this time?

CHAPTER 3

The years after the First World War saw the rise of two new ideologies in Europe. One, communism, was embodied in the newly-born Soviet Union, the brutal realities of whose political system were yet to be revealed. The other was fascism, whose followers seized power in Italy in 1922. Fascism was similar to traditional conservatism in that it was nationalist and authoritarian. But it was also significantly different: in its enthusiasm for economic development and concern with the situation of industrial workers; in the cult of its leader, Mussolini; and in the importance it laid on the Fascist Party itself as a means of controlling society. As it happened, both Italy and the Soviet Union made significant economic progress – starting from a relatively low base, it is true – at a time when Europe's democracies were experiencing severe economic and social problems. As a result, democrats throughout the continent had been pushed onto the defensive long before the 1929 Wall Street crash triggered off the worst depression of modern times.

Change imposed (1917–1931)

The closing years of the First World War brought upheaval to Spain and, to the various forces working for serious reform in the country, one last chance to bring it about. They were unable to take it. For a few more years, the now sclerotic regime first established in 1876 staggered on. Finally, in 1923, it was brought to an end in a familiar way, by a military coup staged by General Miguel Primo de Rivera, who became the country's dictator. His declared intentions – to restore order and bring about the reforms so widely discussed for the last 25 years – meant that his action was generally welcomed by an exhausted country. But he failed to establish a political structure for his dictatorship and, when his reforms ran into difficulties, it fell almost as swiftly as it had risen, dragging the monarchy down with it.

The end of liberal Spain

During 1917 and 1918, a combination of factors gave rise to a series of dramatic developments. Briefly it appeared possible that they would spur the Conservatives and Liberals, the so-called 'dynastic parties' (p10), into taking the sort of radical action that Spain so badly needed. But that was not to be. Instead, the country sank deeper into chaos, which in Barcelona took a distinctly violent turn. That brought the Army back into the centre of public affairs and showed clearly that it was subordinate to civilian politicians only insofar as that suited it.

In fact, events as far back as 1905 had already clarified the true nature of the relationship between Spain's political establishment and the military. In that year, irate officers sacked the premises of a Catalan satirical magazine, ¡Cu-Cut!, after it had published material that allegedly defamed the Army. They and their fellows then demanded that such behaviour be made an offence subject to military law (and also that spending on the military be increased).

That their case should have received the tacit backing of the King was no great surprise. More alarming was the fact that virtually the entire political elite should cave in. Even Canalejas (pp20–1) did not openly oppose the Jurisdictions Act of 1906, which allowed the Army to silence press criticism and to crush opposition to the Moroccan war – so much for the civilian primacy supposedly re-established by the Restoration settlement (p10).

It is thus not surprising that military elements were to play an important part in the dramatic events of 1917–18. Middle-ranking officers of the home-based Army, already disgruntled at the quicker promotion of colleagues serving in Morocco, were among those badly hit by rapidly rising prices during the years of the First World War (p28). In the summer of 1917 some of them set up local Defence Committees (*Juntas de Defensa*). Their demands were essentially selfish and parochial. Nonetheless, couched in the language of 'regeneration' (p18), with talk of army 'reform' and 'modernisation', they struck a chord with the public and turned the Committees' supporters (*junteros*) into standard-bearers of its discontent.

While the government was struggling to deal with what had become a tricky problem, it stirred up another. In trying to assuage popular resentment by a tax on war profits, it provoked the ire of those who had made them, prominent among whom were a number of Catalan industrialists. Francesc Cambó, effective leader of the Regionalist League (p22), decided that the time had come for Catalonia to take the lead in changing Spain as a whole.

He called an unofficial 'National Assembly' to draw up a new constitution, which he hoped to impose on the Madrid politicians. Surprisingly, the pro-Assembly movement (*movimiento asambleísta*) was backed by both wings of the workers' movement (pp25,26). The Committees' supporters kept their distance, however, unwilling to cooperate with Catalan regionalists. Cambó's plan thus rested on an uneasy alliance between the conservative League and the revolutionary Left.

On 19 July the Assembly attempted to meet in Barcelona, only to be broken up by the police. That did not prevent it from drawing up proposals for extensive reforms over the following months. In the interim, though, Cambó appears to have been unnerved by attacks on employers' property during a general strike called by the workers' organisations (p28). When the government predictably rejected the Assembly's proposals, he caved in at once.

Abandoning his allies and their demands for far-reaching democratic reform, Cambó agreed to join a makeshift coalition with second-rank figures from the Liberals and Conservatives. The new government only lasted into the early months of 1918, its collapse provoking the King to threaten abdication. This prospect forced the dynastic parties to close ranks. Even Antonio Maura (p19) was called in from the cold, as the only politician the Defence Committees trusted, to head an administration incorporating all Spain's leading political figures.

For a time, this 'National Government' looked like a real vehicle for 'regenerationist' ideas (p18). Its driving force was Cambó, who, as Minister for Development (*Fomento*), applied the economic policies pioneered by his party in regional government, with considerable success. However, just as his colleagues had done in Catalonia (p22), he ignored social problems, with fatal results. In October the coalition's Liberal members, always suspicious of regionalism, used that omission as the excuse to withdraw support for Cambó's policies. Shortly afterwards, their intrigues forced Maura to resign and the National Government was dead. With it died the last chance of 'regeneration' from within the political establishment.

Maura himself, although still nominally a Conservative, used his formidable appeal to build up a personal following, chiefly among the better-off young. This Maurist movement (*maurismo*) was the first mass organisation of the Spanish right. Yet its leader refused either to turn it into a political party, or to use it as a base to seize power as Costa's 'iron surgeon' (p18), and so it remained impotent.

It is true that Eduardo Dato, Maura's successor as Conservative leader, brought in Spain's first industrial relations and social security legislation. But in 1921 he, like Cánovas (p10) and Canalejas before him, fell victim to an anarchist assassin. Admittedly, too, some Liberal leaders of the early 1920s were influenced by the ideas of the Reformist Republicans (p19). However, by now the alternation mechanism that had allowed a degree of political stability (p10), shaky ever since Maura's challenge to it in 1909, had completely collapsed.

Governments lasted only months so that none was in a position to take effective action, far less implement a coherent reform programme. Moreover, in their weakness they repeatedly ignored Parliament and passed legislation by decree; censorship was also widespread. The democratic facade of the Restoration settlement (p10) was ripped away to reveal the authoritarian reality beneath.

Meanwhile, the end of the First World War brought Spain's uneven wartime boom to a juddering halt. Mismanaged by both government and industrialists, neither of whom had paid any heed to much-needed investment, the economy was in a worse state than ever. Unable to compete despite high tariffs, many firms were forced to close, making thousands of workers redundant. The Asturian coal mines and the shipbuilding industry both suffered greatly.

Once again, however, it was in Barcelona that the resultant desperation took the most extreme form. In 1919 workers at the *La Canadiense* electricity company went on strike over wages. The dispute was actually soon settled by government arbitration but, when the Army refused to release a number of arrested strikers, the anarcho-syndicalists of **CNT** called a general strike. It was broken only after further massive arrests and the declaration of a state of war.

With industrial action now illegal, anarchism's terrorist wing (p26) stepped up the attacks it had already begun on the Catalan business community. No longer

Confederación Nacional del Trabajo (CNT)

National Labour Confederation

Founded in 1911 as the umbrella organisation of Spanish *anarco-sindicalismo* (p26), the CNT effectively operated as the political representative of Spanish **anarchism** in general. Its history was a series of dramatic fluctuations, influxes of support and outbursts of activity alternating with savage repression and declining membership. The CNT reached its greatest strength around 1919, but thereafter suffered defeat in its 'social war' with Catalan employers (p36) and persecution under Primo's dictatorship (p39). During the Second Republic and the Civil War it again achieved mass support, but its loose structure was incapable of surviving more severe repression under the Franco regime, and only fragments survived into the post-1975 democratic era.

See also: **Frente Popular** (p59); **Partido Comunista de España** (p70)

represented by Cambó in government, the industrialists lost faith in the central authorities to protect their lives and property against terrorism. Taking matters into their own hands they set up so-called 'Free Trade Unions' – a cover for hired gunmen – and a private, paramilitary police force, the *Somatén*. For the next four years these waged a vicious 'social war' against the anarchist gunmen.

Its result was never really in doubt. Apart from their inferior resources, the anarchists were handicapped by internal divisions. The CNT leadership had been drawn reluctantly into the 1919 strike and thereafter its supporters were in constant, and sometimes violent, dispute with the terrorists. Moreover, their 1917 rapprochement with the Socialists (p28) had soon collapsed; with relations back to their antagonistic norm, the anarchists got no help from that quarter. Above all, they were faced by an implacable and brutal opponent in General Severiano Martínez Anido, the local army commander, who ignored instructions from Madrid to tread warily and cracked down ruthlessly on terrorists and strikers alike.

By 1923 the anarchists had patently lost. But by then, too, the victorious Catalan elite had other worries. The industrialists' political influence had been undermined by the events of 1918 and, four years later, the Madrid government tried to reduce the protectionist tariffs they regarded as vital (p12). At the same time, Cambó's betrayal of the Assembly movement had been the last straw for many supporters of the Regionalist League (p22), who now deserted it in droves to set up organisations of their own. The largest of these was 'Catalan Action', which demanded a Catalan republic in a loosely federal Spain. Its leader, Francesc Macià, soon became Catalonia's most popular politician, his support outstripping that of the League.

It thus became clear that, however much the Catalan magnates were disillusioned with the existing system, they could expect little to come from its democratic reform either. Their disillusion was shared by some 'regenerationist' intellectuals, notably Maeztu (p18), who had come to see Spain's salvation in the rediscovery of its supposed 'real essence': Castilian, Catholic, and Conservative. He and others linked this reactionary, authoritarian nationalism to Costa's concept of an 'iron surgeon' (p19); some began to look towards soldiers like Martínez Anido to fill the role.

Meanwhile, in July 1921, the Army's prestige had been badly hit by its humiliating defeat at Annual in Morocco (p39). In summer 1923, the parliamentary committee set up to investigate the causes of this disaster completed its report. The findings were to become public once Parliament reconvened in the autumn. Many had good reason to fear them: politicians, who had ignored warnings of inadequate equipment and low morale; the King, who had allegedly encouraged the ill-fated operation; above all, the Army itself, of whose incompetence and even corruption rumours abounded but whose leaders liked to portray themselves as the helpless victims of political inaction. Appropriately enough, given Spanish liberalism's links with the military, it was one of their number who now, at last, put the venerable movement out of its misery.

The 'iron surgeon'

The soldier who took matters into his own hands by staging a military coup on 13 September 1923 was General Miguel Primo de Rivera. He was to be the country's effective ruler for the next seven years, during which time democratic freedoms were suspended. Primo's self-appointed task was that of Costa's 'iron surgeon', administering drastic, emergency treatment to save his country. For a while, at least, he enjoyed some success in it.

Figure 3.1 General Primo de Rivera (left) with Alfonso XIII (right) and members of his first, military government. © Topical Press Agency/Getty Images.

Primo's revolt, which took the classic Spanish form of a declaration (p5), received no direct backing but it met with no real resistance either. Two factors were crucial to its success. One was the Army's anxiety about the forthcoming results of investigations into the Moroccan War (p37). In time-honoured fashion, it staged its own 'negative declaration' and stood aside. That left matters in the hands of the King.

Alfonso XIII himself also had cause to fear the forthcoming revelations. Additionally, he may have seen a monarchical dictatorship as the means finally to apply 'regenerationist' ideas (p18). Whatever the reason, he ignored the lesson drummed into his father by Cánovas (p10) and exercised his prerogative under the Restoration Constitution of 1876 to appoint Primo his Prime Minister.

Spain's new ruler was a man of simple but rather confused beliefs. The strongest was his sense of Spanish nationalism; the 'fatherland' (*patria*) outranked even the traditional institutions of Church and Crown in his scale of loyalties. His modernising tendencies were apparent in his regard for Mussolini. Yet Primo's basically conservative interpretation of his role as 'surgeon' was equally evident in the way he fostered Church influence and in his admiration for Maura, whose concept of 'revolution from above' (p20) he espoused.

Impulsive, with a strong sense of fairness that bordered on sentimentality, Primo approached his task in a highly personalised manner. He issued constant explanations of his actions and motives, and travelled feverishly round the country to address his people. Such direct contact with public opinion, he felt, allowed him to 'rectify' policies based on his own 'intuition' in the light of popular response. For politicians he had only contempt, sharing the increasingly prevalent Army view that they – along with 'separatism' and 'communism' – were the root of Spain's ills, which it was soldiers' mission to cure.

Against that background it is understandable that Primo's regime, at least initially, took the form of an outright military dictatorship, with the government formed by a 'Military Directorate'. Even at provincial and municipal level, civilian authorities were replaced by Army officers. The 1876 Constitution was suspended, a state of siege declared and the press subjected to censorship. Although political parties were not formally banned, all senior civil servants and politicians who had previously held office were debarred, not just from administrative posts but also from directorships in firms awarded government contracts – a key source of business for many large companies.

The most serious problem facing the Directorate was the situation in **Morocco**. Here Primo showed his pragmatic streak. He did not belong to the tightly knit group of officers involved in the fighting there and passionately committed to Spain's role in Africa (*africanistas*). Believing the Spanish positions to be militarily indefensible, he ordered a withdrawal to the coast. However, in 1925 the threat to its own Moroccan interests led France to join in operations against the local tribes. That gave Primo the chance to 'rectify' his policy. He grasped it through a dramatic amphibious operation at the Bay of Alhucemas that opened the way to complete victory.

With his internal enemies, Primo dealt more swiftly. The radical wing of Catalan regionalism (p36), which offered token resistance to his takeover, was crushed with ease. Deeply suspicious of anything that might threaten Spain's unity, Primo did not stop there, however. He banned all political expressions of regionalist feeling in both Catalonia and the Basque Country, and abolished the Catalan regional government established in 1913 (p22).

The anarcho-syndicalist CNT (p36) represented a more formidable foe. But General Martínez Anido, who had been appointed Interior Minister, was given a free hand to extend the repressive policies he had used to win the 'social war' on Barcelona's streets (p36), and during 1924 the CNT's remnants were driven underground. The country was more orderly than it had been for years, if not decades.

The coup had caught the other wing of the workers' movement at a low ebb. The Socialists' return to moderation after 1917 had brought no obvious benefits; indeed, after ending their loose Republican alliance (p27) two years later, they lost even the parliamentary seat that had brought them. Then, in 1921, the creation of a Spanish Communist Party (p70) cost them a number of leading figures (although few supporters as yet). Moreover, to Socialists Primo was no worse than the middle-class politicians he had ousted and they offered no opposition to his takeover. Indeed, when the General showed himself willing, and able, to push

Marruecos

Morocco

Previously confined to the garrison towns of Ceuta and Melilla, Spanish involvement in Morocco as a whole began in 1904, due to pressure to protect mining interests and the desire to prevent French control over the southern shore of the Straits of Gibraltar. Under the Franco–Moroccan Treaty of 1912 Spain was allocated a 'zone' in northern Morocco as a Protectorate, but her hold on the inhospitable terrain was constantly threatened by the resistance of local tribes. In 1921, under the leadership of Abd el Krim, these inflicted a serious defeat on the colonial forces at Annual. By 1927, however, the Protectorate had been fully recovered, and it remained in Spanish hands until 1956 (p90). During this time, the Morocco-based 'Army of Africa' was a breeding ground for extreme reactionary ideas and its officers were among the main instigators of the 1936 revolt against the Second Republic (p67), General Franco being among its most celebrated figures. Spain's involvement in the Maghreb region finally came to an end in 1975, when the strategically less valuable colony of Spanish Sahara further to the south was abandoned.

through reforms, they came to see him as a means of speeding capitalist development, and so the approach of their own revolution (p25).

This view was especially strong in the Socialist trade union federation, the **UGT**, which enthusiastically backed reforms designed to improve working-class conditions, in particular subsidised housing and medical assistance. However, it was Primo's measures to reduce the level of industrial conflict that induced the UGT to cooperate actively with him. It not only agreed to take part in compulsory arbitration to settle labour disputes, but even became a sort of government agency

Unión General de Trabajadores (UGT)

General Workers' Union

The UGT was founded in 1888 as a federation of Socialist trade unions. Unlike the anarcho-syndicalist **CNT** (p36), it long saw its role as the improvement of workers' material conditions through strictly industrial activity, an attitude reflected in its cooperation with the Primo dictatorship. Under the Second Republic, when it acquired considerable influence (p57), the UGT took an increasingly militant political line that culminated in its participation in the uprising of 1934 (p58) and its revolutionary attitudes during the Civil War. Banned by Franco, the UGT briefly regained an important – and moderating – role in the transition that followed his death (p119). Ironically, after its sister **Socialist Party** came to power in 1982 its stance again turned more radical (pp138–9), but – like that of unions in general – its influence is now much reduced.

responsible for operating the statutory code of practice introduced in 1926. Under it, arbitration powers were exercised by joint boards with equal employer and employee representation (*comités paritarios*). The latter was provided by UGT officials, while the union's leader, Francisco Largo Caballero, became a sort of *de facto* labour minister.

The UGT's collaborationist line brought the union considerable dividends, allowing it to consolidate its industrial membership and establish a significant presence in the rural south. Admittedly, the policy also provoked tensions within the Socialist movement as a whole, as well as deepening the rifts with the fledgling Communists and the anarcho-syndicalists. However, the CNT was itself rent by feuds between moderates and extremists, who in 1927 set up the 'Iberian Anarchist Federation' (FAI) as a pure revolutionary organisation, unconcerned with trade union activity. On balance, then, one ironic result of Primo's regime was to strengthen the Socialists' position, both within the working class movement and in the country as a whole.

The measures that the UGT helped to implement enjoyed considerable success, reducing sharply the days lost to industrial conflict. They reflected the dictator's sense of social justice, also apparent in his plans for a single income tax that would hit earnings from capital as well as wages; that proposal, however, met with strong opposition from the banks and had to be abandoned. The other factor behind Primo's economic policy was his nationalism, which led him to see issues essentially in terms of national prestige. Thus his reintroduction of tariffs at a higher level than ever before reflected his view of imports as a slight on Spain's own economic capabilities, to improve which he instigated the country's first large-scale programme of state intervention.

The government's development projects took various forms. The most visible was a massive programme of infrastructure, especially roads, dams and irrigation schemes; electricity was brought to many rural areas for the first time. A number of state-run monopolies were established, sometimes in association with private interests, including the CAMPSA oil and petrol company, the national telephone company (*Telefónica*) and the powerful Water Boards (*Confederaciones Hidráulicas*), as well as a plethora of regulatory bodies to advise on, promote and control activity in a wide range of industries. Finally, to assist in financing development, Primo founded various semi-public banks, covering fields such as overseas trade, house-building and new industries.

Between 1923 and 1928 the Spanish economy showed distinct signs of improvement. Admittedly, that was partly thanks to the favourable international climate. Yet, even so, Primo's measures, social as well as economic, deserve credit for the upswing. Equally, when it was rudely reversed in 1928/29, some of the blame could be ascribed to the first effects of the coming world-wide depression. But the sudden and extreme nature of the downturn in Spain was to a large extent caused by grave flaws inherent in those same measures.

The collapse of dictatorship – and monarchy

The fact is that Primo's entire 'revolution from above' contained the seeds of its own failure. In trying to tackle the grievances of so many different groups simultaneously, he finished up by satisfying none and arousing the animosity of most. Since his attempts at political reform were an unmitigated failure, he never gave his regime a solid basis. When the heat was turned up it simply melted away – and the King with it.

Among the first to be alienated by Primo were those intellectuals who had seen in him the realisation of their ideas. One reason for this was the continuing press censorship, another Primo's tendency to intervene 'intuitively' in individual court cases, using his effectively absolute powers to right specific wrongs without thought for the wider consequences. Especially in a country with such a strong legalistic tradition, this approach soon turned admiration to scorn among the intelligentsia and large sections of the educated classes in general.

Their indignation was heightened by Primo's effective banishment of Miguel Unamuno (p18), for protesting against one of his arbitrary interventions. Students, too, were outraged by this treatment of a highly respected professor. They were already protesting against Primo's proposals to extend Church influence into the higher education sphere, by giving state recognition to the degrees awarded by private, Catholic universities. After Unamuno's exile their demonstrations became a permanent feature of Madrid life, a minor but persistent irritant to the regime.

Another group whose support Primo soon lost was the Catalan business community. Its gratitude at his restoration of law and order turned to anger when he banned the use of Catalan in Church and, especially, at the suppression of devolution (p22). That step was doubly damaging to the industrialists, since it completed the swing of Catalan opinion behind demands for more far-reaching self-government (p36). Along with consolidating Socialism (p40), the other main political effect of the dictatorship was thus to seal the conversion of Catalan regionalism from a conservative, monarchist force into a radical, republican one.

Catalonia was a much more serious enemy than the intellectuals or the old politicians who had never accepted Primo – even Maura, his acknowledged inspiration, refused to back him. Nevertheless, it was not strong enough alone to shake the dictator's hold on power. What did eventually have that effect was Primo's scatter-gun approach to reform, which meant that every section of society which had initially backed him was sooner or later offended by one of his measures. For example, while devout Catholics welcomed his concessions to the Church, they deplored his cooperation with 'godless' socialists.

In the Basque Country, that worked to the benefit of regionalists; elsewhere it merged with a broader conservative reaction against his regime. Thus employers were never reconciled to Primo's labour legislation (pp39–40). Those who failed to profit from the creation of state monopolies were antagonised further, as was much of the financial world. Landowners, the very bastion of conservative opinion, were outraged by Primo's attempt to introduce the mildest of land reforms (p53). Both these groups, who tended to share Primo's brand of Spanish nationalism, were disappointed by his inability to achieve either of his foreign-policy aims: the incorporation of Tangiers into Spanish Morocco (p39) and the granting of a seat on the League of Nations' Security Council.

The resultant spreading disillusion formed the background to Primo's attempts at political reform, which began in 1924 with the establishment of the Patriotic Union (UP). Partly modelled on Mussolini's Fascist Party, the UP promoted a cult of the leader. It rejected representative democracy in favour of a direct relationship between the leader and the people, for instance through the rigged referendums which were a feature of the regime. Yet Primo never intended the UP to be a genuine party, never mind a fascist one. Instead he conceived it as a 'Citizens' League', a social organisation that would allow him to tap into opinion but have no political role.

At heart Primo was a traditionalist, out of tune with fascism's modernising tendencies, and the UP's philosophy was influenced chiefly by Spanish conservatism. Only among Carlists (p2), and the personal following built up by Maura (p35), did it find a faint echo. Instead, the bulk of UP's small membership was made up of those who benefited directly from the regime, such as journalists, hangers-on and public servants – many of whom, especially at local level, had been in post before 1923. Their vested interests put paid to the 1925 Municipal Statute which had been intended to clean up local government along the lines originally proposed by Maura (p20). More generally, too, the UP acted not as an instrument of change but as a brake on it.

The year 1925 did bring some change with the establishment of a new government in the form of a Civilian Directorate (*Directorio Civil*). Its members were appointed by Primo, largely from the ranks of UP. They were professional experts (*tecnócratas*), chiefly lawyers and economists, usually civil servants; their star was the young Finance Minister, José Calvo Sotelo. These new arrangements were prompted by necessity – military government having become impractical – and were intended to be temporary, pending completion of what was now Primo's main project: a new constitution.

The task of drafting the new text was given to an Advisory National Assembly (*Asamblea Nacional Consultiva*) which differed substantially from earlier constituent bodies. Whereas these had been elected, albeit usually under less than free conditions, the members of Primo's Assembly were appointed by him. Moreover, its powers were limited to producing proposals for the dictator's consideration, which it did in 1928. Unsurprisingly, they pandered to his views, in particular granting the prime minister extensive new powers, including the right to nominate half the members of Parliament.

At a time when the regime's popularity was waning fast, the Assembly's proposals were met by a barrage of criticism. Primo showed his political naivety, first by proposing another of his discredited referendums, then by appointing a number of his critics to the Assembly. Naturally enough, they used their new position mainly to restate their objections, reinforcing Primo's distrust of anything that smacked of politics. His enthusiasm for a constitution rapidly faded, and the question of how Spain should be governed was left in mid-air.

In this situation of political vacuum the weaknesses in Primo's expansionist economic policies came home to roost. The original intention had been to finance them by extending the scope of income tax. When that idea was blocked by the banks (p40), Primo resorted to increased public borrowing, concealing the additional interest payments in a separate 'Extraordinary Budget'. In effect, he gambled on an economic take-off generating more revenue from existing taxes. When Spain became a victim of world depression – because of its commercial links with Latin America, one of the first areas affected – Primo lost his bet.

At home recession, combined with the inflation inevitably caused by so much public spending, had disastrous effects, especially for low earners. Abroad, the peseta came under intense pressure. For Primo the currency's value was above all a matter of national pride, and he instructed Calvo Sotelo to defend it at what was now a totally unrealistic level. That strategy merely aggravated speculation and made eventual devaluation all the more drastic, forcing the resignation of Primo's most able lieutenant.

Politically, the recession had even graver repercussions for Primo. His Socialist allies (pp39–40) grew restive at the plight of their own supporters. Devaluation was a further blow to his prestige among the nationalist Right that his own rhetoric had helped to create. Indeed, it was a Conservative politician, Sánchez Guerra, who first tried to channel dissent, in January 1929. Although his amateurish conspiracy was easily put down, it had an important knock-on effect. Coming on top of the proposal by the Assembly to cut his powers, its Republican overtones convinced the King that Primo had become the biggest danger to his throne. Alfonso, too, now started to distance himself from his Prime Minister.

The last nail in the dictator's coffin was the loss of Army backing. Again it was induced by reforms that, in themselves, were perfectly sensible. To improve military efficiency, Primo had insisted that promotion to the rank of general should be based not on seniority but on merit, an attack on military tradition that was bound to ruffle important feathers. On the other hand, his abolition of the Artillery Corps' special privileges was not unpopular in the rest of the Army. But any sympathy evaporated when he reacted to opposition from within the Corps by dissolving it altogether.

Primo's response to the rising tide of discontent was typically impulsive. In January 1930 he spontaneously sought the views of the various Army regional commanders (*Capitanes Generales*). When they evinced a clear lack of enthusiasm for his continuation, he resigned and left the country; he died a few months later. His departure did not immediately threaten the monarchy. Although the King was tainted by his part in Primo's ascent to power (p38), and by having willingly played the dictatorship's figurehead, the continuing use of repression meant that resentment against him was so far unfocused and disorganised. But Alfonso soon contrived to change that.

Ignoring popular and even Army opinion, the King appointed another soldier to replace Primo. His choice, the aged and infirm General Berenguer, proved hopelessly indecisive, first promising to hold a general election, then failing to call it for over a year. While he maintained Primo's legal restrictions on political activity, little or no attempt was made to impose them in practice. His so-called soft dictatorship (*dictablanda*) was to provide perfect conditions for opposition to flourish.

It was channelled mainly by the Republican movement (p8), which had been revived by a new generation of leaders. During 1930 they conducted a campaign that destroyed the King's remaining prestige, at least among the educated classes. In August, they signed a secret agreement with other opposition groups. This **San Sebastian Pact** had some backing from the Army, which blamed Alfonso for failing to save the Artillery Corps. A military declaration was planned for 15 December, but Colonel Galán, its commander in the Aragonese garrison-town of Jaca, jumped the gun and the conspiracy was revealed. The setback proved temporary. Galán's execution gave Republicanism a martyr and the trial of the Pact's leaders was a farce, ending in their virtual absolution. Coming from a military court, the verdict indicated how little control the royal authorities now exercised over events.

> ### Pacto de San Sebastián
> ....
> San Sebastian Pact
>
> The Pact agreed in August 1930 in the Basque resort was a secret agreement to overthrow the monarchy. It was joined by various groups which later became known as the **Left Republicans** (p50); the **Radical Republicans** (p27); the radical Catalan regionalist *Estat Català* set up by Francesc Macià (p36); and by several prominent defectors from the old 'dynastic parties' (p10), including Miguel Maura, son of Antonio (p19), and the ex-Liberal Niceto Alcalá Zamora.

As their last throw they finally called municipal elections, for 12 April 1931. While supporters of the monarchy won most votes, these were concentrated on the land where clientilism still reigned supreme (p11). The provincial capitals, where elections had some meaning, voted massively for Republican candidates. The more responsible of the remaining monarchist politicians realised that the game was up. One of them, Count Romanones, took it upon himself to act as intermediary between the King and the opposition leaders. As a result of the contacts, Alfonso left Spain on 14 April.

Summary of main points

End of liberal Spain

- During 1917 a broad front in favour of change was created under Cambó's leadership. After abandoning it, he became a key figure in a National Government under Maura, the collapse of which marked the effective end of attempts at reform from within the Restoration system.
- From 1919, economic downturn led to renewed hardship for workers. In Barcelona it gave rise to a 'social war' between anarchists and the Army, which had long since shown itself to be outside civilian control.
- Meanwhile, the Catalan industrialists and others were turning increasingly to the idea of an authoritarian solution to Spain's problems.

The 'iron surgeon'

- In 1923 General Primo de Rivera took power in a military coup pledging to restore order and modernise the country; however, his notion of 'modernisation' was confused, simplistic and authoritarian.
- As well as crushing his opponents, who were in any case initially few and weak, he introduced significant social security and employment regulation measures that won him the support of the Socialist trade union, the UGT.
- Along with the improvement in industrial relations, Primo's policy of spending heavily on infrastructure projects contributed to strong, if short-lived, economic growth.

The collapse of dictatorship – and monarchy

- Primo's 'revolution from above' contained the seeds of its own failure. Economically, excessive spending contributed to a sharp economic collapse after 1928; politically, Primo was unable to create any alternative to the discredited structures of the Restoration system.
- Meanwhile, his haphazard approach to reform alienated a succession of groups and institutions that had initially backed him, including intellectuals, moderate Catalan regionalists, industrialists, the King and, most importantly, the Army itself.
- His abrupt departure left a political vacuum that was effectively filled by the resurgent Republican movement.

Exhibit 3.1: Primo de Rivera's manifesto (1923)

Opening of Primo's 'declaration' on the morning of his coup

AL PAÍS Y AL EJÉRCITO ESPAÑOLES

Ha llegado para nosotros el momento más temido que esperado (porque hubiéramos querido vivir siempre en la legalidad y que ella rigiera sin interrupción la vida española) de recoger las ansias, de atender el clamoroso requerimiento de cuantos amando la Patria no ven para ella otra salvación que libertarla de los profesionales de la política, de los hombres que por una u otra razón nos ofrecen el cuadro de desdichas e inmoralidades que empezaron el año 98 y amenazan a España con un próximo fin trágico y deshonroso. La tupida red de la política de concupiscencias ha cogido en sus mallas, secuestrándola, hasta la voluntad real. Con frecuencia parecen pedir que gobiernen los que ellos dicen no dejan gobernar, aludiendo a los que han sido su único, aunque débil freno, y llevaron a las leyes y costumbres la poca ética sana, el tenue tinte de moral y equidad que aún tienen; pero en la realidad se avienen fáciles y contentos al turno y al reparto y entre ellos mismos designan la sucesión.

Pues bien, ahora vamos a recabar todas las responsabilidades y a gobernar nosotros u hombres civiles que representan nuestra moral y doctrina. Basta ya de rebeldías mansas, que sin poner remedio a nada, dañan tanto y más a la disciplina que está recia y viril a que nos lanzamos por España y por el Rey.

Este movimiento es de hombres: el que no sienta la masculinidad completamente caracterizada, que espere en un rincón, sin perturbar los días buenos que para la patria preparamos. Españoles: ¡Viva España y viva el Rey! [...]

TO THE SPANISH PEOPLE AND ARMY

For us has arrived the moment we have not so much awaited as dreaded – for we would have wished always to abide by the law, and for its rule over Spaniards' lives to have remained unbroken. It is the moment to take up the concerns, to obey the clamorous desire, of those Spanish patriots who see no other salvation for their fatherland than to free it from the professional politicians, from those men that, for one reason or another, have been responsible for the sorry tale of misfortune and immorality which began in 1898 and which threatens Spain with an imminent end, as tragic as it would be dishonourable. Even the King's will has been ensnared and trapped in the web woven by these lustful politicians. Often they appear to wish that government be taken over by those they accuse of making it impossible – meaning those who have been the only restraint, albeit a weak one, on their activities, and who have lent to the law and political practice that small element of ethical health, that vague tinge of morality and equity which they still retain. But in reality the politicians are only too happy to succeed each other in rotation, carving up power and deciding the succession amongst themselves.

Very well, now we are going to assume the full responsibility of government ourselves, or civilians who share our morality and our ideas. There will be no more half-hearted rebellions that solve nothing, while doing so much damage to the robust and manly discipline which urges us to rise now for Spain and for the King.

Ours is a masculine movement. Let him who does not feel himself the complete embodiment of manhood stand aside and do nothing to cloud the bright future we are building for our fatherland. Spaniards: long live Spain and long live the King! [...]

Source: La Vanguardia (Barcelona), 13 September 1923.

Exhibit 3.2: Cambó on the roots of dictatorship (1929)

Excerpt from a book written by the political leader of the Catalan bourgeoisie (text in Catalan)

La dictadura espanyola nasqué a Barcelona, la creà l'ambient de Barcelona, on la demagògia sindicalista tenia una intensitat i una cronicitat intolerables. I, davant la demagògia sindicalista, fallaren tots els recursos normals del poder, totes les defenses normals de la societat. Al executiu, davant dels atemptats sindicalistes, no s'acudí altra cosa que organitzar atemptats antisindicalistes; els tribunals de justícia i els jurats, dominats pel terror, consagraren la impunitat de l'assassinat social; la burgesia barcelonina, ni resistí les exigències, el triomf de les quals fou base de la puixança dels sindicats (els negocis anaven molt bé i no es volia una vaga!), ni contrabalançà la coacció que les masses sindicalistes feien als jurats; el govern, no s'atreví ni a suspendre el jurat, ni a modificar la llei d'ordre públic; preferia consentir el terror blanc dels seus representants a Barcelona. El decret del darrer gabinet liberal suprimint el règim de quinzenes governatives, sense la compensació d'una llei d'ordre, augmentà el terror en que vivia el poble de Barcelona.

L'actitud de Barcelona fou evidentement expressió d'un cos d'abúlia, de covardia. Però que no oblidin mai els demagogs, els homes que volen subvertir de sobte i per la violència el règim existent, que una societat els ideals on interessos de la qual són greument en perill per l'escomesa demagògica, es resignarà a tot, per tal de sentir-se emparada. [...]

L'instint de vida i defensa prendrà lloc, i la societat sotraguejada cridarà un dictador i el cridarà sense condicions; no li demanarà que serveixi el seu ideal, ni tan sols que el respecti; li demanar, únicament, que mantingui l'ordre, que li asseguri l'estat possessori ... [...]

I, oh fet extraordinari! Els qui sota un règim de lliberat preparaven amb fúria de posseïts, la més radical i catastròfica de les revolucions polítiques o socials, sota una dictadura militar o burgesa callen i es sotmeten, com si llurs ideals haguessin assolit el triomf! Esperen que a l'horitzó pugin les primeres lluïsors de la llibertat, per a sentir-se de nou demagogs i revolucionaris.

Spain's dictatorship was born in Barcelona, created by the atmosphere of a city where anarcho-syndicalist demagoguery was so intense and so long-lasting as to be intolerable. Against it, all the normal resources of power, all society's normal defences, were helpless. Faced with syndicalist shootings, the only thing the authorities could think of was to shoot syndicalists. The courts and juries, cowed by terror, confirmed the terrorists' impunity. The city's middle classes neither resisted syndicalist demands, the success of which gave the unions their strength (business was going well and no one wanted a strike!), nor did anything to counteract the pressure placed on juries by the syndicalist masses. The government lacked the courage to suspend the jury system or to amend the public order legislation, preferring to connive at the counter-terror measures of its representatives in Barcelona. When the last Liberal government issued its decree suspending the practice of two-week detention without trial, while doing nothing to reform the public order laws, it further increased the state of terror in which the people of Barcelona were living.

Barcelona's attitude was clearly the expression of a loss of will, of cowardice. But the demagogues, those men who seek to subvert, suddenly and violently, the existing order, they never forget that a society whose values or interests are under grave threat from their attacks will put up with anything in order to feel protected. [...]

The survival instinct will take over and the sorely battered society will call a dictator to power without placing any conditions on him. It will not require him to share its values nor even to show respect for them. It will require him solely to maintain order and to assure the status of property. [...]

Yet it is an extraordinary fact that that those who under a regime of liberty work like men possessed to bring about the most radical, the most disastrous of political and social revolutions turn silent and submissive under a dictatorship, whether of the military or the middle classes, as if their values had triumphed. Only with the first signs of returning freedom do they again become the demagogues and revolutionaries of old.

Topics for discussion

- What insights does Exhibit 3.1 give into Primo's worldview?
- How does Primo appear to see the role of the Army in Spain's public life? How does his view compare to that of O'Donnell (Exhibit 1.1)?
- Who does Cambó blame for the dictatorship (Exhibit 3.2)? How does his analysis reflect his own interests and political stance?
- How would you assess the legacy of almost ninety years of liberal rule in Spain?
- Could Primo have succeeded? If so, what would his success have looked like?

CHAPTER 4

A troubled democracy (1931–1936)

The 1930s were the decade of depression in Europe. Millions were plunged into poverty, which the political and economic structures of liberal democracy seemed powerless to relieve. Many looked to the authoritarian regimes which were apparently enjoying greater success in the Soviet Union and fascist Italy. In their different ways, communism and fascism were both international movements and both strove to undermine other, democratic regimes by propaganda and by the street violence of their paramilitary gangs. Germany was especially affected. In 1933, its conservatives attempted to forestall the threat from the Left by taking German fascism into government. Hitler and his Nazis exploited this foothold to establish their own dictatorship, eliminating democratic institutions and cracking down ruthlessly on political opponents. Their rise confirmed the Left's suspicions not just of fascism but of the traditional Right, particularly given that conservatives close to the Catholic Church had imposed their own brand of authoritarian regime in Austria. By 1936 Soviet leader Stalin was sufficiently worried to instruct communists worldwide to change tack and co-operate with socialists and middle-class liberals in an all-out bid to halt fascism.

Even before Alfonso XIII left the country, Spain's Second Republic had been declared by popular acclaim. The country's first attempt at genuine democracy was born in very difficult circumstances, in the midst of world depression and with democracy under growing pressure throughout Europe. Insofar as it shielded Spain from the worst effects of depression, economic backwardness was now, ironically, an asset. But it could not prevent the political tension round about from seeping into Spanish affairs, especially when it resonated so strongly with internal events. For, after a period when its fate lay in the hands of its truest supporters, the Republic's politics were dominated increasingly by two aggressive and antagonistic forces whose commitment to its democratic principles was questionable at best: a resurgent Right and a newly reunited Left.

The reforming years

In the confusion following the King's departure (p44), a Provisional Government was formed. It was composed mainly of the Republicans who had plotted the monarchy's fall, a heterogeneous group who now became the decisive factor in determining the character of the new Republic. They were also the main driving force behind the many and wide-ranging changes of the 'two reforming years' (*bienio de reformas*) that followed.

The Provisional Government's composition was a coalition of the parties that had signed the Pact agreed at San Sebastian in 1930 (p44). Even the one, crucial addition – the Socialist PSOE (p25) – had been represented there by two of its leading figures. All the parties involved in the Pact itself were relatively new, with the exception of the Radical Republicans (p27), now known merely as Radicals. Their leader, Alejandro Lerroux, had been an important secondary player in sham democratic politics before 1923 and it showed, in corruption and in opportunistic attempts to exploit changes in public mood (p54). So, while his party theoretically formed the centre of the Republican bloc, it differed fundamentally from both wings, each of which was genuinely concerned with meaningful reform.

The 'Republican Right' was a party formed by ex-members of the old 'dynastic parties' (p10) who had recently converted to Republicanism. Their main interest was political reform, and they had only limited support. The party's main value to its allies was to reassure the middle classes that the Republic would not damage their interests – hence the choice of its leader, Niceto Alcalá Zamora (p44), to head the new government.

The real core of Republicanism was therefore what, in ideological terms, constituted its left wing. The leader and archetype of these **Left Republicans** was Manuel Azaña. As much an intellectual as a politician, he had close links to the '1927 generation' – the new wave of literary and artistic talent whose leading figure was Federico García Lorca. For Azaña and his colleagues, cultural considerations were of prime importance. They believed strongly in the fundamental importance of education as the basis of social change and were almost fanatically opposed to the social influence of the Church, which they regarded as the main reason for Spain's intellectual and cultural stagnation.

The first task facing the Provisional Government was to draw up a constitution for the Republic. It was assigned to the constituent parliament (*Cortes constituyentes*) that emerged from the elections in June, in which the PSOE and the Radicals led the field and the government parties in conjunction won an overwhelming victory. As a result, most major issues were settled without great dispute.

Spain was formally declared a Republic and its citizens constitutionally assured of a long list of rights and freedoms. Sovereignty

---

Republicanos de izquierdas

Left Republicans

The Left Republicans were a loose grouping of several small parties during the Second Republic. They inherited the concern for practical reform of the **Reformist Republicans** (p19), from which most had emerged, but also the anticlericalism historically associated with **Republicans**. The group's main components were the Radical Socialists (*Partido Republicano Radical Socialista*) led by Marcelino Domingo, the Galician Republicans (ORGA) of Casares Quiroga, and Manuel Azaña's short-lived 'Republican Action', later replaced by the confusingly named 'Republican Left' (p58), also led by Azaña. See also: **Frente Popular** (p59) was placed in the hands of their representatives: a single-chamber parliament to be elected by universal adult suffrage, both male and female. This house would, in turn, elect the president, whose mainly ceremonial powers would include that of appointing a prime minister – now assumed, wrongly as it turned out (p55), to be a mere formality.

Where compromise proved impossible was over the religious issue, since the Left Republicans, the third largest grouping in Parliament, joined the Socialists in taking a hard anticlerical line. Consequently, Article 26 of the new Constitution not only decreed freedom of worship for all creeds, but also broke all links between Church and state, including government funding of clerical salaries (p4). The Catholic Church's position became that of a voluntary association, subject to the law and to taxation but also to certain special restrictions, including a ban on involvement in education.

Article 26 was to become the focus of widespread conservative opposition (pp53–4). For the moment, however, its main impact was within the government itself, whose more right-wing members, including Alcalá Zamora, resigned in protest at its provisions. Yet the differences were patched up and, once the Constitution had been approved in December, Alcalá Zamora was elected the Republic's first president. He was replaced as Prime Minister by Azaña, under whom the government set about implementing a series of ambitious reforms.

In some areas these built on measures introduced by Primo de Rivera, whose system of joint industrial relations boards (p40) was retained and extended, albeit under a new name (*jurados mixtos*). Similarly, the Socialist Prieto continued Primo's programme of infrastructure investment (p40), to good effect. He could do so thanks to an overhaul of public finances that massively increased government income by tightening up tax collection and administration – and incidentally showed how inefficient they had been previously. Taxes themselves remained very low, with the top rate on income under eight per cent. This approach had the benefit of avoiding offence to the better-off, but it also meant that the funds available for reform were severely restricted.

In other respects, such as social policy, the Republic made a sharp break with the past, notably in the legalisation of divorce. The most significant initiatives, though, came in the education field. A large-scale school-building programme was begun, aimed at bringing education to the masses for the first time. Teacher training was also greatly expanded. In line with Left Republican ideas, too, was the attempt to bring cultural experience to impoverished rural areas, through such initiatives as the establishment of libraries, and the provision of subsidies for Lorca's travelling theatre company, '*La Barraca*'.

Another innovation was the government's policy towards the regions, or more precisely Catalonia. There, the regionalist leader Macià (p36) had declared an independent republic on Alfonso's departure before being persuaded to back down by the Provisional Government. His payoff came in 1932, when a regional government (*Generalitat*) was established with much wider powers than its predecessor (p22). Regional autonomy was now underpinned by a Catalan parliament. At the first

Esquerra Republicana de Catalunya (ERC)

Catalan Republican Left

Formed in 1931, immediately before the declaration of the Second Republic, ERC was an alliance of left-leaning regionalist groupings. It was led by the charismatic Francesc Macià (p39) until his death in 1933, when he was replaced by Lluís Companys, the man largely responsible for ERC's creation. Despite its talk of independence, ERC was content to settle for the devolution granted by the Republic, under which it dominated Catalan politics and ran the regional government. It was suppressed by the Franco regime and, although it re-emerged thereafter, lost its leadership of the regionalist movement to the newly formed **CiU** (p145). From the 1990s it enjoyed something of a revival that culminated in 2003, when it became the key partner in a centre-left regional executive (p157). Despite subsequent turbulences (p177), it has retained that role up to now (autumn 2008).

See also: *Frente Popular* (p59)

election Macià's new party, **Catalan Republican Left**, won an easy victory. While this sealed Catalonia's support for the Republic, at the same time it awakened concerns among Spanish conservatives that their country was starting to break up.

Right-wing concern was also aroused by Azaña's military reforms. These were designed to create a modern Army, which inevitably meant reducing the excessive number of officers and making promotion more dependent on ability. They were also supposed to involve modernising outdated equipment, but in the absence of a true tax reform there was no money for that. Inevitably, this aggravated the dissatisfaction caused by the other changes, and by rumours that promotion was now dependent on pro-Republican views. In August 1932 a group of right-wing officers led by General Sanjurjo attempted a coup, but it was quickly suppressed by loyal troops.

The coup attempt came while the government was struggling to pass legislation not only on Catalan devolution but also on an even more controversial issue. Although the need for **land reform** was recognised in principle by all the government parties, its details were another matter. In the summer of 1932 discussions had reached deadlock, but the coup attempt gave them renewed impetus and measures were agreed soon after. Unfortunately they were badly flawed.

Part of the problem was that Socialist support had to be bought by allowing estates owned by the aristocracy to be expropriated. As a vindictive reaction against the coup's suspected supporters, the move set an unhappy precedent (pp55–6). It was also a meaningless gesture since, while estate owners were eligible for compensation, the government had no funds with which to pay them. In addition, the understandable emphasis on the plight of landless labourers in the south meant that the problems of northern smallholders were largely ignored. Most important of all, the extent of reform was modest in the extreme.

The land reform fiasco turned discontent on the left of the political spectrum into a major problem for the government. Throughout 1932 it repeatedly had to dispatch the security forces to deal with those who attempted, in a long-standing anarchist tradition, to take land redistribution into their own hands (pp26–7). The clashes reached a tragic climax in January 1933 at the Andalusian hamlet of Casas Viejas, when 25 villagers were shot dead after they had killed several Civil Guards.

Azaña's coalition was fatally weakened, and the Socialists increasingly distanced themselves from it under pressure from their left (p57). With utter hypocrisy, the Right – which previously had criticised it for being too mild in dealing with such outbreaks – also used the incident to berate the government as authoritarian. Lerroux, sensing he was aboard a sinking ship, joined in their attacks. In November, unable to command a majority in Parliament, Azaña resigned and a general election was called. Abandoned by the Republican Right, the Socialists and the Radicals, the Left Republicans also fell victim to the electoral system,

> ### reforma agraria
> land reform
>
> While referring, as elsewhere, to changes in the pattern of landownership and to landholding in general, in Spain land reform is especially associated with the break-up of the large estates (*latifundios*) commonly found in poorer parts of the country's centre and south, many of which were notoriously underused for agricultural purposes. As a result, land reform became an extremely emotive issue for both wings of the workers' movement, as well as a particular aim of many **'regenerationists'** (p18). See also: ***colectivización*** (p69)

which effectively ensured that only the two largest groupings in each provincial constituency could win seats. They were decimated, Azaña's own party obtaining just five seats. The reforming years were over.

The rise of the Right

The main feature of the 1933 election was a strong swing to the Right. This reflected the extent to which the government's various reforms, and above all its religious legislation, had provoked a fierce backlash among the more traditionalist sections of Spanish society. As a result, the parties that now took over the Republic's government were concerned to undo the work of their predecessors. Indeed, there was widespread suspicion that the largest of them wished to overthrow the democratic regime itself.

In 1931 the Spanish Right barely existed as a political force. Primo de Rivera's single party (p42) had melted away with its creator. The old 'dynastic' parties had withered under his rule, a process completed by the discredit of their *raison d'être*, the monarchy. Nor was the Church the bulwark it had been. The Papacy's depression-inspired concern with social issues sat uneasily with the reactionary views of the Spanish Right. Within the country many parish priests, finding their own financial circumstances precarious, were sympathetic to social reform. When the head of Spain's Church, Cardinal Segura, viciously attacked the newly proclaimed Republic and was banned from the country as a result, the support he received from Catholics was lukewarm.

This decline in the Right's fortunes was abruptly reversed by the adoption of the new Constitution, whose strongly anticlerical provisions (p51) alienated all shades

Confederación Española de Derechas Autónomas (CEDA)

Confederation of the Right

An alliance of various right-wing parties, the most important of which was José-María Gil-Robles' People's Action (*Acción Popular*), the CEDA was set up in 1933. Under Gil-Robles's leadership the CEDA grew rapidly, topping the poll at the next year's general election. However, the dubious compatibility of its ideas with democracy made even conservative Republicans distrustful. As a result it was excluded from power until October 1934, when its admission to government sparked off an attempted left-wing revolution (p58). Defeated at the 1936 election, the CEDA disintegrated once Civil War broke out later that year.

of Catholic opinion and gave a target against which conservatives could campaign. Further steps in the same direction, including a ban on the Jesuits, only increased their indignation and resolve. For the first time, the Right was able to mobilise supporters *en masse* at rallies over large areas of the country, something which only the workers' parties had previously managed, and then only in particular urban areas.

The catalyst for this transformation was a new political organisation, the **CEDA**, intended by its leader, José-María Gil-Robles, to become a mass party capable of defeating the Left in a free election. Its philosophy was also new to the Spanish Right, reflecting as it did the Christian Social ideas now in favour with the Vatican, which emphasised the state's role in providing for the less well-off. However, the CEDA had other features that made it the object of deep distrust among its opponents.

Part of the problem was Gil-Robles' refusal to make clear his attitude to the Republican form of government. His own fervent monarchism, and the fact that he had rich backers hostile to the Republic, was well-known. Yet he refused to say whether he wanted to restore the monarchy, declaring his policy to be one of adapting to circumstances (*accidentalismo*). Even more worryingly, he displayed open sympathy with developments in Austria, where his fellow Christian Socials had imposed a virtual dictatorship. The government's alarm at the CEDA's rise is thus understandable. But attempting to have the party banned and its meetings broken up represented a clumsy over-reaction that only increased the CEDA's appeal to the swelling ranks of those unhappy with the course of reform.

By 1933 these included employers resentful at the extension of labour regulation (p51) and much of the middle class, concerned that even limited land reform (pp52–3) might herald a threat to their own property. By no means all were particularly conservative; many were convinced Republicans, and suspicious of the Church. Their unease, along with the antagonism evoked in Castile by Catalan devolution, was picked up by the sensitive antennae of Lerroux, who swiftly positioned his Radicals to exploit it by ratting on his government colleagues (p53).

For the 1933 election the Radicals and CEDA formed an alliance, which also included smaller right-wing groups, notably the Agrarians, who enjoyed strong support among the smallholders of Old Castile. With the help of the electoral system (p53) the allies won a solid parliamentary majority. The CEDA was the biggest winner of all, and became the largest single party. However, President Alcalá Zamora shared the widespread suspicions of its intentions and declined to appoint Gil-Robles as Prime Minister. As a result, during its second phase the Republic was run mainly by weak coalitions of centre parties, Radical-led but dependent on the CEDA's parliamentary support.

Known to the Left as the 'two black years' (*bienio negro*), from the colour associated with the Church, this period saw a concerted attempt to reverse the Azaña government's policies, in particular its anticlerical legislation. Thus, as well as repealing some social measures, such as wage regulation, and some aspects of land reform, the Radicals also reintroduced government support for the clergy's salaries – ironically, given that the Church was one of their traditional bogeys (p27).

Another, regionalism, was anathema also to the CEDA's fierce Spanish nationalism and became a further target for the programme of counter-reform. In the Basque Country, that involved blocking devolution proposals put forward by the Basque Nationalist Party (PNV), previously a firm supporter of the Right. In fact, on many issues the PNV's ideas were very similar to those of the CEDA (p24) but now, on the promise of devolution from a future government of the Left, it began campaigning alongside its traditional Socialist enemies against the central government.

In Catalonia, too, the Right was driven onto the defensive. There, the old Regionalist League (p22) had recovered some of its former strength in 1933, but at the subsequent regional election it was again crushed by the more radical ERC (p52), this time for good. Emboldened by this triumph, the regional government moved to help one of its key constituencies, the small tenant farmers who had been hit by the effects of economic depression.

The Smallholdings Act (*Ley de Cultivos*) was designed to give them greater security by bolstering their rights *vis-à-vis* landowners. However, its implications for property rights in general alarmed both the Catalan bourgeoisie and the Madrid government, which referred the Act to the Constitutional Court. By doing so it turned a class issue into something much more emotive; a national conflict between Spain and Catalonia. When the Court threw out the Act in autumn 1934, the ERC reacted in correspondingly heated terms.

The ERC's anger was directed chiefly at the Radicals, who had already been weakened by the defection of a faction, led by deputy leader Martínez Barrio, which objected to the party's U-turn on religious policy. Sensing an opportunity, Gil-Robles brought the government down and made the CEDA's entry into its successor the price of his continuing support. It was a fateful decision, being used by the Left to justify an attempted revolution (p58). That in turn set off a spiral of increasingly undemocratic behaviour on both sides of the political spectrum, which ended in war.

Already Lerroux had set a bad example. Pardoning former Primo supporters banned from politics by the Azaña government could be interpreted as a gesture of reconciliation: his amnesty for those involved in the 1932 coup attempt (p52) could not. But the new, CEDA-dominated administration's reaction to the 1934 'revolution' plumbed new depths of vindictiveness and bias. Thousands of ordinary workers were put on trial, many for relatively minor offences, while the left-wing press was

monarquistas

monarchists

While technically it also included **Carlists** (p2), the term 'monarchists' was usually understood to mean those who supported the abolition of the Second Republic and the restoration of Alfonso XIII (*alfonsistas*). For the most part strongly Catholic, some supported the **CEDA** (p54), while others joined the smaller, more reactionary Spanish Renewal (*Renovación Española*); later they all gravitated towards the 'Nationalist Bloc' set up by José Calvo Sotelo. During the Franco era monarchists were among the regime's most prominent supporters (p85), but they also formed part of the 'legal' opposition (p104).
See also: *familias* (p84), *aperturistas* (p107)

censored and Catalan autonomy suspended. Efforts were even made to implicate Azaña (p50) in the rising, when in fact he had tried to calm the situation. Yet the many, and manifestly well-founded claims of Army brutality were not even investigated.

The CEDA's performance in other areas of government was initially less partisan. In some – public works, the status of leaseholders, provision of low-cost rented housing – its Christian Social ideas inspired policies that were little different from those of the Azaña era. However, as the effects of depression, and Gil-Robles' insistence on maintaining military spending, made budget cuts inevitable, his party's line hardened, with education suffering badly. But it was above all the complete reversal of land policy, which now blatantly favoured big landowners, that made the CEDA look downright reactionary. At the same time, Gil-Robles' promotion of extreme right-wing generals, and his talk of a 'revolution' to return Spain to its roots, gave weight to the Left's argument that it did not merit treatment as a democratic party.

For some on the Right, though, the CEDA was too cautious. Nominally they were **monarchists** but, for most, the real issue was not so much the Republic's lack of a king as its reformist nature. Their feelings lacked a vehicle until, in May 1934, the charismatic José Calvo Sotelo returned from exile (p43). He gave the far Right a new impetus with his vicious verbal attacks, not just on the Republic but also on Gil-Robles for 'treacherously' propping it up. Like his contacts with seditious generals, they made the undemocratic nature of his intentions plain to all, supporters and opponents.

Gil-Robles' plans were now approaching fulfilment. The four-year moratorium imposed by the Constitution on amendments to its text would soon be up, and he could move to repeal Article 26. But his moment never came. In late 1935 Lerroux's political career was ended by financial scandal; without their leader the Radicals fragmented and the government fell. And, once again, President Alcalá refused to countenance a CEDA-led administration. Instead, he called an election for February 1936. Although the Right obtained more votes in total than it had done in 1933, its parliamentary strength was decimated, since the enmity between Gil-Robles and Calvo Sotelo prevented the close cooperation between their parties that the electoral system made essential (p53). The centre parties, including the Radicals, suffered a similar fate as a resurgent Left swept back to power.

The reunification of the Left

In 1936, the forces of the Left reaped the reward of standing as a united bloc, in contrast to their fragmentation of three years before. That had been caused by the workers' disillusion with Republican reforms, and by its increasingly radical expression. The process of radicalisation was accelerated by the election of a right-wing government and culminated in an attempted revolution. Its failure, and the government's brutal reaction to it, opened the way for the Left's reunification.

In the changing pattern of relations within the Left the Socialists played a crucial role. Given the absence of an anarchist party (p26), they were the only means by which the Left's working-class support was represented in the Parliament, which had become the centre of political life. They were also the link between the workers' movement as a whole and the Republicans, with whom anarchists mainly refused to talk.

The main channel for such contacts was the Basque Socialist leader Indalecio Prieto, one of those who attended the signing of the San Sebastian Pact (p50). Thereafter, he persuaded the PSOE to drop its policy of non-cooperation with middle-class parties (p26) – overcoming the reservations of party leader Julián Besteiro, among others – and to join the Republic's Provisional Government. Prieto argued that the Republic would bring in the modernising reforms the PSOE had always seen as the prerequisite for a revolution (p25). Yet his real reason for cooperating with it was pragmatic: that the alternative was much worse.

Pragmatism also weighed heavily with the Socialist movement's trade union wing, the UGT, which found that state-sponsored labour regulation brought the same advantages as under the Primo regime (pp39–40), only in greater measure; civil service jobs for union officials, and the title as well as the functions of Labour Minister for the UGT leader, Francisco Largo Caballero. As a bonus, it was able to secure a further rise in membership by offering workers access to – often favourable – arbitration procedures.

Such access remained the preserve of the UGT because Spain's other large labour organisation, the anarcho-syndicalist CNT (p36), continued to boycott arbitration. Its attitude was dictated by the traditional anarchist view that all governments, dictatorial or democratic, were equally bad. Even so, amidst the euphoria of 1931 many anarchists forgot their disdain for '*bourgeois*' elections and voted, mainly for the PSOE. In the same year a group of prominent anarcho-syndicalists led by Angel Pestaña issued a manifesto in which they argued against an immediate revolution. But they and their supporters (*treintistas*) overwhelmingly lost the internal debate and were subsequenrly expelled from the CNT.

For the next two years, anarchism was in thrall to its terrorist tradition, represented by the Iberian Anarchist Federation (p40). Attacks on property were common, often accompanied by waves of political strikes; Barcelona, Seville and Saragossa were especially affected. With the government's failure to legislate an effective programme of land reform, the focus of violence shifted to the countryside (p52). In 1932 the Alto Llobregat area of Catalonia was briefly 'liberated' from government control. Andalusia was another hotbed, with the tragic incident at Casas Viejas (p33) merely the worst of many.

Its attitude hardened by the government's tough response to such activities, in 1933 the CNT urged its followers 'Don't vote', an injunction most were happy to obey. In theory, the right-wing government their abstention helped to elect was meant to provoke a spontaneous revolution. In practice, its effect on most anarchists was another bout of the periodic disillusion to which their movement had always been prone.

In the meantime, the failure of land reform had affected Socialists as well, provoking the PSOE to leave the government. The UGT, terrified of losing rural members to the CNT, changed its line even more dramatically. Abandoning his habitual caution, Largo Caballero began to talk of an imminent workers' revolution. After the Right's election victory he set up a semi-secret Workers' Alliance (*Alianza Obrera*), with the aim of uniting militants from both wings of the workers' movement under UGT leadership. He also stepped up his inflammatory rhetoric, warning that he would regard the CEDA's admission to government as a fascist takeover. When it occurred (p55), he was forced to back his words with deeds.

Largo Caballero's call for a 'revolutionary strike' was catastrophic. Dispirited anarchists mainly ignored it, with particularly damaging effects in Catalonia. There, the ERC regional government had also boxed itself into a corner with intemperate attacks on the Madrid authorities (p55) and was dragged along in Largo's wake. The regional premier, Lluis Companys, reluctantly declared Catalonia a free Republic within federal Spain, but few workers rallied to his support and, even worse, the Catalan police controlled by his own party helped to crush those who did. 'Free' Catalonia survived less than a day; in most of Spain the uprising was over even more quickly.

Only in Asturias did the 'October revolution' get off the ground. There not only anarchists but also Communists, who were well represented among the local miners, backed Largo's Alliance. For a week its supporters controlled the coalfield area. Even when the government sent in hardened units of the Moroccan army, the miners put up determined resistance which ended only after several thousand had been killed or wounded. Their heroics gave the Left a powerful symbol. But it derived more concrete benefit from the government's over-reaction to events (pp55–6), which not only drew workers together but also unleashed a wave of sympathy for them among Left Republicans (p50).

The 1934 uprising thus provided a foundation on which to rebuild the unity of 1931, a process initiated by Azaña. Founding a new party, 'Republican Left', he toured the country speaking in favour of a renewed alliance. He found a willing ally in Prieto, who swung chastened Socialists behind the notion of a **Popular Front** to fight the 1936 election. Its programme was simple: resumption of reforms, release of imprisoned strikers and an amnesty for those involved in the 'October revolution'. On that platform the Front won a narrow lead in votes, which was converted by the electoral system (p53) into a large parliamentary majority.

Although the Front as a whole was broader than the alliance that had formed the 1931 Provisional Government (p50), its Republican component was markedly depleted. Its real strength lay in the working-class support that the CNT had, unprecedentedly, helped to mobilise by calling on its supporters to vote. But, as before, that backing was represented almost exclusively by the PSOE. It was therefore disastrous that pressure from Largo Caballero prevented his party from entering the new government.

Without the Socialists it looked like a minority administration, its only parliamentary base being that of the Republican MPs, whose meagre numbers actually over-represented their popular support. Even worse, its main law and order instrument was the Assault Guards (*Guardias de Asalto*). Set up in 1931 because of doubts about the existing security forces' loyalty to the Republic, these had fallen under the control of the Socialists, becoming a sort of party militia. As a result, a succession of weak cabinets were constantly attacked by the Right as unrepresentative and partisan.

The new government provided grounds for such charges by following the bad example of its right-wing predecessors. The 'revolutionaries' of 1934 were not just pardoned but feted; censorship was aimed almost exclusively at the conservative press. As well as allowing such actions Azaña succumbed to the mood of hysteria, talking of radical reform in terms calculated to alarm even moderate conservatives. But he remained the Republicans' greatest asset, and when they appointed him President in place of the officious Alcalá Zamora they only worsened their plight. Day-to-day government was left in the charge of Santiago Casares Quiroga (p50), who was quite inadequate for the task.

> ### *Frente Popular*
> Popular Front
> ---
> Based on the notion of a broad alliance of all progressive forces to oppose fascism, or the far Right in general, the Spanish Popular Front (more correctly, People's Front) was formed in late 1935. It was made up of: middle-class Republican parties – the **Left Republicans** (p50) and Martínez Barrio's dissident Radicals (p55), renamed 'Republican Union'; regionalist parties – the Catalan **ERC** (p52) and the Basque **PNV** (p24); and elements of the workers' movement – the Socialist **PSOE** (p25), the **Communist Party** (p70) and the 'Syndicalist Party' founded by the renegade anarcho-syndicalist, Angel Pestaña (p57). Once the Civil War started it was extended by the inclusion of the anarcho-syndicalist **CNT** (p36) and FAI (p40).

By this time, in any case, the government was no longer in control of events. Admittedly Catalan autonomy was restored (p56) and work began on similar devolution for Basques and also Galicians; even land reform (p53) was restarted and pursued with some vigour. But the real force for change on the land now was the seizure of estates by farmworkers convinced that the Front's victory meant that revolution had come. The Socialists made little attempt to disabuse them. In the cities, too, politics was becoming a spiral of street violence between organised gangs, including those of the openly fascist Falange (p66). Their appearance indicated how the division into two camps apparent in 1933 had been widened and polarised.

On the Left this could be seen in the growing strength of the Communists, to whom the Socialist youth organisation defected *en bloc*. Largo Caballero was speaking of revolution in fierier terms than ever; on May Day he presided over a massive parade whose banners demanded a workers' government and lauded the Soviet Red Army. Meanwhile, on the Right, Gil-Robles' gradualist strategy (p54) was in ruins; his own party's youth wing defected to the Falange and his leader's mantle passed to the more extremist Calvo Sotelo (p56), who had plans in place for a military-backed coup. On 13 July 1936 they were pre-empted when Calvo Sotelo was murdered by Assault Guards avenging a colleague killed by the Falange. It was the spark that set the country alight.

Summary of main points

The reforming years

- The Republic's 1931 Constitution was mostly uncontroversial and impeccably democratic, but its religious provisions (Article 26) imposed significant restrictions on the Catholic Church that were, at best, ill-judged.
- Like the Constitution, the next two years of the Republic's course were effectively determined by an alliance between Left Republicans and the Socialists, under the leadership of Azaña.
- During this time a range of significant reforms were carried out, most notably a massive expansion of the education system and the granting of devolution to Catalonia. However, neither military nor land reform was carried through successfully; while the first alarmed the Right in principle, the disastrous failure of the second alienated much of the Left and led to the government's fall.

The rise of the Right

- The Right, moribund at the Republic's outset, was revived by opposition to the Constitution's anticlerical provisions. As a result, the CEDA became the first Spanish right-wing party to attract a mass support.
- Despite winning the 1933 election, the CEDA initially remained outside government because of – justifiable – suspicions that it was anti-democratic. But for the next two years it was the driving force behind attempts to dismantle and reverse many of the earlier reforms, and behind reprisals after the failed 1934 'revolution'.
- Even so, many 'monarchists' considered the CEDA to be too moderate; the resultant split led to the Right being defeated at the 1936 election.

The reunification of the Left

- In 1931 the Socialist PSOE joined the new government, while even some anarchists supported it. However, both groups were alienated by the failure of land reform and split with their Republican allies.
- The Right's 1933 victory led to a further radicalisation; the following year the Socialists, along with Catalan regionalists, staged the disastrous 'October revolution', which was brutally crushed.
- The failure of this uprising, and the government's vicious reaction to it, laid the basis for a renewed and broadened alliance between the workers' movement as a whole, regionalists and Republicans.
- This Popular Front won the 1936 election, but once in power proved unable to stem either anarchist land seizures or street-fighting fomented by extremists on both sides.

Exhibit 4.1: Programme of the CEDA (1933)

Extracts from the first two sections

I. RELIGIÓN

1. *La Confederación Española de Derechas Autónomas declara que en el orden político-religioso no puede ni quiere tener otro programa que el que representa la incorporación al suyo de toda la doctrina de la Iglesia católica sobre este punto. Las reivindicaciones de carácter religioso deben ocupar, y ocuparán siempre, el primer lugar de su programa, de su propaganda y de su acción. [...]*
2. *CEDA formula su más enérgica protesta contra el laicismo del Estado y contra las leyes de excepción y de la persecución de que se ha hecho víctima la Iglesia católica en España. [...]*
3. *La CEDA [...] se atendrá siempre a las normas que en cada momento dicte para España la Jerarquía eclesiástica en el orden político-religioso.*

II. RÉGIMEN POLÍTICO GENERAL
[...]
3. *Se ha de organizar la representación nacional de modo que las Cortes reflejen el verdadero sentir del pueblo español, tanto en los estados de opinión política manifestados por los individuos, cuanto en la organización corporativa que responda al carácter orgánico de la sociedad.*
4. *Robustecimiento del Poder ejecutivo, en la medida que sea necesario, para que desenvuelva eficazmente la función que le corresponde dentro de la organización fundamental del Estado. [...]*

I   RELIGION

1. The Spanish Confederation of the Right (CEDA) declares that, as regards the relationship between politics and religion, the only course that it can, or wishes to follow is to adopt as its own all the Catholic Church's teaching on this issue. Demands of a religious nature must, and always will, take pride of place in its programme, in its communication with the voters and in its actions.
2. The CEDA opposes, with its utmost strength, the separation of Church and State, and those exceptional and discriminatory measures of which the Catholic Church in Spain has been the victim.
3. The CEDA […] will, at all times, obey whatever instructions may be issued by the Church authorities with regard to the relationship between politics and religion in Spain.

II   POLITICAL SYSTEM
[…]
3. The nation's political representation shall be organised in such a way as to ensure that Parliament reflects the true feelings of the Spanish people, in terms both of the political opinions expressed by individual Spaniards and of the associations that embody the organic nature of society.
4. Strengthening of the executive branch of government, as far as is necessary to ensure that it can effectively discharge the functions that correspond to it within the basic structure of the State. […]

Source: Artola, M. (1991) *Partidos y programas políticos 1808–1936: Tomo II.* Madrid: Alianza.

Exhibit 4.2: The '1934 Revolution' in Asturias (1934)

Statement issued by one of the 'provisional revolutionary committees' established in the province

COMITÉ REVOLUCIONARIO DE ALIANZA OBRERA Y CAMPESINA DE ASTURIAS A TODOS LOS TRABAJADORES
Compañeros: Ante la marcha victoriosa de nuestra revolución, ya gloriosa, los enemigos de los intereses de nuestra clase utilizan todas sus malas artes e intentan desmoralizar a los trabajadores asturianos que en magnífico esfuerzo se han colocado a la cabeza de la Revolución proletaria española.

Mientras en el resto de las provincias se dan noticias de que en Asturias está sofocado el movimiento, el Gobierno contrarrevolucionario dice en sus proclamas a los trabajadores de nuestra región que en el resto de España no ocurre nada y nos invita a entregarnos a nuestros verdugos.

Hoy podemos decir que la base aérea de León ha caído en poder de los obreros revolucionarios leoneses y que éstos se disponen a enviarnos fuerzas en nuestra ayuda. Contra la voluntad indomable del proletariado asturiano, nada podrán las fuerzas del fascismo.

Estamos dispuestos, antes de ser vencidos, a vender cara nuestra existencia. Tras nosotros, el enemigo sólo encontrará un montón de ruinas. Por cada uno de los nuestros que caiga por la metralla de los aviones, haremos justicia con los centenares de rehenes que tenemos prisioneros.

Sépanlo nuestros enemigos. ¡Camaradas: un último esfuerzo por el triunfo de la revolución! ¡Viva la revolución obrera y campesina!

MESSAGE FROM THE REVOLUTIONARY COMMITTEE OF THE ASTURIAN WORKERS' AND PEASANTS' ALLIANCE, TO ALL WORKERS
Brothers: Faced with the victorious advance of our glorious revolution, the enemies of our class interests are using all their evil ploys and attempting to undermine the spirit of the Asturian workers, whose magnificent efforts have placed them in the vanguard of Spain's proletarian revolution.

Thus in the rest of the country reports are circulating that here in Asturias the uprising has been suppressed, while at the same time the counter-revolutionary government announces to the workers of our region that elsewhere in Spain all is quiet and invites us to hand ourselves over to our executioners.

Today, though, we can report to you that the airbase at Leon has fallen to the revolutionary workers of that region, who are preparing to send forces to assist us. Against the unbreakable will of the Asturian working class the forces of Fascism are powerless.

Rather than be defeated we are ready to sell our lives dearly. To the enemy we will leave only a heap of ruins. For each of us who falls, cut down by the machine guns of their planes, we will exact justice on the hundreds of hostages we hold captive.

Let our enemies beware. Comrades: one last effort for the triumph of the revolution! Long live the workers' and peasants' revolution!

Source: Ruiz, D. (1975) *Asturias contemporánea (1808–1936)*. Madrid: Siglo XXI.

Topics for discussion

- What does the CEDA appear to regard as the ultimate political authority (Exhibit 4.1)? Does its view have any precedents in modern Spanish history?
- What sort of political regime does the CEDA appear to want? What does it have in mind when it refers to the 'true feelings of the Spanish people'? Do its views in this respect presage any future developments?
- What sense does Exhibit 4.2 give of the political climate in Spain in 1934?
- What, if anything, do the views expressed there have in common with those of the CEDA?
- Was the Republic doomed to failure?
- Why were the various Republican parties so easily marginalised over the course of the Republic?

CHAPTER 5

An unequal struggle (1936–1939)

In July 1936 Spain was shaken yet again by a military revolt. This time, however, the uprising met with fierce opposition, triggering off a three-year civil war. The conflict's course reflected a shifting balance of advantage, as the initial edge afforded the Republic's defenders by superior popular support was first eroded and then reversed by their own divisions and the rebels' growing cohesion. Foreign intervention from various sources also played a key role. For, while it helped to stiffen the Republican authorities' resistance, it crucially enabled the insurgents to survive the failure of their coup attempt. It also contributed to their grinding progress to victory, which went hand-in-hand with the rise to supreme power of General Franco.

The Nationalist rebels

The 1936 rebellion was the result of planning by both soldiers and civilians. But circumstances dictated that it was essentially another old-style military declaration, with no clear leader. Like most of its forerunners the coup failed, but the rebels were rescued by a new factor in such situations: outside intervention. Thanks to this help the Nationalists, as they had become known, were soon in control of a large part of Spain, in which they established what amounted to a separate state.

In the late 1930s European affairs were dominated by the rise of the extreme Right, whose grip on several countries, including Portugal, tightened. There was concern, above all, at the growing strength and aggressiveness of Nazi Germany, which in November 1936 signed the 'Axis' agreement with Italy. This fascist alliance was seen by Stalin as a grave threat not only to Russia's own security but to communism worldwide. In response, he intensified his efforts to form an anti-fascist alliance, confirming communist backing for Popular Fronts such as that which briefly ruled France in 1936 and again in 1938, and seeking international allies. In that regard, too, France offered his best hope. But the French were held back from a Soviet alliance by pressure from their own Right and from the other western power, Britain, whose rulers regarded communism as a greater threat than fascism. The British policy of appeasing Hitler's territorial demands reached its peak in 1938, when the Munich Agreement effectively handed him Czechoslovakia. Its terms convinced Stalin of the futility of seeking security in the West; instead he began to think in terms of accommodation with Germany.

Comunión Tradicionalista

Traditionalist Party

Formed in 1932, the Traditionalist Party brought together the two divided branches of the **Carlist movement** (p2). Although its nominal aim was to restore the monarchy in the person of the Carlist claimant, the Traditionalists were in reality more concerned about Carlism's broader principles: authoritarian rule in a highly personalised form, extreme social conservatism and subjugation to the tenets of the Catholic Church. In 1937 the party was forcibly amalgamated with the **Falange** to form the Francoist single party (p74).
See also: *familias* (p84)

In the increasingly tense and polarised conditions of 1936 (pp59–60), various right-wing groups abandoned all notion of regaining power by democratic means and began conspiring to overthrow the Republic's government. Notable by its absence was the party that had spearheaded the Right's recent political rise, the CEDA, since the ambivalent attitude of its leader made it as suspect to the plotters as to democrats (p54). Instead, the principal civilian conspirator was José Calvo Sotelo, who was backed by most of those anxious to see Alfonso XIII return to the throne. These monarchists (p56) controlled considerable wealth and influence but as a political force they were heavily dependent on their leader, and so were effectively neutralised by his assassination (p60).

Also involved in the plot were the **Traditionalists**, the heirs of the old Carlists (p2). Unlike Alfonso's supporters, they could call on an element of mass support in the Carlist heartland of Navarre, where drilling of Traditionalist volunteers (*requetés*) was under way well before war broke out. Yet, while they represented an important fighting resource for the rebels, in other respects the Traditionalists' value to the uprising was limited; outside Navarre the extreme reactionary nature of their ideas was as likely to frighten off supporters as attract them.

The **Falange** party's main assets were its charismatic leader, José Antonio Primo de Rivera, and the street-fighting experience of its student gangs (p59). But at the February election it had failed to win a single seat and, despite having grown since, its popular backing remained tiny. Moreover, it was an uneasy alliance between well-off students and a limited number of the workers and peasants to which its leader's romanticised

Falange

Falange

Founded by José Antonio Primo de Rivera, son of ex-dictator Miguel (p38), the Falange was composed chiefly of upper-class young men (*señoritos*), many of them students. After merging with two other small groupings on the far Right, its membership widened and its official title became *Falange Española y de las Juntas de Ofensiva Nacional-Sindicalista (FE y de las JONS)*. The Falange's ideas were basically fascist; its members embraced technical and economic progress and notions of social justice, while being aggressively opposed to the Left. In 1937 it was forcibly amalgamated with the **Traditionalists** to form the Francoist single party (p74), also known colloquially as the Falange.
See also: *familias* (p84); *Movimiento Nacional* (p90)

brand of fascism was intended to appeal. Doubts concerning the compatibility of this new approach with the traditional conservatism of the Right in general meant that José Antonio agreed to join the conspirators only at the last minute.

Given the weakness and diversity of these civilian elements, the uprising became in essence a matter for disgruntled generals, among whom each party had its sympathisers, even the Falange. Along with a desire for minimal political interference in Army affairs, the military plotters shared two grievances against the Republic. One was the collapse of law and order, for which they held it responsible. The other was a nebulous but powerful conviction that it was destroying a 'true Spain' whose foundation was not 'artificial' democracy but respect for authority and which was threatened by equally 'artificial' regionalist claims. Their beliefs led the rebellion's leaders to style their enterprise a 'National Movement', and in the war that followed their side became known as Nationalists (*nacionales*).

The rebels' nominal head was General Sanjurjo, who had been exiled in Lisbon since the failure of his 1932 coup attempt (p52). But, even before his death in an air crash on 20 July 1936, age meant that his authority was far from uncontested. Thereafter a number of generals harboured ambitions to replace him, the most obvious candidates being Emilio Mola, who had been responsible for organising the uprising inside Spain, and Francisco Franco, whose task was to assume command in Morocco (p39), where he had served with great distinction. The issue was a touchy one and, given that all the generals expected a quick victory, they tacitly agreed to shelve any decision until it had been achieved.

Their expectations were shattered as soon as the revolt got under way, prematurely, on 17 July in Morocco, and one day later, as planned, elsewhere. In terms of popular backing it suffered from the fact that most barracks were located in towns, while mass support for the Right was concentrated in the northern countryside, above all in Old Castile (p11), where the coup met with little resistance. In other regions its success was limited to a few larger cities where individual commanders acted decisively and rode their luck, most spectacularly General Queipo de Llano in Seville. Elsewhere, and crucially in Madrid and Barcelona, the revolt was crushed (p69).

Even within the armed forces support was patchy. The paramilitary Civil Guard proved much less enthusiastic than anticipated, while the bulk of the fledgling Air Force remained loyal to the government. Within the Army itself reactions were mixed, though most of the lower ranks – mainly conscripts drawn from the social groups most solidly behind the Popular Front government – were hostile. In Morocco, the elite troops of the Army of Africa rebelled and quickly established control. However, since the naval uprising had been a complete failure – those officers who did attempt to rebel were soon overwhelmed – there was no immediate way the North African forces could be brought into action in mainland Spain. As a result, the coup's leaders were staring defeat in the face.

They were saved by the first outside intervention of the war. Both Hitler and Mussolini responded to Franco's pleas by sending air force units to Morocco to airlift his troops across the Straits of Gibraltar to Andalusia. There they linked up with

Queipo de Llano's forces to advance on Madrid from the south-west, while other columns under Mola's command approached the capital from the north. Whereas Mola's inexperienced soldiers and Traditionalist militiamen were halted with relative ease, the battle-hardened Army of Africa advanced inexorably through Extremadura, so that soon all rebel-held territory was joined in a single 'zone' stretching in an arc from Cadiz to the Pyrenees.

At this point the problems of coordinating action on several fronts spurred the Nationalist generals into establishing a single command structure. Franco's control of the Moroccan Army now gave him an unanswerable claim to primacy and, at a meeting in Salamanca on 21 September, the generals appointed him to be their Supreme Commander (*Generalísimo*). They also gave him the title of 'Head of the State', for the duration of the war as they thought, but this restriction was omitted from the official announcement on 1 October. For the rebels' purpose was more than military. They were claiming, above all to foreign observers, that the territory they had overrun had the same status as the legitimate Spanish state, whose resistance had turned out to be stronger than expected.

The Republic's defenders

From the moment of the uprising, the term 'Republicans' was used to denote all those involved in resisting it. This involved not only the old Republican parties but also their allies in the workers' movement. Indeed, it was the latter that bore the brunt of the war effort, even though it was sharply divided over what the war was about, and about how it should be fought. The key role in this debate was played by the Communists, whose growing influence was the main reason why unity among the Republic's defenders inexorably crumbled.

Despite persistent rumours of a right-wing plot, the July uprising caught the government off-guard and almost entirely unprepared. The Republicans – in the pre-war sense – of which the government was made up were demoralised by the course of events since the Popular Front's election victory (p59), as was evident in their reactions to the coup. Casares Quiroga, the weak and ailing Prime Minister, simply resigned. His successor, the more conservative Martínez Barrio (p55), sought to negotiate with the rebels. Only when he, in turn, was replaced by José Giral did the government opt unambiguously for resistance.

While its supposed guardians dithered, the Republic was saved by three factors. The

---

milicia

militia

Groups of volunteers raised to defend the interests of a particular group or party, militias were a feature of Spanish politics from the first half of the nineteenth century (p5). During the Civil War they fought on both sides, but for the Republicans the term acquired special overtones. It implied the absence of conventional military hierarchy and discipline, both within units and in their relations with others and with the overall Republican command; in that sense it was associated with **anarchist** influence (p26).

first was the indecisiveness shown by the insurgents in a number of centres, the second the loyalty of many Army and Civil Guard commanders (p67), without which their rebel colleagues might well have succeeded. The third was a massive display of opposition to the coup from ordinary Spaniards, especially urban workers, who took to the streets and demanded that the government give them arms to defend it. This Giral eventually agreed to do. His action allowed the hasty formation of **militia** units by the various workers' organisations, which in several places, including Madrid and Barcelona, played an important part in suppressing the rising.

Spontaneous resistance to the coup was part of a wider phenomenon; the belief among many on the Left that it offered an unparalleled opportunity to stage their own revolution. Their conviction had a variety of effects, including a wave of violence directed against the rich and, especially, against the Church's buildings and personnel. This was largely the work of so-called mavericks (*incontrolados*) acting on their own initiative and soon died down. Altogether more important in determining the course of the war was the open debating of revolutionary ideas as to how the country should be run, ideas shared at least in part by some leading figures not just in the anarcho-syndicalist CNT (p36), but also in the Socialist trade union, the UGT (p40).

In a number of towns and cities revolutionary committees (*juntas revolucionarias*), composed of workers' representatives, were set up to administer public services instead of, or alongside the official authorities. At the same time, widespread and often successful attempts were made at **collectivisation** of economic activity. The advocates of immediate revolution also insisted that the militias were not merely an emergency recourse, but should form the basis of the Republic's defence in the longer war now looming.

It was the militias' ineffectiveness against Franco's experienced regulars (p68) that highlighted the practical problems of these revolutionary policies, and crystallised a very different view of the war among other sectors of the Left. To much of the Socialist Party (PSOE), and even the top leadership of the CNT and UGT, the war was not an opportunity, but a mortal threat both to the '*bourgeois*' Republic and to workers. That view, which had also underlain the formation of the Popular Front (p59), now led to its revival in strengthened form when, in September 1936, a new government was formed.

The new Prime Minister was the UGT leader Largo Caballero (pp57,58), the figure best placed to unite both sections of the workers' movement. Socialists also filled the majority of cabinet posts. The middle-class

> ### *colectivización*
> collectivisation
>
> Whereas in Soviet Russia collectivisation involved the imposition of large-scale, centrally controlled units of production, in Spain it was associated with **anarchist** ideas of work on a small scale, involving autonomy and participative management, and consequently opposed by the **Communist Party** (p70). During the early phase of the Civil War it was implemented in some parts of the Republican zone, both on the land, as a sort of spontaneous **land reform** (p53), and in commerce and industry, especially by supporters of the anarcho-syndicalist **CNT** (p36).

Partido Comunista de España (PCE)

Spanish Communist Party

Founded in 1921 by dissidents from the Socialist **PSOE** (p25) and anarcho-syndicalist **CNT** (p36), the PCE was banned under the Primo dictatorship and achieved little success during the Second Republic. Strictly obedient to Soviet instructions, in 1936 it reversed its refusal to cooperate with 'bourgeois' parties and backed the **Popular Front** (p59). During the Civil War it acquired significant influence on the Republican side, but the tactics it used to do so alienated many of those who belonged to other parties on the Left. The PCE played a leading part in opposition to the Franco regime (p102), but after 1975 proved unable to capitalise on the prestige that its action had brought. Since 1986 it has been the main component of the United Left alliance, which has also failed to make a significant electoral impact. The PCE is unusual among Communist parties in that its operations do not cover the whole country, Catalonia having its own Communist party known as the Catalan United Socialist Party (PSUC).
See also: **Comisiones Obreras** (p102); **consenso** (p119)

---

parties were reduced to two ministers, although Azaña (p50) remained the Republic's President and figurehead. Two posts each went to the **Communist Party** (PCE) and to the Front's regionalist members, the Catalan ERC and the PNV, whose support was sealed by granting Basque devolution. A month later the CNT and, astonishingly, the Iberian Anarchist Federation (p40), abjured their principles and also accepted cabinet posts, so that the government now included representatives from all sections of the Republic's support. The most significant aspect of these changes was the inclusion of the Communists, who at the start of 1936 had been little more than a sect.

Since then, however, two factors had greatly increased their importance. One was the fact that, as Franco's column bore down on Madrid (p68), the Soviet Union – unlike the Western Powers (p72) – came to the Republic's aid. From the autumn of 1936 it sent large quantities of tanks and planes, and – through the international communist movement – recruited most of the volunteers (*brigadistas*) who formed the International Brigades. These reinforcements played an important part, first in the successful defence of Madrid and then in defeating two further assaults on the capital at the battles of the Jarama and Guadalajara. The crucial intermediary between the Republican authorities and the source of this precious support was the PCE.

However, the party's ascent also reflected another change; its adoption of pragmatic policies in response to Stalin's decision that the overriding priority was to defeat the Right. Suddenly, the Communists became fervent opponents of revolutionary activity that might alienate middle-class backing. As the only force on the government side solidly behind such moderation, they attracted support from those whose enthusiasm for the Republic did not extend to wanting their own property to be collectivised. Their approach also brought them significant influence among the Republican leadership, not least because it was broadly shared by the PSOE's majority faction, led by Indalecio Prieto (p57).

Together, the PSOE and the PCE were responsible for the new government's efforts to bring revolutionary enthusiasm under control in the interests of the war effort. Law and order were imposed, where necessary by force. The revolutionary committees were disbanded, agricultural collectives suppressed, and industry made increasingly subject to central planning and control. Most controversially, the government moved to integrate the militias – whose weaknesses were again highlighted by the fall of Malaga in early 1937 – into a new People's Army (*Ejército Popular*), organised on the more conventional lines favoured by the Communists.

Resentment at these steps was widespread, above all in Barcelona, where the revolutionaries were especially strong. Conscious that it could not defy them, the regional government had agreed to run the city in tandem with an Anti-Fascist Militia Committee. In May 1937 the third major force in regional politics, the Communist-dominated PSUC, moved to disband the Committee. Its action was resisted by the POUM, a communist splinter group with anarcho-syndicalist leanings, and by grassroots anarchists. After several days of confused street fighting the revolutionaries were completely defeated and pragmatic policies were imposed in Catalonia, too.

Their proponents used the disorder in Barcelona as an excuse to replace Largo Caballero as Prime Minister with Juan Negrín, a Socialist close to Prieto (p57). Under his leadership, resistance continued for another two years, despite the loss of the vital northern industrial areas over the summer of 1937. On several occasions, most notably in the battles of Teruel (winter 1937/38) and the Ebro (autumn 1938), the People's Army even managed significant local advances. However, it could not reverse the general pattern of defeats, in which the collapse of Republican unity played a key part.

While the Barcelona clashes were not the start of that process, they did accelerate it markedly. First of all, they fatally undermined Catalan enthusiasm for the Republic, not only among workers but also among a middle-class alarmed at the regional government's manifest inability to control events. In addition, Largo's removal prompted the CNT and FAI representatives to withdraw from the government, further weakening its credibility among workers. That same step also added to growing suspicion of the party that, along with Prieto, had engineered it; the PCE.

Doubts had already been aroused by the party's constant efforts to increase its influence, particularly within the People's Army, and by the ruthless nature of its methods. Now the first revelations about Stalin's rule in Russia were mirrored by the Communist secret police's murderous pursuit of the defeated POUM and other opponents. Another favoured PCE tactic was to mount scurrilous attacks on opponents in their own press, one of which drove Prieto out of government after he attempted to resist PCE influence. As with the resort to terror tactics, the move was ultimately self-defeating. For, even accompanied by the CNT's return to government, Prieto's departure inevitably alienated much of his substantial support within the PSOE.

The chief charge against Prieto was defeatism; like PSOE leader Besteiro (p57), he had questioned the point of continuing with increasingly hopeless resistance.

Quite apart from the fact that the Nationalist leadership had no intention of negotiating (p75), though, the two timed their public musings badly, just as the Czech
crisis seemed, at last, to offer the prospect of Western aid. To encourage it the
Republican government disbanded the International Brigades, hoping to quell
British fears of Communist influence; the last volunteers left in November 1938. By
then, however, the Munich agreement had dashed hopes of an anti-fascist alliance,
and also hastened the ending of Soviet support. Now the Republic really was lost.

Its end came tragically with another, pathetic Army uprising. The revolt was led
by Colonel Casado, a soldier who had stayed loyal in 1936 and now commanded
what remained of the People's Army, Communist interference in which he deeply
resented. He was also convinced, quite wrongly, that the sole barrier to a negotiated
end to the fighting was the PCE's presence in Negrín's government, which he therefore attempted to overthrow. His futile action succeeded only in sparking off six
days of street fighting in Madrid, at the end of which the capital lay undefended. The
war was over, as a triumphant Nationalist communiqué announced on 1 April 1939.

Franco's triumph

Although it was signed by a number of generals, the announcement was issued in
one name alone, that of General Franco. It was a graphic illustration of the importance he had assumed during the war's progress. Of course, there were several
reasons for the Nationalists' victory. Franco's leadership was only one of these, but it
was crucial in determining the nature of his side's triumph and in linking that indis-
solubly to his own person.

To some extent victory was due to factors beyond the Nationalists' control,
such as their opponents' divisions, and the stunted economic development of
Spain's main industrial region, Catalonia, which rendered its factories ill-suited for
conversion to munitions production. Nor could they claim credit for the realities of
economic and political geography that left the arms-producing industries of the
North an easy prey, and placed Spain's main food-producing areas in their hands
from the war's outset. The rather fortunate capture of Seville (p67) was also vital, as
it gave the rebels control of the poor southern areas where the Left had solid
support and collectivisation (p69) might have been received as a boon rather than a
threat (p54).

Above all, there was the balance of foreign intervention, which was clearly in the
Nationalists' favour even before 1938, when France stopped turning a blind eye to
smuggling across the Pyrenean frontier and Soviet supplies (p70) tailed off. Once
Hitler and Mussolini had thrown their support behind the insurgency (p67) they were
determined to avoid the propaganda setback its defeat would have meant. Indeed,
common interest in a Nationalist victory helped prompt their formal alliance of
November 1936. Thereafter, both sent substantial aid to Franco's troops, virtually
unhindered by the **Non-Intervention Pact** they had signed with the Western Powers.

In quantitative terms, the greater contribution came from Italy. The Italians
had supplied most of the Spanish Air Force's existing machines. Now they pro-

Pacto de No Intervención

Non-Intervention Pact

Signed in 1936 by Britain, France, Germany and Italy, the Pact was an agreement to refrain from intervening in the Civil War. Its legal basis was questionable – it effectively accepted the Nationalists' spurious claim to be given equal treatment with the Republican government (p68) – and its practice was downright fraudulent. It was respected by the two Western Powers, thus denying the Republic French aid and impeding supplies to it from third countries. However, since Britain was determined to stay out of conflict, in Spain or elsewhere, the Pact did virtually nothing to prevent Hitler and Mussolini from supplying the Nationalists as they wished.

vided further supplies and back-up to the Nationalists, while denying vital spare parts to the Republicans. Mussolini also committed substantial numbers of ground troops, including armoured units, although they turned out to be of limited value; while they led the capture of Malaga, they failed badly at Guadalajara (p70). Hitler's support was more limited in quantity but of higher quality, consisting of elite air units, including that responsible for the bombing of **Guernica**.

Aid from the Axis powers was undoubtedly crucial in establishing Nationalist military superiority, above all in the air. Ultimately, though, the war was won on the ground, and there the rebels' success in building up an effective Army was vital. The lukewarm response from the armed forces to their initial coup (p67) left them little better off in that respect than the Republicans. Even so, the Nationalists had significant assets in the greater experience of their leaders, especially in Morocco, and the Army of Africa itself; they also had the benefit of German and Italian advice. Above all, the nature of their uprising and the support it had received meant that there was minimal resistance to the imposition of standard military practices in training and action; the Traditionalist and Falange militias (p66) were integrated into a single Nationalist Army without any of the problems experienced on the other side.

As well as its primary role at the front, the rebel Army also served as the chief instrument of organised terror within the Nationalist zone. From an early stage these tactics were associated particularly with Franco. One of the most notorious mass executions occurred at Badajoz during his initial march on Madrid. Once he was established as effective ruler of rebel-held Spain such killings and other forms of brutality were routinely used against known or suspected government supporters. As a result, there was little of the uncertainty that wracked

Guernica (Basque: Gernika)

Guernica

Because of its associations with their **traditional privileges or 'old laws'** (p3), Guernica is of enormous symbolic importance to Basques. In 1937, during the Nationalist northern offensive, it was the target of a bombing raid by the German Condor Legion that caused heavy civilian casualties, tactics which were to be perfected in the Second World War. The Basque Statute of Autonomy was signed there in 1979 (p123).

Republican Spain, where the better-off were constantly suspected of mere 'geographic loyalty' and rumours abounded of a 'fifth column' of traitors within.

Franco's insistence on stamping out opposition in captured areas before proceeding to a further offensive was one reason why, in strictly military terms, the war lasted longer than necessary. Several times, too, Franco chose tactical options that almost certainly prolonged it. Most glaringly, having defeated the Republicans' Teruel offensive, he ignored the obvious course of a direct attack on Catalonia, instead advancing on Valencia through the difficult terrain of the Maestrazgo district. But such moves were not unintended errors. They were part of a deliberate strategy of attrition (*desgaste*), designed – like the use of terror – quite literally to eliminate his opponents.

Imposition of this approach, which was unmistakably his own, was a mark of Franco's new status as the Nationalists' undisputed leader. The emergence of such a figurehead was assisted by the military ethos of the insurgency, with its emphasis on hierarchy and obedience. Franco's elevation to the role in October 1936 (p68) was partly due to the disappearance of all other contenders in the space of a year; following the deaths of Calvo Sotelo (p60) and Sanjurjo (p67), José Antonio Primo de Rivera (p66) died in a Republican prison in late 1936, while Mola (p67) was killed in another air crash the following summer. But Franco himself also manoeuvred to ensure his pre-eminence, halting his march on Madrid to relieve the rebel garrison besieged in the fortress (*alcázar*) at Toledo, and then exploiting the feat to bolster his own prestige.

Moreover, once installed as effective ruler of Nationalist Spain, Franco worked single-mindedly to consolidate his position, which rested on three pillars. The first was his tremendous standing within the Army. The second was a new political organisation, whose creation reflected his conviction that the main reason for Spain's decline lay in the fractious squabbling of party politics. Determined to avoid any such development in his fief, he decreed the merger of the two largest parties among his support: the Falange and the Traditionalists (p66). All other political organisations were outlawed forthwith.

The clumsy title given to the merged party (p90) betrayed the fundamental incompatibility between Traditionalism and the modernising, socially minded ideas of the Falange. Franco quickly crushed the resultant discontent, imprisoning José Antonio's successor as party leader, Manuel Hedilla. But such methods soon became unnecessary. Membership of the new single party – still known colloquially as the Falange – was a requirement for public office in the Nationalist zone, not to mention an invaluable badge of loyalty. New recruits flocked to it in order to secure their material interests, their sheer numbers drowning out dissent from purists, whether of the Traditionalist or the Falangist variety.

The new Falange was to some extent modelled on the parties created by Mussolini and Hitler, and performed some of the same functions. With its members spread throughout society in the Nationalist zone, it enabled the authorities there to exercise close control over the population. It was also used to promote, through relentless propaganda, a fascist-style leadership cult. Yet the Falange never exercised the control over other institutions, notably the Army, typical of true fascist parties. Nor did Franco assume its leadership, a task he left to his brother-in-law and faithful subordinate, Ramón Serrano Suñer. Instead, his status as *Caudillo*, the nation's hero and predestined leader, rested ultimately on the support of a very different organisation, the third pillar of his authority.

Outside the Basque Country and Catalonia, the Catholic Church solidly backed the Nationalist cause from the outset. Even the lower clergy, initially more sympathetic to the Republic's cause, had been alienated by its religious legislation (p51) and by anticlerical violence once war broke out (p69). Franco, for his part, was a firm believer of the traditional school and regarded the Church as one of the foundations of the 'true Spain' he sought to restore. To that end he quickly set about re-establishing its social role, especially by handing it control over education.

In return, the Church threw its moral authority enthusiastically behind him and the cult of his leadership. Spanish bishops gave their blessing to the elaborate and deliberately old-fashioned ceremonies which became a feature of public life in the Nationalist zone, and which appeared to give Franco a status close to sainthood. The clergy also sanctioned and promoted his notion of the war as a 'crusade', consciously evoking the country's reconquest from the Moors (ppxiii–xiv) – and conveniently overlooking Franco's use of Muslim Moroccan troops, especially in terrorising civilians. The idea was a powerful one in the context of civil war, submerging divided loyalties under the powerful appeal of patriotism.

While the 'crusade' notion fostered growing unity among Nationalists, it was deeply divisive of the country as a whole. For it implied unmistakably that the Nationalists' opponents were not truly Spaniards at all, but inherently hostile to 'true Spain'. Indeed, in Franco's eyes the Republicans embodied an 'anti-Spain' which must be utterly defeated, if not annihilated; at no time would he countenance negotiations with its representatives. His view of them was encapsulated in an extraordinary measure he decreed as the war drew to a close. This 'Political Responsibilities Act' effectively declared all those who had served the Republic – Spain's legitimate government – in any capacity to be guilty of treason. It set the tone for the much of what was to follow.

Summary of main points

The Nationalist rebels

- The 1936 rebellion was motivated by distaste for democracy and regionalism, and by ideas of authority and Spanish national unity; hence the designation 'Nationalists' for its supporters.
- Although it enjoyed some influential civilian support – from monarchists, Traditionalists (Carlists) and the Falange – the revolt was overwhelmingly a military affair. Even in the armed forces support for it was far from universal.
- As a result, the initial coup attempt failed. However, assistance from the fascist dictators Hitler and Mussolini enabled the rebels to seize half of Spain and declare their own 'state'.

The Republic's defenders

- The initial coup's defeat owed little to the traditional Republican parties and a great deal to the spontaneous resistance of ordinary people, especially workers. Subsequently, the task of defending the Republic fell mainly to the parties and unions of the Left.
- The Left itself was divided over how to regard the war. Some, especially grass-roots anarchists, saw it as the opportunity for a social revolution; others, including the Socialist Prieto and his supporters, as a struggle for survival.
- The main proponents of this second view were the Communists, who were crucial in organising effective resistance to the rebels. But their ruthless and vicious methods were also the main cause of the splits that contributed to the Republican government's defeat.

Franco's triumph

- The Nationalists won the war for various reasons, including their control of economically important regions, the support they received from Germany and Italy, and the possession of a disciplined army with relatively experienced officers.
- Another important factor was the undisputed leadership of Franco, whose personal attitudes were reflected in the savagery and vindictiveness displayed by the Nationalists towards their opponents.
- In turn, Franco used his position as war leader to cement his authority, which rested on the support of three institutions: the Army, the new single party created by amalgamating Falangists with Traditionalists, and the Church.

Exhibit 5.1: The Communist view of the War (1936)

Extract from manifesto issued by the PCE in December

> [...S]i queremos ganar la guerra, no basta ya la improvisación de nuestras Milicias, ni el heroísmo que nuestras fuerzas armadas han demostrado en tantas batallas, sino que es preciso transformar éstas en un gran ejército popular, dotado de la disciplina y de los medios técnicos que exige la guerra, una guerra como ésta que se nos impone contra ejércitos imperialistas bien pertrechados por sus respectivos países. Por esto, la realización de la consigna de crear un ejército popular, férreamente disciplinado, obediente a los mandos y con sólida estructura, consigna lanzada desde los primeros días por nuestro Partido, es hoy de una necesidad imperiosa si queremos ganar rápidamente la guerra. [...] Urge acabar con las fuerzas dispersas, con las Milicias sindicales, de partido, regionales, etc, que si en los momentos iniciales de la lucha fueron la forma obligada para encuadrar rápidamente las fuerzas armadas que hubieron de improvisarse para batir al fascismo, ahora que tenemos enfrente no sólo moros, legionarios, requetés y falangistas, sino un ejército orgánico, formado por tropas alemanas, italianas, portuguesas, ya no bastan, pues, para vencer a este ejército, también nosotros necesitamos un ejército regular, superior al enemigo en armamento, en disciplina, en moral y en combatividad.

[…I]f we want to win the war, it will take more than our improvised Militias, or the heroism that our troops have displayed in so many battles. What is needed is to transform our forces into one great people's army, possessing the discipline and equipment demanded by a war like the one we are engaged in, against imperialist armies each properly equipped by its own government. Under those circumstances, if we want to win the war quickly there is no option but to create a people's army, strictly disciplined, obedient to its officers, and properly organised – an idea our Party has championed from the outset. […] We need urgently to do away with small, dispersed units, with Militias organised on the basis of trade unions, parties, regions or whatever. In the early days of the fighting they may have been the necessary means of mobilising rapidly the armed forces which had to be improvised in order to combat the Fascists. But now we are facing not just Moroccans, foreign legionaries, Carlists and Falangists, but a well-organised army of German, Italian and Portuguese troops. And to defeat such an army our Militias are not enough. We too need a regular army, superior to the enemy's in armaments, in discipline, in morale and in the capacity to fight.

Source: Vázquez, M. & Valero, J. (1978) *La Guerra Civil en Madrid*. Madrid: Tebas.

Exhibit 5.2: The Church and the Nationalist uprising (1937)

Extract from a pastoral letter issued jointly by the country's bishops

Demos ahora un esbozo del carácter del movimiento llamado "nacional". Creemos justa esta denominación. Primero, por su espíritu; porque la nación española está disociada, en su inmensa mayoría, de una situación estatal que no supo encarnar sus profundas necesidades y aspiraciones; y el movimiento fue aceptado como una esperanza en toda la nación; en las regiones no liberadas sólo espera romper la coraza de las fuerzas comunistas que le oprimen. Es también nacional por su objetivo, por cuanto tiende a salvar y sostener para lo futuro las esencias de un pueblo organizado en un Estado que sepa continuar dignamente su historia. [...]

El movimiento ha fortalecido el sentido de patria, contra el exotismo de las fuerzas que le son contrarias. La patria implica una paternidad; es el ambiente moral, como de una familia dilatada, en que logra el ciudadano su desarrollo total; y el Movimiento Nacional ha determinado una corriente de amor que se ha concentrado alrededor del nombre y de la sustancia histórica de España, con aversión de los elementos forasteros que nos acarrearon su ruina. Y como el amor patrio, cuando se ha sobrenaturalizado por el amor de Jesucristo, nuestro Dios y Señor, toca las cumbres de la caridad cristiana, hemos visto una explosión de verdadera caridad que ha tenido su expresión máxima en la sangre de millares de españoles que le han dado al grito de "¡Viva España!", "¡Viva Cristo Rey!"

Let us outline the nature of the 'national' movement, as it is known. We believe the epithet to be correct, firstly because of the movement's nature. For the vast majority of the Spanish nation feels no sympathy with a system of government that was incapable of embodying its fundamental needs and aspirations, and the movement was accepted as bringing hope to the nation as a whole; in those regions which have not yet been freed it will very soon break the hold of the communist forces of oppression. The movement is national, too, in its aim, in that it wishes to save, and to preserve for the future, the essence of a people, under a form of state capable of maintaining with dignity its historical traditions. […]

> The movement has strengthened the notion of fatherland, in the face of the alien ideas espoused by the forces that oppose it. Fatherland implies fatherhood; it is a moral climate, like that of an extended family, in which each citizen can develop fully, and the national movement has generated a flow of love focused on the name and the history of Spain, in contrast to the foreign ideas that led us to disaster. And as the love of fatherland, once transformed by the love of Jesus Christ, our Lord God, reaches the very heights of Christian charity, we have witnessed an explosion of true charity whose ultimate expression is the blood of those Spaniards who, in their thousands, have raised the cry of 'Long live Spain', 'Long live Christ the King'.

Source: Aguirre Prado, L. (1964) *La Iglesia y la Guerra Española.* Madrid: Servicio Informativo Español.

Topics for discussion

- What are the key points made in Exhibit 5.1?
- How does the way they are expressed compare with earlier left-wing documents of this kind, in content and in style (cf. Exhibits 2.2, 4.2)?
- What themes of Nationalist propaganda are reflected in Exhibit 5.2?
- How would you interpret the notion of 'charity' described in the final lines?
- Could the Republicans have won the Civil War? Would they have been better off without Soviet aid?
- What were the bases of popular support for the Nationalists, initially and as the war progressed?

CHAPTER 6

From 1939 to 1945, Europe outside the Iberian Peninsula was embroiled in the Second World War. Initially, its course favoured the fascist Axis powers, Germany and Italy. In 1942, however, the balance of forces changed decisively with the intervention of the United States and Hitler's attack on Russia. Thereafter the Allies slowly but surely turned the tables, achieving complete victory in 1945. Almost immediately the Soviets imposed Communist rule in Eastern Europe and by 1949 the Cold War between the two superpowers had begun, giving rise to new security fears in western Europe. Economically, though, the region had begun a remarkable recovery, greatly helped by US aid under the Marshall Plan. Indeed, it now formed part of an American-dominated western economy. The foundations had been laid at the 1944 Bretton Woods Conference, which established the World Bank and the International Monetary Fund. Along with the Organisation for European Economic Cooperation (later to become the OECD), and the links that culminated in the formation of the European Economic Community in 1957, these bodies provided a framework for steady growth throughout the bulk of western Europe.

Back to the future (1939–1959)

General Franco's victory in 1939 ushered in a period of 36 years during which Spain's history was determined ultimately by his own distinctive attitudes. Even so, the nature of his rule underwent significant changes. Thus, while in the early 1940s his regime flaunted its fascist side, by the 1950s it was attempting to present a democratic face to the outside world. Nevertheless, one thing remained constant throughout both decades: the regime sought its inspiration in the past, be it the Civil War period or an earlier one. For a long time the regime's survival was threatened by the isolation from the contemporary world which, in various senses, that implied. Only when it was relaxed was Franco able to fully entrench his rule. But, at the same time, he was brought up against the harsh realities of modern international relations, especially the economic ones.

The 'New State'

The form of government imposed by Franco throughout Spain after his triumph in the Civil War was essentially a continuation of arrangements in the Nationalist zone during the conflict. The name he gave it emphasised its affinity with fascism, as did the special status enjoyed by the Falange. Although to a large extent a reflection of

Franco's own ideas, its economic policy also had fascist overtones. By the late 1940s it had brought the regime to the verge of collapse.

The wartime character of the new regime was evident from the very top down. The unity of command established in 1936 (p68) was retained, with Franco acting as Head of State, Head of Government and – last but far from least – Supreme Commander of the Armed Forces. Moreover, his pronouncements made quite plain that the legitimacy of his rule – its ultimate justification – derived not from any constitution or traditional rights, but quite simply from his victory over the Republic. Hence the constant glorification of the uprising (*alzamiento*), as the 1936 rebellion was now known, and the date (18 July) associated with it (p67).

Nor did the cessation of hostilities mark the end of Franco's 'crusade' against those he regarded not just as his enemies but as Spain's (p75). Rather it provided an opportunity to strike at those of them who previously had been beyond his reach, in the government zone. Initially, his revenge took the form of savage violence; tens of thousands of Republican sympathisers were shot, and many more sentenced to prison terms, often lengthy. The survivors suffered systematic discrimination in access to state benefits and employment, which, like the use of brutality and torture against dissenters of all sorts, continued right to the end of his life.

More generally, the policies pursued by the **Franco regime** favoured those sections of society that had supported the 1936 revolt, in particular large landowners and financiers. Conversely, industrial workers saw their trade unions banned along with other basic freedoms, including those of association and expression, and their wages held down. Regionalists, Franco's other great *bête noire*, also suffered. Devolution was revoked and stern measures taken to stamp out notions of local or regional distinctiveness. Even then, the Civil War was the ultimate yardstick. The so-called 'rebel' Basque provinces of Guipúzcoa and Vizcaya – which had in fact remained loyal to the country's legitimate government – were stripped of the financial privileges agreed in 1876 (p9): neighbouring Navarre and Alava, which had largely backed his own anti-constitutional revolt, were allowed to retain theirs.

Another relic of wartime was the continuing high profile of the armed forces, especially the Army. In part that reflected the extent and severity of repression. But the forces' role went considerably further; indeed, the new regime flaunted its military character, contrasting its 'virility' with the alleged feebleness of its civilian prede-

---

franquismo

Franco era; Franco regime; Franco's political philosophy

As well as the period during which General Franco ruled, from 1939 to 1975, the Spanish term is used to mean his regime and the ideas that underlay it. Its main features in that sense were: his own supreme authority; an authoritarian, traditionalist concept of Spain based on an idealised image of its past; and an aggressive nationalism, directed less against external enemies than against his opponents, real and imagined, inside Spain.

cessors. Military men consistently made up a large part of Franco's cabinet (*Consejo de Ministros*), in the early years often filling up to half the portfolios. In the administration, both central and local, their presence was equally marked, with officers even taking up key posts in business. Military courts, too, were given wide jurisdiction to deal with civil offences.

Bizarrely, Franco's own preferred designation for the reactionary dictatorship he had imposed was the 'New State'. Yet the name was easily understood in terms of the world situation. For its overtones were clearly fascist and so in tune with what, up to 1941, seemed likely to be a new European order. Anxious to place himself in the victors' camp, Franco made the fascist salute obligatory in Spain and, echoing Nazi ideas, developed a keen interest in the notion of a Spanish 'race'.

Franco also played up Spain's indigenous version of fascism, the Falange. Within the larger single party – also called the Falange, for short (p74) – into which Franco had merged it, the party had been bent to his will during the war. Now the dictator felt confident enough to give it a prominent role in his regime. Thus the Falange emblem, consisting of an arrow and bundle of rods, or fasces, was displayed at the entrance to every town and village. The party's anthem, 'Face the Sun' (*Cara al sol*), was sung at official occasions and school assemblies. Its founder, José Antonio Primo de Rivera (p66), acquired martyr status and his motto, 'Spain; One, Great, Free', was adopted by Franco. The blue fascist-style shirts worn by Falange members became a common sight: a 'Blue Division' was sent to fight alongside the Nazis in Russia.

The Falange also took on roles typical of a fascist-style party, most obviously in controlling the government propaganda machine. Directed from 1939 to 1941 by the poet Dionisio Ridruejo, the 'Spanish Goebbels', it ran numerous newspapers and radio stations. Their unvarying themes were the regime's triumphs and the evils of its foes at home and abroad, allegedly linked in a conspiracy of communists, freemasons – and Jews. The Falange was also in charge of the strict censorship to which all other media organs were subjected. Meanwhile its network of subsidiary organisations, including the Women's Section (*Sección Femenina*), disseminated the regime's message throughout Spanish society and provided a means of snuffing out any sign of dissent.

> ### *sindicatos verticales*
>
> government-controlled trade unions
>
> ---
>
> Based on the ideas of the **Falange** (p66), which rejected the 'horizontal' notion of class underlying the workers' movement, the 'vertical' unions included all those who worked in a particular industry – managers, workers and even employers. Their importance to the **Franco regime** was reflected in the term it used to describe its own philosophical basis in the 1940s: National Syndicalism (*nacionalsindicalismo*). In practice, they acted as a means of government control over workers, although from the 1960s on they were increasingly infiltrated by opponents of the regime (p101). They were dissolved shortly after Franco's death.
> See also: ***democracia orgánica***
> (p83)

In government, too, the Falange played an important part, being the second main source of ministers in Franco's early cabinets after the military. But its main power base lay in the **government-controlled trade unions** and their central 'Syndical Organisation'. Established by the 1938 Labour Charter (*Fuero del Trabajo*), these were the only form of industrial organisation allowed by law, since all independent action by workers in common, including collective bargaining, was banned. As well as their control function, the unions also provided a degree of job security through the system of Labour Tribunals (*Magistraturas de Trabajo*) they ran, which were in some ways reminiscent of arrangements under the Primo regime and the Republic (pp40,51). They were also behind the introduction of a mild form of social insurance.

All these measures reflected the influence of fascist ideas, which could be seen also in the economic field. There, the regime's strategy of autarky (*autarquía*) – running the economy in isolation from the outside world – was to some extent dictated by the World War. Initially, too, it had the attraction of being associated with Nazi Germany. Yet it was also in part a deliberate choice, as was shown by Franco's adherence to it well past fascism's final defeat. It corresponded to his delusion that Spain was well-endowed with resources, and hence naturally rich. But perhaps above all for a simple soldier like Franco, self-sufficiency was a matter of national pride. Hardship – especially when borne chiefly by his enemies – was greatly preferable to dependence.

In its efforts to achieve self-sufficiency, the regime intervened in the economy on a massive scale. Spain's already high tariff barriers were raised still further, as were restrictions on foreign investment. Movement of persons both in and out of the country was strictly controlled. Wages, and some prices, were set by official decree; rationing was introduced. Business activity, in particular the establishment of new firms, was subject to a mass of regulations. The promotion of new industry became chiefly a matter for government, the concern of another Falange stronghold, set up in 1941: the National Industry Agency (*Instituto Nacional de Industria*).

Coming on top of all the damage wrought by the Civil War, the effects of ham-handed intervention were disastrous. Production failed to reach pre-war levels, themselves low by European standards. A thriving black market (*estraperlo*) brought quick riches to a few while millions scraped a bare existence. Deaths from starvation and malnutrition were commonplace, so that the early 1940s became known as the hungry years (*años de hambre*). Conditions in the cities were so hard that Spain experienced a phenomenon unparalleled in modern Europe: a return to the land.

In fact, this extraordinary development was actively encouraged by a National Land Settlement Agency (*Instituto Nacional de Colonización*), in a desperate attempt to increase food production by re-cultivating marginal areas. This was a plan more typical of the Third World, as part of which the UN officially classified Spain towards the decade's end. In any event, it failed to solve the country's grave problems; for several years a genuine famine was kept at bay only by shipments of wheat from Argentina, sent on favourable financial terms. The need for such charity laid bare the abject failure of autarky.

Its origin was equally revealing, however. For, since the defeat of fascism, Argentina under the dictatorship of General Juan Perón was the only significant country favourably disposed to Spain. Most of the world seemed happy to see his regime starved into submission (p87). The concept of the 'New State' itself, with its strongly fascist overtones, had become a millstone round Franco's neck.

Politics without parties

As soon as it became clear that the western democracies were going to prevail in the World War, Franco began to downplay the fascist side of his regime. At the same time, he started to introduce elements of what he called democracy. It was a cosmetic exercise. Certainly politics existed, in the sense of a struggle for influence, but it continued to be played out between groups with no democratic basis. Yet below the surface, as it were, significant changes were taking place in the balance of power between them.

Franco distanced himself from fascism in a variety of ways after 1942, and more rapidly after 1945. Thus, the raised-arm salute was dropped, as was the name 'New State' (p81). The Falange's representation in government was cut and its presence in public life generally reduced. Its social measures, too, were watered down. In Labour Tribunals (p82) the dice were loaded increasingly in the employers' favour. And, although land settlement measures (p82) included a system of fixed rents, it was large landowners who gained most from the project as a whole. Other aspects of the Falange's social programme were simply abandoned, to the disgust of the party old guard (*camisas viejas*).

The regime's first concession to the forms of democracy also came in 1942, when Franco issued a 'Creation of Parliament Act' re-instituting the Spanish Parliament (*Cortes*). However, as the Act's title implied, the new, single-chamber assembly bore little relation to previous bodies with the same title, or to the principles on which they had been based. Thus most of the new Parliament's members were appointed by Franco himself, the remainder being indirectly elected by institutions under the regime's control, such as the trade unions and local authorities. Up to half of the representatives (*procuradores*) were government-employed civil servants. In any case, they were given only advisory powers. Their real function was to play the part of Franco's rubber stamp and they performed it faithfully.

> ### *democracia orgánica*
> 'organic' democracy
>
> Adopted by the **Franco regime** in 1945 as a description of its philosophy, 'organic' democracy – as opposed to the 'inorganic', liberal variety – was based on the theory that individuals' interests were best represented, indirectly and collectively, through bodies that were well-established in society. Such natural 'organs' included the **government-controlled trade unions** (p81), professional associations, the Church and, latterly, the family (represented by its male 'head'), but not political parties. The notion bore some resemblance to the ideas of the Austrian Right in the 1930s (p54); as then, it was a cover for dictatorship.

Then, in 1945, Franco unveiled his Spaniards' Charter (*Fuero de los Españoles*). In it he disavowed his own previous description of his regime as 'totalitarian'; instead he used a new term, **'organic' democracy**. The name was deliberately misleading. The Charter did nothing to prevent continuing discrimination against, and repression of former Republican supporters (p80). Instead, it consolidated censorship and the denial of basic rights; in effect, Spaniards had the 'right' to express their views, provided they were in agreement with those of the regime! In particular, the ban on political parties was confirmed.

Yet, although overt political activity was banned, jockeying for power and influence continued behind the scenes. Indeed, Franco subtly encouraged it, as it allowed him to play interests off against each other and thereby protect his own authority. Never formally organised, these interests nonetheless formed loose groupings that, at least initially, corresponded to the various elements that had supported the 1936 rising. Their existence, though officially unmentionable, was an open secret. They were commonly known as the regime's **clans**.

In many ways the most crucial clan was the military, including not just the three main forces but also the paramilitary Civil Guard and armed police; as before, Army officers were the key group. Indeed, the end of the Second World War further strengthened the military's already considerable importance (pp80–1), bringing as it did the prospect of international action against a regime that had made no secret of its backing for the Axis. In the event, however, nothing of the sort occurred and the only attempted invasion was a fiasco (p87). Thereafter, the military's security role reverted to the suppression of occasional strikes and, at a later stage, student demonstrations.

> ### *familias*
> ....
> clans
> ___
> Lacking in any official status or formal organisation, the clans – often also termed 'families' in English – were loose groupings of Franco's supporters and servants. Based on broadly shared aims or interests, they competed for influence within and over his regime. The main ones are usually considered to be: the military; the **Falange** (p66); the Church and its satellite organisations; the **monarchists** (p56); the **Traditionalists** (p66); and, latterly, the civil service (p89). See also: *tecnócratas* (p98)

Politically and socially, the military retained a strong influence. Franco's cabinets always contained a military presence, and not merely in the ministries responsible for the forces – when he eventually relinquished the post of prime minister it was to an Admiral (pp106,107). But in some ways the forces fared surprisingly ill; like military spending in general, officers' salaries were kept low, because their loyalty did not need to be bought. Shut off from civilian society in special living quarters and by habitual intermarriage, fed on a constant diet of regime propaganda, the officer corps and their families remained stuck in the 1930s, convinced that only Franco stood between Spain and disaster. In clan politics they took the initiative only in order to block the proposals of others.

Despite its downgrading by Franco, the Falange remained a player in the game. Falangist ministers continued to serve in government, notably José Antonio Girón de Velasco, who as Labour Minister long controlled the powerful unions (p81), and José Luis Arrese, responsible for the introduction of subsidised housing (*viviendas de protección oficial*). Its supporters also kept a strong presence in the media. Yet after 1945 the old-style, fascist-inspired Falange never enjoyed the same influence as before. Instead, it was supplanted by groups connected with traditional Spanish institutions, popular respect for which could help to bolster Franco's authority, as an association with international fascism had before.

Thus Franco's interest in a possible restoration of the monarchy strengthened the position of its many supporters among senior Army officers, large landowners and financiers. Some of these monarchists were Traditionalists (p66) but most backed the claim of ex-King Alfonso. With his death in 1941, their attention – and Franco's – focused on his exiled son, Juan de Borbón. However, Don Juan – as the Prince became known – had his own mildly liberal agenda. He was also aware of his potential symbolic value to the dictator, both domestically and internationally, and his advisers had already had talks with exiled Republicans (p87). In 1945, he offered to assume the throne in agreement with Franco – but only as a constitutional monarch.

That was too high a price to pay for restoration in Franco's eyes, and even in those of most influential monarchists; the dictatorship had brought them too many other benefits. Moreover, as the danger of outside action against the regime receded (p88), so too did Don Juan's worth as a proof of its non-fascist nature. In 1947 Franco felt confident enough to pass an 'Act of Succession' ruling out any compromise with him. While it declared Spain to be a kingdom (*reino*), it also made Franco himself Regent for Life, effectively suspending the monarchy until his death. Moreover, it empowered him to nominate who should then ascend the throne, subordinating the principle of heredity to the authority of Franco. He, the Act also stated, was responsible only 'to himself and to God'.

Realising that his bluff had been called, Don Juan decided on an accommodation with Franco. In 1948 he agreed that his son, Juan Carlos, should be educated under the dictator's supervision. In return, the monarchists' leading paper, *Abc*, was allowed to reappear, giving them privileged, if limited, access to public opinion. Moreover, governments continued to contain a good proportion of ministers who sympathised with their ambitions. But the monarchists had lost the chance to exert real leverage over Franco. From now on their influence was increasingly usurped by the partisans of an even more venerable and conservative institution.

Franco's alliance with the Church, immensely helpful to him during the Civil War (p75), had remained strong. For all the fascist-style rhetoric of the New State era, the restored Church influence already apparent in the Nationalist zone had been extended and intensified. All school education was placed under its control, which for the first time reached to the universities. Social mores were governed by strict traditional principles; divorce was again banned. In 1945 a further aspect became apparent; with the appointment of Alberto Martín Artajo as Foreign Secretary.

Martín Artajo was a prominent member of the National Catholic Propaganda Association (*Asociación Católica Nacional de Propagandistas [ACNP]*), one of a growing network of Catholic lay organisations. Over the next decade, it was to achieve considerable success in its explicit purpose of extending Church influence into the political sphere, with several more leading figures becoming ministers. Another important Catholic pressure group was 'Catholic Action', which in 1946 set up a section to work among industrial workers, the Workers' Brotherhood (*Hermandades Obreras de Acción Católica*). Thanks to the work of these and other satellite organisations, by the 1950s the Church had become clearly the most powerful influence on the regime; tellingly, the favoured term to describe its philosophy was now Catholic Nationalism (*Nacionalcatolicismo*).

Like the regime's other clans, of course, militant Catholics were ultimately subordinate to Franco's authority. That had been demonstrated in 1942, when embarrassing scuffles between their followers resulted in the summary dismissal of Falange party boss Serrano Suñer (p75) and the downgrading of Traditionalist leader General Varela. Fourteen years later, following similar inter-clan squabbles, Education Minister Ruiz Giménez's ACNP membership did not save him from the sack along with Suñer's successor. In the interim, the new Concordat signed between Spain and the Vatican to replace that of 1851 (p4) had given Franco considerable power over the nomination of Spanish bishops and implicitly guaranteed that his regime – and the dictator personally – would continue to be bathed in a benevolent aura of religiosity (Figure 6.1).

Figure 6.1   Franco's ceremonial exit from the requiem for Alfonso XIII in 1941, a scene combining the key elements of his regime at the time: the Church, the military and fascism. © Hulton-Deutsch Collection/Corbis.

Yet, on balance, the 1953 agreement was extraordinarily favourable to the Church: Spain was declared a confessional state, guided by Catholic precepts; no other religion could be practised in public; and Canon, or Church Law was integrated into the state's Civil Code. These concessions were not just a mark of Franco's religiosity, or even the price of Church backing for his regime within Spain. Primarily, they reflected the dictator's desperate need for the outside approval that 'organic' democracy had so far failed to bring.

International acceptance – and its price

For some time after 1945 the Franco regime's survival was far from assured. While domestic opposition was negligible and the western Allies held back from intervention, the international isolation they imposed threatened the regime with collapse. Yet, slowly the economic situation improved and in the 1950s isolation was eased by the new circumstances of the Cold War. That assisted the regime to consolidate, but it also meant that Franco's options were greatly constrained, as he soon discovered.

Among Franco's opponents, the defeat of his former Axis backers in the World War raised hopes of support from the victorious allies to overthrow him. The Communist Party was sufficiently encouraged to mount a mini-invasion across the Pyrenees in 1945. But no support was forthcoming and it was defeated almost before it got under way. Thereafter internal opposition virtually disappeared, crushed by repression, propaganda and the parlous living conditions of most Spaniards (p82). Occasional – illegal – strikes occurred, as in 1947, but they were an expression of economic desperation, not political resistance.

Nor did the former Republican leaders who had fled Spain prove any more of a threat, since their chronic divisions had been aggravated by the bitterness of defeat. Because of resentment over Communist behaviour during the Civil War (p71), the government-in-exile set up under José Giral (p68) excluded the group which, despite the setback in 1945, remained best placed to organise underground resistance. It was further divided by the attempts of its leading figure, Indalecio Prieto (p71), to negotiate with the right-wing leader José María Gil-Robles (p54), now an adviser to the monarchist pretender. When Don Juan reached an accommodation with Franco in 1948 (p85), the exiles were left in complete disarray.

By then, too, it was clear that the victorious western powers had no intention of overthrowing Franco by force. However, they did seem prepared to impose their will on him by another means: isolation. In 1946 the French closed the Pyrenean frontier. Later the same year Spain was refused admission to the newly formed United Nations on the grounds of its tacit support for Nazi Germany. Almost all countries then followed a UN injunction to withdraw their ambassadors from Madrid, the sole exceptions being Argentina, Portugal, Switzerland and the Vatican. Another sanction that had real material effects was Spain's exclusion from the Marshall Plan, in 1947.

Even these measures failed to shake Franco; indeed, in some ways they actually helped him. For isolation gave real force to his regime's propaganda about an international conspiracy against it, just as the 1945 invasion had been grist to the mill of its anti-communism. Isolation also allowed Franco to justify, even glorify, his strategy of economic self-sufficiency, which had brought Spain to the verge of starvation. That very real threat slowly receded, thanks to continuing Argentinean food aid (p82), until eventually, with the help of a bumper harvest in 1951, it was dispelled altogether. Even so, a wave of strikes that same year was a reminder that the country's appalling economic state continued to threaten the regime's stability.

These various pressures explain the yearning for international acceptance, towards which the 1953 Concordat with the Vatican (pp86–7) was a small but important step. Later the same year came a much more crucial one, the background to which was the outbreak of the Cold War and the development of new weaponry. Long-range strikes against the Soviet bloc were now technically possible, and Spain constituted an excellent potential base for them. The US was determined to secure it. Ignoring the continuing reservations of their European allies, the Americans began attempts to woo Franco. When he rejected their offer of cheap loans, they raised the stakes by offering a full-blown treaty.

Formal recognition by the world's most powerful country was too great a prize to sacrifice on the altar of self-sufficiency. In 1953 Franco signed the series of accords known as the **Defence Agreements**. Although their direct material benefits proved disappointing, that was more than compensated by the acquisition of such a powerful friend. In 1955 the advantages of the agreement were amply illustrated when Spain was admitted to the UN, the objections of a decade earlier now overlooked, even if the regime itself ascribed the success to the skills of its Foreign Minister, Martín Artajo (pp85–6). Moreover, without the backing of the world's leading economic power there was no question of an effective trade embargo against the regime.

Having swallowed his national pride, Franco now accepted the financial support he had previously scorned. This provided the Spanish economy with a significant boost, as did the general upswing in the world economy during the early 1950s, especially once the regime slightly relaxed its trade restrictions towards the middle of the decade. Coupled with the policy of state-promoted industrialisation (p82) – and the fact that its starting point was so low – these external factors enabled the country to enjoy a sudden burst of growth. For some years production rose at around six per cent annually, so that pre-war levels were finally surpassed. Living standards rose appreciably, especially for a small but growing middle class.

Insofar as public satisfaction was increased, growth had a stabilising effect. But it also had other, less positive implications for the regime. Reversal of the drift

Acuerdos para la Defensa

Defence Agreements (of 1953)

Signed in 1953 between the Spanish and US governments, the Defence Agreements, or 'Pact of Madrid', permitted the Americans to set up and operate four military bases on Spanish soil. They were renewed on a five-yearly basis up to 1978, but thereafter the issue was caught up in the furore surrounding Spain's entry to NATO (pp133–4). After lengthy negotiations a further, partial renewal was agreed in 1988, under which the US retained only the naval base at Rota, near Cadiz.

back to the land (p82) revealed the grave lack of adequate urban housing; many poorer Spaniards were condemned to live in shanty-towns (*chabolismo*) which became a breeding-ground for discontent. Prices rose sharply, to the discomfort of workers whose wages continued to be controlled by law. Among the better-off young, on the other hand, prosperity awakened the desire for greater personal freedom. When the Education Minister, Ruiz Giménez, was prompted to partly relax conditions in the universities in 1956, the result was an outbreak of student unrest that cost him his job (p86).

That same year also saw the largest strike wave yet, but this time it did not elicit the usual response. Employers whose businesses were at last getting off the ground were reluctant to have them disrupted and also had the funds to meet wage demands. They found an ally in Labour Minister Girón (p85), who saw a chance to re-assert the Falange's credentials as defender of worker interests (p82). In some industries the government was persuaded to concede wage rises of up to 30 per cent.

This policy pacified the strikers, certainly, but for the economy as a whole the effects were disastrous. Inflation was pushed still higher, increasing the already dangerous disparities between different sectors of the economy and further reducing the competitiveness of Spanish goods on world markets. This was especially serious given that, as the economy took off, Spanish manufacturers had begun to demand more sophisticated plant and machinery. Yet it was precisely these capital goods that the country could not produce. The result was a soaring import bill and a widening trade gap, which Spain's exports of agricultural produce and low-grade manufactures were quite incapable of closing.

The rapidly worsening situation alarmed the country's new trading partners, of which the US was now the most important. Worried that Spain might be unable to pay its debts, the Americans brought their influence to bear on the IMF and the OEEC. The two international bodies agreed to provide further substantial loans, but only in return for changes in economic policy. Spain was required to abolish the system of multiple exchange rates it had used to restrict imports in contravention of international trade guidelines. Franco had no option but to take a second gulp of nationalist pride and agree to devaluation of the peseta.

His reaction to these developments came in 1958 in legislation ostensibly concerned with the single party, long a bulwark of his power (pp81–2). Even so, its function had changed considerably since the 1940s, when repression and propaganda were primary tasks of his governments. Now their overriding concern was to run the apparatus of a modern state. In the absence of democratic politics, that gave enormous influence to civil servants, who had emerged as a new, and very influential, clan within the regime (p84). Moreover, the party's title evoked unfortunate memories of fascism. It was accordingly renamed the **National Movement** and the use of 'Falange' officially banned.

However, that was the only concession to change made by the 'Principles of the National Movement Act'. In general, it restated the regime's underlying tenets in fundamentalist terms. Admittedly, it defined Spain not just as a 'traditional, Catholic

Movimiento Nacional

National Movement

First used as a self-description by
the insurgent side in the Civil War
(p67), 'National Movement' was
adopted in 1958 by the **Franco
regime** as the official designation
of the sole political organisation
permitted under its rule, replacing
the original title of *'Falange
Española Tradicionalista y de las
Juntas de Ofensiva Nacional
Sindicalista'* (*FET y de las JONS*).
All government employees,
including military officers, were
required to be members. It was
assured representation in
government – its secretary-
general was automatically a
minister – and in Parliament, of
which its own National Council
functioned as an unofficial upper
house. The Movement controlled
important sectors of Spanish life,
in particular the media and the
trade unions (p81), in both of
which old-style Falangists (p66)
retained some influence. As a
whole, however, it was dominated
by bureaucrats, many of the
technocrat type (p98). It was
officially dissolved on 1 April
1977.
See also: **UCD** (p117)

monarchy', but also as a 'social and representative' one. Yet the basis for doing so was
still the 'organic' brand of democracy
dreamed up by Franco in the 1940s (p83). All
legislation was required to conform to the
'spirit' of the Movement, whose National
Council was given the task of checking that it
did so. The Movement itself was defined as
the 'communion of Spaniards united by
belief in the ideals which gave life to the
Crusade' – in other words, as one side in the
Civil War to which the very name harked
back.

In effect, Franco was saying that, as far
as he was concerned, nothing had changed.
But it had. The partial integration into the
world community that had helped the
regime to consolidate also meant it was no
longer master of its own fate. Indeed, the
regime had already tacitly acknowledged
this fact: in 1956, by quietly surrendering
the Moroccan protectorate that was Spain's
last claim to 'greatness', in the imperial
sense dear to Franco (p39); and, a year later,
in changing its economic tack at America's
behest.

The mild changes introduced then failed
to produce the desired effect, however, and
Spain came under renewed pressure. In
1959, US President Eisenhower arrived in
Madrid to speak personally with Franco,
whose regime lauded the visit as a signal of
acceptance into the US-dominated western economic order. It preferred not to dwell
on the other image evoked by the celebrated embrace with which Eisenhower
greeted his fellow general; that of a bear-hug.

Summary of main points

The 'New State'

- The 'New State' established by Franco was essentially a peacetime extension of arrangements during the Civil War. It discriminated harshly against groups and individuals who had supported the Republic, and was to a considerable degree run by the Army.
- It also had markedly fascist features, including the important role of the single party (commonly still known as the Falange), especially in social and labour policy.
- Both fascist ideology and Franco's own ideas led his regime to strive for autarky (self-sufficiency) by intervening extensively in the economy. The results were disastrous; in the 1940s Spain even experienced serious food shortages.

Politics without parties

- After 1942 Franco distanced his regime from fascism, including the social measures associated with it. But moves to introduce aspects of democracy were a sham; basic freedoms continued to be curtailed and political parties remained banned.
- Meanwhile, different groups among the regime's supporters jockeyed for influence. The most important of these so-called clans were the Army, the Falange, Monarchists, Traditionalists, and the Church with its related organisations.
- Although even it remained subordinate to Franco's supreme authority, by the 1950s the Church had emerged as the most influential clan. Its position was further strengthened by the Concordat signed with the Vatican in 1953.

International acceptance – and its price

- For a period in the aftermath of World War II, Spain was almost entirely shut out of the international community. This made it hard to improve the country's appalling economic situation.
- Isolation was effectively ended in 1953 by the US, whose support was decisive in improving the country's situation both diplomatically and economically.
- However, economic growth soon led to various forms of social and economic disruption within Spain, as well as a serious balance of payments deficit. Yet Franco refused to respond to these changed circumstances by altering the regime's nature in any significant way.

Exhibit 6.1: The Principles of the National Movement Act' (1958)

The second last of Franco's 'Basic Laws' (final article omitted)

Yo Franciso Franco Bahamonde, Caudillo de España,
   Consciente de mi responsabilidad ante Dios y ante la Historia, en presencia de las Cortes del Reino, promulgo como Principios del movimiento Nacional, entendido como comunión de los españoles en los ideales que dieron vida a la Cruzada, los siguientes:

I

España es una unidad de destino en lo universal. El servicio a la unidad, grandeza y libertad de la Patria es deber sagrado y tarea colectiva de todos los españoles.

II

La Nación española considera como timbre de honor el acatamiento a la Ley de Dios, según la doctrina de la Santa Iglesia Católica, Apostólica y Romana, única verdadera y fe inseparable de la conciencia nacional, que inspirará su legislación.

III

España, raíz de una gran familia de pueblos, con los que se siente indisolublemente hermanada, aspira a la instauración de la justicia y de la paz entre las naciones.

IV

La unidad entre los hombres y las tierras de España es intangible. La integridad de la Patria y su independencia son exigencias supremas de la comunidad nacional. Los Ejércitos de España, garantía de su seguridad y expresión de las virtudes heroicas de nuestro pueblo, deberán poseer la fortaleza necesaria para el mejor servicio de la Patria.

V

La comunidad nacional se funda en el hombre, como portador de valores eternos, y en la familia, como base de la vida social; pero los intereses individuales y colectivos han de estar subordinados siempre al bien común de la Nación, constituida por las generaciones pasadas, presentes y futuras. La Ley ampara por igual al derecho de todos los españoles.

VI

Las entidades naturales de la vida social: familia, municipio y sindicato, son estructuras básicas de la comunidad nacional. Las instituciones y corporaciones de otro carácter que satisfagan exigencias sociales de interés general deberán ser amparadas para que puedan participar eficazmente en el perfeccionamiento de los fines de la comunidad nacional.

VII

El pueblo español, unido en un orden de Derecho, informado por los postulados de autoridad, libertad y servicio, constituye el Estado Nacional. Su forma política es, dentro de los principios inmutables del Movimiento Nacional y de cuanto determinan la Ley de Sucesión y demás Leyes Fundamentales, la Monarquía tradicional, católica, social y representativa.

VIII

El carácter representativo del orden político es principio básico de nuestras instituciones públicas. La participación del pueblo en las tareas legislativas y en las demás funciones de interés general se llevará a cabo a través de la familia, el municipio, el sindicato y demás entidades con representación orgánica que a este fin reconozcan las leyes. Toda organización política de cualquier índole, al margen de este sistema representativo, será considerada ilegal.

Todos los españoles tendrán acceso a los cargos y funciones públicas según su mérito y capacidad.

IX

Todos los españoles tienen derecho: a una justicia independiente, que será gratuita para aquéllos que carezcan de medios económicos; a una educación general y profesional, que nunca podrá dejar de recibirse por falta de medios materiales; a los beneficios de la asistencia y seguridad sociales, y a una equitativa distribución de la renta nacional y de las cargas fiscales. El ideal cristiano de la justicia social, reflejado en el Fuero de Trabajo, inspirará la política y las leyes.

X

Se reconoce al trabajo como origen de jerarquía, deber y honor de los españoles, y a la propiedad privada, en todas sus formas, como derecho condicionado a su función social. La iniciativa privada, fundamento de la actividad económica, deberá ser estimulada, encauzada, y, en su caso, suplida por la acción del Estado.

XI

La Empresa, asociación de hombres y medios ordenados a la producción, constituye una comunidad de intereses y una unidad de propósitos. Las relaciones entre los elementos de aquélla deben basarse en la justicia y en la recíproca lealtad, y los valores económicos estarán subordinados a los de orden humano y social. [...]

I, Francisco Franco Bahamonde, Caudillo of Spain:

Conscious of my responsibility before God and before History, in the presence of the Parliament of the Kingdom, proclaim the following to be the Principles of the National Movement, which being the communion of Spaniards in the ideals that gave birth to the Crusade:

I

Spain's destiny in the world order is one and indivisible. The service of the fatherland's unity, greatness and freedom is a sacred duty and a collective undertaking for all Spaniards.

II

The Spanish nation regards it as a mark of honour to obey the law of God, according to the doctrine of the Holy Catholic Apostolic and Roman Church, the sole true church, whose faith is an integral part of the nation's consciousness and shall inspire its legislation.

III

Spain, the root of a great family of peoples, to whom she feels bound in indissoluble brotherhood, aspires to the establishment of justice and peace between all nations.

IV

The unity which binds the land and men of Spain is inviolable. The country's physical integrity and independence are supreme priorities of the national community. Spain's

Armed Forces, as the guarantor of her security and the expression of our people's heroic virtues, shall possess the strength required to serve the fatherland optimally.

V

The national community is founded on man as the bearer of eternal values, and on the family as the basis of social life; but individual and collective interests are always to be subordinated to the common good of the nation, which is made up of past, present and future generations of Spaniards. The law shall protect the rights of all Spaniards equally.

VI

The natural entities of social life – the family, the municipality and the trade union – are the basic structures of the national community. Such other types of institutions and corporations as meet the general needs of society shall be protected, so that they may contribute efficaciously to achieving the national community's aims.

VII

The Spanish people, united under the rule of Law and informed by the notions of authority, freedom and service, make up the National State. In accordance with the immutable principles of the National Movement, and the provisions of the Act of Succession and the other Basic Laws, its form shall be that of the traditional, Catholic, social and representative Monarchy.

VIII

The representative nature of the political order is the fundamental principle of our public institutions. Public participation in the legislative process and other tasks of general interest shall take place through the family, the municipality, the trade union, and such other bodies representing the basic organs of society as the law may recognize for that purpose. All political organizations of whatever kind that lie outside this system of representation shall be deemed illegal.

All Spaniards shall have access to public offices and functions according to their merits and abilities.

IX

All Spaniards are entitled to: an independent system of justice, which shall be available free to those lacking financial means; general and vocational education, which none shall fail to receive through want of material means; the benefits of social services and security; and an equitable distribution of the national income and of the burden of taxation. The State's laws and actions shall be inspired by the Christian ideal of social justice, as reflected in the Labour Charter.

X

Work shall be recognized as the basis of Spaniards' rank, duty and honour, and private property in all its forms as a right conditioned by its social function. Private enterprise, the basis of economic activity, shall be encouraged, channelled and, where necessary, supplemented by State intervention.

XI

Business enterprises, which are associations of men and resources for the purpose of production, constitute communities of interests with common aims. The relationships between their various components shall be based on justice and mutual loyalty, with economic values being subordinated to those of a human and social nature.

Topics for discussion

- To which institutions does Exhibit 6.1 refer, explicitly and implicitly? What roles are they assigned by the Act?
- What attitudes does the Act reflect towards:
  (a) liberal democracy;
  (b) capitalism; and
  (c) regionalism?
- What evidence is there of a desire to improve relations with the outside world?

- What similarities and differences does the Act suggest between Franco's ideas and those of earlier representatives of the Spanish Right (cf. Exhibits 1.2, 2.1, 3.1, 4.1, 5.2)?
- How new was the 'New State', in Spanish terms? Which aspects of it were retained after the designation itself was dropped in the later 1940s?
- What significant changes occurred in Spain, and in the Franco regime itself, between 1939 and 1959?

CHAPTER 7

The bottle half-uncorked (1959–1975)

Throughout the Western world the 1960s were a period of economic growth. It was underpinned by the network of trans-Atlantic institutions set up in the 1940s and extended, in 1961, by the creation of the Organisation for Economic Cooperation and Development (OECD). In western Europe a further support was the European Community (EC), as the European Economic Community (EEC) became in 1967; six years later it acquired three new members, including Britain. The decade also saw a trend in favour of social and personal freedom, which, with the liberalising decisions of the Second Vatican Council, even affected the Catholic Church. In 1968 the pressure for change boiled over in widespread protests, especially among the young, many of whom were heavily influenced by new interpretations of Marxist ideas. In Italy, these led to the emergence of a so-called eurocommunism that rejected the authority of the Soviet Union. The uncertainty caused by these developments was heightened by the collapse of the Bretton Woods system of fixed exchange rates in 1971 and, two years later, by the first oil shock, a massive price increase imposed by the producer countries.

At the end of the 1950s the Franco regime was faced with a choice. It could bow to American pressure for radical changes in its economic policies. Or it could risk a return to the conditions of the early 1950s, something not even Franco was prepared to contemplate. He therefore entrusted his regime's fate to a group of its supporters who felt that the changes were actually in its interest. To a degree events proved them right; the spectacular economic development brought by the new policies did indeed increase Spaniards' material living standards. Yet it also triggered changes that fomented opposition among certain groups, as well as a more general, if muted dissatisfaction, which some within the regime sought to counter by relaxing its authoritarian nature. As their leader neared his end, however, they once again lost influence in favour of reactionary hardliners determined to resist reform at all costs. Spain was left like a champagne bottle from which the cork had been half removed, on the point of explosion.

Uneven development

For some of its supporters, the grave situation faced by the Franco regime in the late 1950s was not a crisis but an opportunity. They believed

tecnócratas

technocrats

Perhaps better described as 'professional experts', the technocrats were the highly trained specialists, mainly in economics and finance, who acquired decisive influence in the late 1950s. Many were under the influence of the **Opus Dei**, including Mariano Navarro Rubio, appointed Finance Minister in 1957, and Alberto Ullastres, who took over the Trade portfolio at the same time. Other leading technocrats were Gregorio López Bravo, Minister for Industry and subsequently Foreign Minister, and Laureano López Rodó, another Opus member, who co-ordinated the 1959 measures known as the 'Stabilisation Plan' and the various subsequent Development Plans.

that economic change could and should be managed, in order to equip the regime for survival in the contemporary world. Their ideas formed the basis of Spain's astonishing economic development in the 1960s. However, that success also triggered off substantial social changes which were barely compatible with the regime's snail-paced political evolution.

The domestic impetus behind the new course came largely from elements of the civil service elite, which by now had become very influential (p89). These **technocrats** were influenced by – and in some cases members of – the **Opus Dei** organisation, which believed that the survival of a conservative, Catholic regime could only be assured by satisfying the popular desire for

Opus Dei

Opus Dei

Founded in 1928 by the Aragonese priest José María Escrivá de Balaguer, Opus Dei (Latin: God's Work) is a lay organisation dedicated to preserving conservative Catholic principles in the face of economic modernisation. Under the **Franco regime** the Opus, as it is frequently known, acquired considerable power, its members and sympathisers filling many top ministerial and administrative posts from 1957 on. Although its political influence was dented by the 1969 Matesa scandal (p107) and, more severely, by Franco's death, the Opus continues to be strongly represented in business, finance and higher education; a number of leading figures in the **People's Party** (p162) are believed to be members. See also: *inmovilistas* (p108)

better living standards. The necessary economic growth, they believed, was best achieved by allowing market forces free rein through the ending of government intervention in the economy (p82). By contrast, they favoured continued strong control over society, to prevent it from going along the liberal, secular road it had taken elsewhere in the West.

The technocrats' influence dated from 1957, when some of the group's leading figures were brought into government to oversee changes in economic policy. When the inadequacy of those changes gave rise to US pressure for more (p90), they were able to persuade Franco to give them a virtually free hand over economic strategy. The U-turn is now usually associated with 1959, the year in which most of the measures making up the so-called 'Stabilisation Plan' were enacted, while the 'Plan' itself is often seen as being essentially an exercise in cutting intervention and red tape. But, though some deregulation did occur, it was neither new – most price controls had been abolished in 1956 – nor by any means complete. As a result, when Franco died, by modern western standards his government was still playing a large economic role.

In the event, two other aspects of the technocrats' strategy proved to be more crucial. One was a standard package of deflationary measures (*medidas de ajuste*), introduced in agreement with the OECD and the International Monetary Fund, to which Spain was admitted in 1960. Wages were frozen and public spending reduced. The result was a sharp slowdown in the economy, with severe effects on employment and earnings. But the package achieved its aims of bringing down inflation, eliminating many uncompetitive firms and forcing the survivors to become more efficient.

The final plank in the technocrats' strategy was the one most resisted by Franco, since it involved finally abandoning any idea of autarky (p82). The opening up (*apertura*) of Spain's economy that followed had two key aspects. On the one hand, controls on inward investment were relaxed. Foreign capital was now permitted to acquire a controlling stake in companies in all but the most politically sensitive industries such as defence. On the other hand, restrictions on the movement of persons were eased. Tourism, previously accepted grudgingly at best, was promoted, while Spaniards were allowed, even encouraged, to seek work outside the country.

The effects were dramatic. Investment poured into the country, attracted by low production costs and the helpful industrial relations framework – in plain English, the absence of normal trade union freedoms. Spain launched, at last, a full-blooded process of industrialisation, which now affected not only Catalonia and the Basque Country, but also Madrid and its rapidly growing satellite towns, as well as a number of other regional centres, notably Valladolid. At the same time tourism took off, so that within a few years Spain had become the world's leading provider of beach holidays. The result of these twin stimuli was the period of very rapid growth which brought the word 'boom' into the Spanish language and marked the beginning of what became known as the development years (*años de desarrollo*).

Nor was it just growth that was achieved. Soaring receipts from tourism, combined with the remittance payments (*remesas*) sent by emigrants to their families at home, were more than sufficient to make up for Spain's trade deficit, and so soothe the concerns of its trading partners (p89). Emigration also solved the problem of unemployment inherent in such massive structural change; in effect, it was simply exported. Back home remittances also helped ensure that, although wage-earners paid the vast bulk of taxes, the material benefits of growth were felt almost throughout society, at least in the rapidly expanding cities.

To a degree, rising prosperity had the effect envisaged by the technocrats. Television sets and cars might not necessarily turn workers into enthusiastic supporters of the regime, but they often meant that the resigned resentment of its early years transmuted into apathy. Such indifference was constantly fed by the official media, with its comparisons between 'Franco's peace' and the 'anarchy' that had allegedly preceded it. To those who, for the first time, had significant material possessions to lose, it could seem a powerful argument, especially if they were too young to have their own memories of how 'peace' had been achieved (p80).

Yet development also had other effects. The decline of agriculture, and the attraction of city jobs, led to depopulation of the countryside on a massive scale (*éxodo rural*). Even in Francoist Spain, urban life brought a wider range of experience, especially for the young, many of whom were increasingly resentful of the constraints imposed by strict Catholic morality (p85). Not only that; tourism and emigration meant that more and more Spaniards were coming into contact with outside influences. They became aware that life in other western countries bore no resemblance to the way it was portrayed by the regime's propaganda; instead, it seemed to involve not only higher living standards but also greater personal freedom – and more fun.

These trends contributed to the growth of opposition in the 1960s (pp101–2). It was kept in check by the repression that the technocrats, like Franco himself, regarded as the essential complement to their economic liberalisation. Harder to deal with, since it could not be combated by the security forces, was the less intense but increasingly widespread discontent that represented a potential breeding ground for future protest. It was this longer term threat which led some within the regime to propose a form of liberalisation that went beyond the economic sphere (*aperturismo*).

In most cases such liberalisers were also motivated by dislike of the technocrats. Thus one proposal came from José Solís Ruiz, Secretary-General of the National Movement (p90), an old-style Falangist (p66) deeply distrustful of the new course. For him, liberalisation meant making the government-run unions (p81) attractive to workers in the face of competition from illegal alternatives. To do so he proposed the free election of union representatives, and even a limited right to strike. His ideas were blocked but some leading civil servants opposed to the technocrats were more successful. Their principal representative was the Minister of Information, Manuel Fraga Iribarne, author of the 1966 'Press Act'.

The Fraga Act, as it became known, brought big changes in the regime's control over the media, including the abolition of prior censorship, i.e. the requirement for editors to get material approved in advance of publication. Instead, they now had to judge for themselves what would, and would not, prove acceptable. For those who guessed wrongly, the Act retained harsh punishments, in the form of suspensions and fines. It was also insidious, imposing as it did a form of self-censorship. But its application by Fraga's Ministry was relaxed enough to allow a number of mildly critical journals to appear. For the first time in 30 years a form of public debate was possible, albeit confined to the economic sphere; political criticism was still strictly taboo.

Some apparent political relaxation was included in the last of the regime's **basic laws,** promulgated in 1967. As well as a degree of religious freedom – for the first time since 1939 faiths other than Catholicism could be practised publicly – this 'Organic Law of the State' (*LOE*) also provided for parliamentary elections. In fact, though, they were as big a sham as earlier aspects of 'organic' democracy (p83). The electorate was restricted to – male – heads of households; the elected representatives remained a small minority in Parliament, the bulk of whose members continued to be appointed; and the elections were subject to strict control by the authorities, to ensure that only approved candidates were successful.

The LOE was thus proof of how Spain's political evolution continued to lag far behind its economic development. That had not gone unnoticed by her neighbours who, less compliant than their American allies (p88), had rejected her application to join the EEC in 1962 – on the specific grounds that she was not a democracy. The decision was a severe blow to the technocrats, who knew that continuing growth could only be assured by access to wider European markets. More immediately, the gap between political and economic development had the drawback of stimulating opposition of various sorts within Spain itself.

> ### leyes básicas (del franquismo)
>
> (Franco regime's) basic laws
>
> In the absence of a constitution, the basic ground rules of government under the **Franco regime** (p80) were set out in legislation passed over a period of almost 30 years. The first of these basic laws were decrees issued in the Nationalist zone during the Civil War, in particular that which, in 1936, installed Franco as Head of State and Government (p68) and the 1938 Labour Charter (p82). There followed the 1942 Creation of Parliament Act (p83), the Spaniards' Charter of 1945 (p84), and the 1947 Act of Succession (p85). The most important of the basic laws were the Principles of the National Movement Act, passed in 1958 (pp89–90), and the 1967 'Organic Law of the State' (pp100–1).

The emergence of opposition

Overt opposition to the regime had never been completely eliminated; indeed, the 1950s had seen several waves of strikes. But it was only in the next decade that unrest among industrial workers became persistent and widespread. The 1960s also saw an upsurge of opposition from regionalists and, ironically, from the institution which had been the regime's chief support: the Church. Indeed, although it rarely turned to anything stronger, by the end of the decade wide sections of Franco's core support were exhibiting signs of discontent.

It was in reaction to earlier industrial unrest that, in 1958, the regime took what turned out to be a fateful decision. It allowed a degree of collective bargaining over pay, on the condition that the negotiations would take place under the wing of its own trade unions (p81). Yet precisely that stipulation gave an unwitting spur to a process that was already under way; infiltration of the unions by organisations set up by workers themselves in defiance of the regime. At first these **Workers' Commissions** operated locally, but in the 1960s they established a nationwide network, thereby greatly increasing their capacity for effective action.

At the same time, economic growth was changing the status of workers and their own expectations. Skills shortages in key industries greatly increased their

Comisiones Obreras (CCOO)

Workers' Commissions

The original Workers' Commissions were illegal associations of workers, created to give employees an alternative form of representation to the Franco regime's own **tightly controlled unions** (p81). The first was set up in 1957. Initially created by separate local initiatives, the Commissions soon came together to form a nationwide underground organisation. Their founders were inspired by widely varying political views, including liberal Catholic ideas (p104), but in the 1960s the Commissions fell under the influence of the **Communist Party** (p70). In the late 1970s they grew dramatically to become Spain's largest labour organisation. Thereafter, their appeal to workers was constrained by their militancy and, later, by their Communist ties. Even so, they remain a major player in Spanish industrial relations.

bargaining power. Successful businesses, especially those engaged in export, wanted quick solutions to labour problems, and therefore preferred to deal with representatives who could deliver the agreement of employees as a whole – which increasingly meant the Commissions. Moreover, rising wages meant that many workers now had a small financial cushion, and so were readier to undertake strike action if their demands were not met. All these factors strengthened both workers' militancy and the Commissions themselves.

By the mid-1960s these had effectively fallen under the control of the Communist Party, whose ideas were well-suited to underground operation – and whose objective was to bring down the regime. This contributed to a change in the nature of industrial action, which increasingly focused on political issues. The regime itself also helped the process along. Strikes were routinely suppressed by the security forces, often with considerable brutality, and tended to turn into battles of attrition. This violence bred resentment, and from there it was only a step to political protest. By the time Franco realised the danger and attempted to crack down on the Commissions (p107), they were far too well established to be rooted out of his own union apparatus.

Neither of the two main strands of the pre-Civil War workers' movement took any significant part in these developments. The anarcho-syndicalists (p36) had been virtually eliminated by repression in the regime's early years. The Socialists' abstention from infiltrating the official unions, on the other hand, was a deliberate choice, prompted by fears that they would be accused of collaborating as they had done under the earlier Primo dictatorship (pp39–40). Ironically, industrial strife reached its highest levels in the Basque Country, a traditional Socialist stronghold. However, that was due to other developments since Franco came to power.

Despite Franco's clampdown on regionalism (p80), the Basque movement did not initially attempt to oppose his regime. It shared some of his conservative ideas and its supporters often benefited economically from his rule. Moreover, his attempts to stamp out the Basque language meant little in the urban areas, where it had long since effectively disappeared. Regionalism's core, the banned Basque Nationalist Party (p24), showed little appetite for organising resistance.

The situation was changed irrevocably by the economic growth that had begun in the 1950s and accelerated in the next decade (p99). It brought a second wave of industrialisation to the region, which penetrated beyond the Bilbao area into the countryside of Guipúzcoa. There it caused enormous social upheaval in the tightly knit rural communities that were the last major stronghold of the Basque language, whose future now looked bleak indeed. They now became the main recruiting ground for a new and very different regionalist organisation; **Euskadi ta Askatasuna (ETA)**.

Part of ETA's efforts were devoted to establishing a network of clandestine Basque-language schools (*ikastolak*) as a means of preserving the language. But its fundamental desire was to strike back at the regime, which led it to get involved in industrial action and – a new departure for Basque regionalists – to establish close links with Spanish workers' organisations of the Left. The conjunction of appeals to national and class solidarity proved a potent mixture, leading to repeated waves of strikes in the region. In response, the regime imposed frequent states of siege and exception, during which indiscriminate brutality by the security forces was the order of the day.

The government's reaction backfired completely, merely serving to bear out ETA's contention that the Basque Country was 'occupied' by a hostile Spanish state. This sense of national conflict was intensified after ETA turned to violence in 1968. From then on its attacks on the security forces, and their persistent over-reaction, fostered the notion of a 'war' in which it acted as the Basque 'army'. Moreover, its links with the Left meant that national sentiment was not only deepened but also extended to new sections of Basque society. By the end of the decade ETA had become the standard-bearer of a radicalised and immeasurably strengthened movement.

Euskadi ta Askatasuna (ETA)

Basque homeland and liberty

Formed in 1959 by younger members of the **PNV** (p24) to oppose the Franco regime's assault on Basque culture, ETA later adopted a vague form of 'revolutionary' socialism to go with its demand for Basque independence. In 1968 it turned to violence, which was directed initially against the security forces and others closely linked to the dictatorship. In 1974 it split into 'military' and 'politico-military' branches, the second of which disappeared in 1982 (p142). After Franco's death, and despite the granting of Basque autonomy, ETA refused to moderate its demands or abandon violence. It became a significant danger to stability, both in its own right and as the potential excuse for a coup (p124). In the early 1990s it appeared to be on the verge of defeat. That it survived was in good part thanks to revelations about a government-sponsored dirty war carried out against it in the 1980s (p153). In 1998 ETA announced a truce but resumed killing little more than a year later (p155), a pattern repeated in 2005–2006 (p178). In recent years its attacks have been directed increasingly against civilians, especially politicians and others who oppose its activities publicly.
See also: **Herri Batasuna** (p143); **caso GAL** (p140); **Pacto de Lizarra** (p155)

The situation in Catalonia was less dramatic, but no less serious for the regime. The business community (p22), the historical core of regionalism, was alienated by Franco's removal of self-government, by his simplistic economic policies (p82) and by the isolation from Europe to which his political ones led (p101). Moreover, much of the middle class deeply resented his attempt to stamp out the Catalan culture, to which they felt strong ties.

Culture certainly formed the initial focus of early underground activities in the region but, as in other cases, the severity with which the regime cracked down on them broadened the scope of protest. A group led by Jordi Pujol (p144) began the work of nation-building (Catalan: *fer país*), a long-term strategy of establishing contacts throughout Catalan society and building a consensus on its future once the regime eventually came to an end. By the end of the 1960s virtually all opinion in Catalonia was agreed, not just that democracy had to come, but that it must bring devolution with it.

In both the Basque Country and Catalonia, as in the past, these regionalist protests received backing from the local clergy. Altogether more surprising was the critical stance increasingly adopted by the Spanish Church in general towards the regime. When the Spanish bishops criticised the 1959 Stabilisation Plan (pp98–9) for paying too little attention to the weakest in society, they showed which way the wind was blowing. In the next decade it became a gale.

Part of the cause of the bishops' intervention lay in the Second Vatican Council, which aligned the Church worldwide with demands for human rights and against authoritarian regimes. To Franco this line was as unacceptable as it was inexplicable; he refused to allow one of the Pope's pronouncements to be read in Spain on the grounds that it was heretical. However, despite his powers under the 1953 Concordat (pp86–7), he was unable to prevent the Vatican filling senior positions in the Spanish Church with men whose rejection of his regime was more or less explicit.

Among the lower clergy such attitudes were already common. By the 1960s, references to the Civil War no longer cut much ice with younger Spanish clerics. They were more concerned with issues affecting their parishes in the present, such as the lack of basic freedoms and, in many areas still, abject poverty. Many became involved in more-or-less clandestine political and industrial activity, mainly through the legal Catholic workers organisations, the HOAC (p86) and its offshoot, the Young Catholic Workers (*Juventudes Obreras Católicas*), although some even joined the Workers' Commissions. The Vatican Council and its aftermath meant that these activities often enjoyed the broad support of their superiors.

Meanwhile, lay Catholics led by the former Education Minister, Joaquín Ruiz Giménez (p86), had established an informal Christian Democrat grouping. Taking advantage of the relaxation of censorship in 1966 (p100) it brought out the journal *Cuadernos para el Diálogo*, which became an important arena for debate. It was tolerated by the regime, as were two other mildly critical groups: the monarchists led by José María Gil-Robles (p87) and the so-called 'Social Democrats' set up by a former propaganda chief, Dionisio Ridruejo (p81). They termed themselves jointly a 'democratic' opposition, to emphasise that they would have nothing to do with Communists.

These groups were often accused of being Franco's stooges, and they undoubtedly played into his hands in some ways. By sticking to the unspoken limits of their criticism, they allowed him to claim that his regime accommodated dissent. And they sometimes gave the regime's propaganda machine a soft target, as when in 1962 they met in Munich and publicly urged the EEC to reject Spain's application to join (p101). The official media had a field day, condemning the treachery of what they dubbed the Munich conspiracy (*Conturbernio de Munich*). Yet, at the same time, the legal' opposition's existence and criticisms, both widely known, helped to sustain a growing sense of dissatisfaction among what had once been the bedrock of the regime's support; the middle classes.

Middle-class discontent took various forms. The most visible was student protest, which intensified after a number of dissident academics, including the popular Professor Enrique Tierno Galván, were dismissed in 1965 for criticising the regime; it got a further boost from the events of 1968. More generally, the better-off young were increasingly unhappy at being denied the personal freedoms enjoyed by their peers abroad. Not a few joined the Communist Party, usually because it was the only group organising serious underground opposition rather than for any great belief in its ideas. Finally, exclusion from Europe in another sense – economic – led some business leaders to conclude that there must be political change of some sort. However, like the vast majority of the population, they had tacitly accepted that this was impossible while the dictator lived.

Death throes of dictatorship

In 1970, as his regime entered its fifth decade, Franco was 78. Clearly his death could not be far away and he had begun making arrangements for it, determined that it should not be a prelude to significant change. In response, his opponents also prepared for outright confrontation. That in turn encouraged his hard-line supporters to dig in deeper. With the regime, quite literally, in its death throes, those who hoped for some form of gradual relaxation were left with little influence.

By this time, Franco had long since ceased to determine the day-to-day operation of his regime. Indeed, his arms-length approach to government, exemplified by the lengthy shooting holidays he spent with cronies, was common knowledge. But his ultimate authority, which continued to rest essentially on his personal standing, remained uncontested. His forthcoming disappearance thus posed a two-fold threat to his regime, and Franco himself was well aware of the need to make preparations for a world without him (*posfranquismo*).

The planning began in earnest with the 1967 'Organic Law of the State' (pp100–1), which established that the new King would be essentially a figurehead without real power, a Head of State but not of Government. Two years later, Franco at last formally settled the question of who would ascend the throne on his death (p85). In reality, his choice had been clear ever since his 1948 agreement with the

Figure 7.1 Franco attending a service in memory of Falange leader José Antonio Primo de Rivera, accompanied by three key figures for the survival of his regime, Admiral Carrero Blanco, Torcuato Fernández-Miranda and Prince Juan Carlos, on 20 November 1972 – three years to the day before his death. © Agencia EFE.

legitimate heir Don Juan, whose son had thereafter been carefully groomed by Franco as future King (p85). Prince Juan Carlos, for his part, had given every indication that he knew what was expected of him, to the extent that he had become publicly estranged from his less compliant father. Nevertheless, Franco did not intend to leave him too much option.

Thus, also in 1969, the dictator appointed as deputy Prime Minister his trusted servant Admiral Luis Carrero Blanco, a die-hard conservative who had allied himself with the technocrats and their patron, the Opus Dei (p98). Carrero was clearly earmarked to succeed Franco as Head of Government, a position from which he would be able to exercise tight control over the King. Admittedly, Juan Carlos would have powers of his own in some areas, such as military affairs or designation of the prime minister and other senior figures. But Franco made sure they were subject to ratification by bodies stuffed full of his own appointees: the Parliament (p83), the National Council of the Movement (p90) and, particularly, the Council of the Kingdom (*Consejo del Reino*), a shadowy committee whose powers were greatly extended in 1967. The dictator's confidence in these arrangements was reflected in his assurance that he had left everything 'all tied up' (*atado y bien atado*) (Figure 7.1).

Franco's determination that his regime should continue unchanged (*continuismo*) was also evident in his reaction to an outbreak of bickering in its ranks, caused by various proposals for mild liberalisation (p100). They had been bitterly opposed by the regime's most conservative supporters. In 1969 a leading **liberaliser**, Manuel Fraga (p100), retaliated by leaking details of a business scandal, the so-called Matesa affair (*caso Matesa*), involving a number of prominent conservatives. As in the past, Franco used the opportunity to exert his authority (p86), sacking both Fraga and National Movement leader, José Solís Ruiz. But this time his judgement was also a clear blow to the liberalisers, among whom, at the time, Solís was counted (p100).

aperturistas
liberalisers
Never formally organised, the liberalisers favoured making some concessions to genuine democracy without abandoning the basic authoritarian conservatism of the **Franco regime** (p80). Unlike the so-called democratic opposition (p104) they were members of, or close to the regime, and were to be found in several of its **clans** (p84); their ranks included public servants, **Falangists** (p66) and businessmen.

The new government marked a return to the strategy of 1959 (pp98–9). Several leading technocrats were recalled or promoted, their task being to revive the economic growth whose slowdown had led to business dissatisfaction and an increase in industrial conflict. At the same time, Carrero Blanco – who in practice now headed the cabinet – was joined by several other hardliners, with the intention of cracking down on the emerging opposition. Specifically, efforts to stamp out the Workers' Commissions (p102) were intensified. The union's premises were raided and shut down, many activists arrested and a number, including its leader Marcelino Camacho, given long prison terms.

At the same time, a major anti-ETA offensive was launched and numerous suspected activists arrested. In 1970, sixteen of them were tried by a military court in Burgos; six were sentenced to death. Franco's decision to commute their sentences to life imprisonment did little to still domestic and international outrage, which was prompted as much by the nature of the proceedings as by the verdicts. Both aspects provided further targets for Church criticism of the regime (p104), which had already become more outspoken with the Pope's appointment of Cardinal Enrique y Tarancón as Bishop of Toledo and head of the Spanish clergy.

Nevertheless, it was in the Basque Country itself that the results were most dramatic. Pro-ETA demonstrations multiplied and were increasingly joined by workers as, following a brief recovery in 1971/72, the economy faltered once again. The resultant clashes with the security forces only heightened public support for ETA, giving a major boost to its activities. Bank robberies, kidnappings and attacks on the security forces all increased. Most spectacularly, in December 1973 ETA struck a major blow to Franco's plans when it assassinated Carrero Blanco, who had finally been appointed prime minister just six months before, by exploding a bomb under his official car as it was driving along a busy Madrid street.

By now Franco's health was deteriorating visibly and his opponents in general had begun to make preparations for his demise. These were furthest advanced in Catalonia, where the high degree of consensus already achieved (p104) had made it possible to set up a clandestine Assembly including representatives of virtually all opinion in the region. Elsewhere, however, such cooperation proved impossible, the problem being the Communist PCE. It had by far the strongest underground organisation of any opposition group but was deeply distrusted by the others for its ambivalent role during the Civil War (pp70–1).

In an attempt to overcome such reservations, the PCE's leader, Santiago Carrillo, announced his party's conversion to eurocommunism. The move was partly successful. In July 1974 the PCE established a Committee for Democracy (*Junta Democrática*), in which it was joined not only by the Workers' Commissions already under its influence (p102), but also by groups ranging from liberal monarchists to the People's Socialist Party (*Partido Socialista Popular*) recently set up by Professor Tierno Galván (p105). However, Carrillo's gesture failed to overcome the suspicions of the much older and more deeply-rooted Socialist Party (PSOE) (p25).

The PSOE itself was finally emerging from its long lethargy (p102). At a conference held in the French town of Suresnes, also in 1974, control over the party was wrested from its ageing leadership in exile by a group of mainly younger activists from within Spain. These were keenly aware of how badly the Socialist organisation had been neglected and had no desire to be swallowed up by the better-prepared PCE and its Committee. In June 1975 they formed a rival 'Platform of Democratic Convergence' together with the Basque Nationalist PNV, the 'legal' Christian Democrats led by Ruiz Giménez (p104) and a number of smaller groups. On one thing, though, Platform and Committee were agreed. Given that the regime showed no willingness to change, there could be no question of compromising with Franco's appointed successors.

inmovilistas

(Francoist) die-hards

United by their fierce opposition to any relaxation of authoritarian rule after Franco's death, the die-hards formed a loose alliance of convenience in the last years of his regime. They included a number of old-style **Falangists** (p66), such as long-time Labour Minister Girón de Velasco (p85) and the one-time **liberaliser** Solís Ruiz (p100), some **technocrats** close to **Opus Dei** (p98), the openly Fascist Blas Piñar, who later set up his own 'New Force' party, and many Army officers.

These various forms of opposition served to entrench attitudes among the regime's **die-hards**, especially the military officers who were ETA's main target. All the greater was their fury at a speech by Carlos Arias Navarro, Carrero's successor as PM, on 12 February 1974. For Arias appeared to promise a degree of liberalisation, floating the idea of a 'Statute of Associations' that would allow some sort of political debate, albeit within strict limits. But the 'spirit of 12 February' did not last. Its promoter was a colourless figure with none of Carrero's prestige within the regime. Nor was he helped by the April coup in Portugal, which sent a shiver through all its supporters. Soon the die-hards were firmly back in charge.

The first indication came in October, when Pío Cabanillas, Fraga's successor at the Information Ministry (p100) and the last liberaliser left in government, was dismissed. The move prompted several other leading administrators with links to the financial and intellectual communities to resign in despair. Cabanillas's offence had been to persevere with the more relaxed censorship policies of his predecessor, as a result of which pornography began to appear on Spanish bookstalls for the first time – to the outrage of both ultraconservatives and Franco himself. Then, in December, the die-hards' renewed ascendancy was confirmed when the eagerly awaited draft of Arias' Statute was finally published. It provided that 'associations' would have to be approved by the National Council of the Movement, a clear sign that no real dissent was to be permitted.

Events in 1975 did nothing to damp the atmosphere of confrontation. When Bishop Añoveros of Bilbao spoke out in favour of Basque nationalist aspirations, he was placed under house arrest; the result was a stand-off between regime and Vatican. Industrial unrest reached new heights as Spain was hit by the effects of the 1973 oil shock. ETA's violence continued unabated. In August, in another triumph for the hard-liners, an 'Anti-Terrorist Act' introduced mandatory death sentences for political killings. A month later, two ETA activists and one from the left-wing FRAP group were executed under its terms. When Franco finally died on 20 November, the chances of a tranquil handover of power looked minimal.

Summary of main points

Uneven development

- Around 1959, so-called technocrats – leading civil servants often associated with the Opus Dei – gained decisive influence over the regime's policies. As a result, Spain's economy was opened up to the outside world in various ways.
- The new strategy led to rapid economic development, which helped to reduce popular resentment. But it also led to new social tensions and to more generalised, lower-level dissatisfaction difficult to combat by outright repression.
- As an alternative response, during the 1960s some moves were made towards mild liberalisation, but they lagged far behind the rate of socio-economic change.

The emergence of opposition

- The economic growth of the 1960s created the conditions for increased labour militancy, channelled mainly through the illegal Workers' Commissions.
- Industrial conflict was most severe in the Basque Country, where it became linked to a nationalist movement greatly strengthened and radicalised by the creation of ETA, and by the regime's brutal response to it.
- In Catalonia regionalism, although less militant, came to enjoy even broader support.
- Large sections of the Church and its followers also turned against the regime,

some as part of a tolerated 'democratic opposition', others more clandestinely. Parts of the middle classes and business community, too, became disillusioned with the effects of dictatorship.

Death throes of dictatorship

- Franco made detailed plans for the continuation of his regime. Prince Juan Carlos was designated his successor as Head of State but real power was to remain with the dictator's most trusted supporters.
- Around 1970 the regime tried to crack down on the resistance of workers and regionalists, with limited success. Indeed, his opponents both inside and outside Spain became increasingly organised and united.
- As Franco's death approached, the liberalising tendencies within his regime were largely suppressed and influence returned to the die-hard reactionaries determined to prevent change of any sort.

Exhibit 7.1: Manuel Fraga's early political philosophy (1968)

Extract from one of the leading liberaliser's best-known works

> *[...] En [las Cortes] se han procurado conjugar las más valiosas enseñanzas de nuestra tradición multisecular con las exigencias debidas al mundo en que vivimos y a la realidad política actual de nuestra nación.*
>
> *Por eso, cuando esta realidad política lo aconsejaba, se han introducido algunas modificaciones en el sentido de un mayor perfeccionamiento en el mecanismo representativo, uniendo en este alto Cuerpo representativo junto a la representación de los productores la de los consumidores, a través de la Familia, que es la célula básica del consumo en la economía moderna.*
>
> *Este perfeccionamiento no es, por otra parte, sino un eslabón más en la cadena de mejoras que nos permite un Régimen siempre abierto y previsor de unas instituciones que sirvan fielmente al imperativo de los tiempos. Este realismo político que ha impulsado los pasos del nuevo estado, ha producido ya resultados que a la vista de todos están. Entre ellos son de citar la nueva Ley de Prensa e Imprenta y, sobre todo, la Ley Orgánica del Estado, con toda la serie de perfeccionamientos que prevén los más variados órdenes de nuestra vida política tales como las leyes sobre la Libertad Religiosa, el mundo sindical, el procedimiento electoral, el Régimen Local, así como la reforma de algunas de las Instituciones fundamentales de nuestro Estado [...].*

[...] In [the Spanish Parliament] it has proved possible to combine the most valuable lessons of our history that date back so many centuries with the requirements of the world in which we live and of our country's current political situation.

Thus, whenever that situation made it advisable, changes have been made to enhance still further the system of representation, by bringing together in this top-level representative body the representatives not only of producers but also of consumers, through the agency of the family, which is the basic unit of consumption in today's society.

At the same time, this is merely one in a line of improvements granted to us by a regime always open to new ideas and ever ready to envisage institutions which faithfully fulfil the needs of the time. This political realism, which has inspired the actions of the New State, has already produced results that are evident to all. As examples one should point to the recent Press and Publishing Act and, above all, to the Organic Law of the State, as well as all the enhancements brought by a wide range of measures governing our political life, such as the laws on Religious Liberty, the trade unions, the electoral system and local government, and also the reform of some of our state's basic institutions […].

Source: Fraga Iribarne, M. (1968) *Horizonte español*. Madrid: Héroes.

Exhibit 7.2: The regime promotes itself (1969)

Opening of a typical work issued by the regime's propaganda service

EL MILAGRO DE FRANCO
A lo largo de este año español, tan español que va de 18 de julio a 18 de julio, [...], Francisco Franco, que desde aquella inolvidable jornada burgalesa del día primero de octubre de 1936 – con un sol dorado y con toda España metida en las calles de la pequeña ciudad, pequeño rincón de aquella Patria tan dura, tan pequeña también y tan llena de esperanzas – rige con pulso sereno nuestros destinos nacionales, cumplió sus primeros setenta y seis años. La gran aventura de su vida, puesta desde adolescente al servicio de España, siempre en los lugares de mayor riesgo y la mayor responsabilidad, encontró en este aniversario un eco unánime de felicitación popular. Incluso en grandes sectores de la Prensa extranjera, por regla general y constante histórica, tan atrabiliaria a la hora de juzgar a los hombres de España y, por supuesto, a España misma, bajo cualquier signo que la presida, se inició una conversión de frente – entrañable en algunos, admirativa en muchos, fría, pero objetiva, en otros – respecto a este veterano general y estadista que ha dado a los españoles la paz más larga que conoce su Historia y también su tranco político más lleno de realizaciones, prosperidad y posibilidades de futuro. [...]

THE MIRACLE THAT IS FRANCO
In the course of this year in the life of Spain, so Spanish in that it ran from one 18th of July to the next, […], Francisco Franco celebrated his 76th birthday. The same Francisco Franco who has been presiding, in all serenity, over the fate of our nation, ever since one unforgettable 1st of October in Burgos[1] – a day of golden sunshine, when it seemed that all of Spain was pressed into the streets of the little city, into one small corner of a Fatherland so harsh, so small too, but so full of hope. The new milestone in the great undertaking that is Franco's life, placed since adolescence at Spain's service, present always where the risks and responsibilities were biggest, was greeted with unanimous popular celebration. Even in large sections of the foreign press, in general and traditionally so mean-spirited in its opinions of Spaniards and, of course, of Spain herself, whoever its ruler might be, began to show a new attitude – of affection in some cases, of admiration in many, of cold objectivity in others – towards the veteran general and statesman who has gifted Spaniards the longest period of peace in their history, and that stage in their political evolution most replete with achievements, prosperity and opportunities for the future. […]

[1] 1 October 1936, when Franco was invested as 'Head of State' of the zone then controlled by his Nationalist forces

Source: Servicio Informativo Español (1969) *Crónica de un año de España*. Madrid.

Topics for discussion

- How could Fraga's work (Exhibit 7.1) be understood as an argument in favour of change in the Franco regime as it then existed?

- What role did the family play in most Francoist thinking? What role is it assigned by Fraga in this text?

- What arguments, explicit and implicit, does Exhibit 7.2 use to glorify Franco? What connotations would the word 'miracle' in the title have had?

- Who would have read such a text in 1969? How credible would it have been to most Spaniards?

- Who benefited from the 'boom' of the 1960s, and how?

- To judge by much of what one reads and hears nowadays, opposition to Franco's regime was very widespread towards the end of his rule. How is that impression to be reconciled with the regime's survival until 1975?

CHAPTER 8

A delicate operation (1975–1982)

Like Primo's departure 45 years before, Franco's death in November 1975 left Spain to emerge from dictatorship at a time of economic recession. This time, though, the international political environment was much more helpful. Ironically, the delicate process was eased most of all by the fact that Franco's regime was a much sturdier edifice than Primo's and did not immediately collapse. Consequently change, when it came, was initiated from within the old regime, whose structures could thus be dismantled without provoking the wrath of extreme conservatives. That, in turn, made it possible to begin constructing a new system in cooperation with the left-wing opposition. Only then was the operation threatened by an attempted coup, whose failure provided the renewed impetus required to conclude successfully Spain's transition to democracy.

The Right outmanoeuvred

So long awaited, with apprehension and hope, Franco's death proved rather an anticlimax. Initially, the arrangements he had put in place appeared to work smoothly, with power remaining firmly in the hands of the hard-line conservatives who had exercised it in the dictator's last years (p109). Although pressures for change

In the second half of the 1970s the economies of western Europe experienced major problems, aggravated by a further oil shock in 1979. To try and maintain growth the European Community (EC) established an Exchange Rate Mechanism to tie its members' currencies more closely together. In particular Germany, the EC's economic powerhouse, began to eye with interest the prospects offered by the relatively undeveloped markets of southern Europe. There the EC was also keen to ensure that stable democracies emerged from the processes of change that began with the overthrow of right-wing dictatorships in Greece and Portugal during 1974, in the latter case under Communist leadership. Contrary to western – especially American – fears, that turned out to mark the furthest leftward swing of the political pendulum which had begun in the previous decade. Now it moved steadily back towards the Right, accelerated by the election of aggressively free-market, anti-communist governments in Britain (1979) and America (1980). In 1979 the trend was given a further boost by the Soviet invasion of Afghanistan and the renewal of the Cold War. Indeed, the only challenge to the ascendancy of the 'New Right' came in 1981, with the election in France of a Socialist government pledged to resist the advance of extreme free market policies.

were building up, there seemed to be no way of releasing them while Franco's institutions remained intact. Yet that was precisely what happened from mid-1976 on.

The dictator's plan for the survival of his regime (*continuismo*) was triggered immediately on his death, beginning with the proclamation of King Juan Carlos I (p106). Admittedly, in his investiture speech the new monarch spoke of a desire not just for opening up (*apertura*) but for 'democratisation'. With his encouragement, the first cabinet of the King's reign included several leading liberalisers, notably Manuel Fraga Iribarne (p100). But their room for manoeuvre, and that of Juan Carlos himself, remained tightly circumscribed by the hold that Franco's die-hard supporters (p108) exercised over a range of key institutions (p109) as well as the judiciary and, crucially, the armed forces.

As a result, Juan Carlos had little option but to retain Franco's appointee, Carlos Arias Navarro, as Prime Minister. Arias was seen in some quarters as a liberaliser, but that view said less about him than about the mentality of the die-hard reactionaries who espoused it. His notions of a distinctively Spanish democracy (*democracia a la española*) were firmly based on the 'organic' variety devised by his former master (p83), for whom Arias retained an unswerving admiration. Nonetheless, the fact that he held them at all suggested that, unlike the die-hards, he had some inkling of the pressures on him.

To a large extent these were the delayed result of the 1973 oil shock, the initial impact of which had been muffled by Spain's substantial economic progress in the 1960s. In any case, successive governments had been too preoccupied with the political situation to worry about the country's extreme dependency on foreign oil. Now Spain paid the price for their inaction. Recession in western Europe shut off the safety valve which, for a decade and a half, had released pressure on Spain's labour market (p99); emigration ceased, and those who had left to work abroad began flooding back to their homes in Spain. Unemployment rose steeply, as did prices, fanning the campaign of industrial unrest mounted by the trade unions (p118).

The unions also demanded political change and they were not alone. An alarmed business community lobbied for political concessions to reduce industrial tensions in the short term and, looking further ahead, to allow access to the benefits of EC membership (p101). Externally, the Community itself was anxious for Spain to fulfil the conditions to join, while the Americans were desperate to prevent a repeat of the Communist takeover in Portugal. Both pressed for significant political reform and discreetly supported those who favoured it.

Largely as a result, Arias took some hesitant steps in that direction. Along with a pardon for some political prisoners and a vague commitment to future reforms, he announced the removal of restrictions on the press. Although officially political parties remained banned, in practice they were permitted to begin operation. These moves were bitterly resisted by the most extreme die-hards who hankered after a return to full-blooded dictatorship (*nostálgicos*), especially the military officers among them (*búnker*). Throughout the first half of 1976 they blocked all moves towards further change as pressure, domestic and external, steadily built up.

Something had to give and in June it did. When Parliament rejected the central plank in Arias's strategy of minimalist reform – his proposals to legalise political parties under strict conditions – he resigned. Here, clearly, was a chance to break the deadlock. Hopes were high that Juan Carlos would appoint someone with the moral authority and drive to push through real changes. Hence the disappointment and astonishment when, on 1 July, he named Adolfo Suárez, a senior Francoist bureaucrat with no liberalising track-record. That, though, was a prime attraction to the King's adviser, Torcuato Fernández Miranda, an enigmatic figure who had given long and loyal service to Franco, but who now played a key role in persuading the institutions left by his old boss to dismantle themselves.

No one was better qualified than the new Prime Minister to implement that strategy, firstly because he had been secretary-general of the National Movement (p90). That gave him, on the one hand, credibility with the reactionaries and, on the other, a deep knowledge not just of the workings of Franco's institutions but also the personal histories of their members. Secondly, he had served as head of the state-run television service and understood like no other Spanish politician how the medium could be used to influence opinion. Finally, unlike most of the regime's grey functionaries, he was telegenic and too young to evoke negative memories of the Civil War and its aftermath.

Suárez's appointment marked the real start of Spain's transition to democracy (*transición democrática*). The key to the operation was that change should be initiated without opposition help, partly because its promoters wanted to prevent change from going too far, partly because external support would alert the reactionaries. To carry it out Suárez relied on a group of close allies, former Francoist bureaucrats like himself, who wanted limited, controlled change in order to avoid anything more drastic. The most prominent – Rodolfo Martín Villa, Fernando Abril Martorell and Leopoldo Calvo Sotelo – took up key posts in his cabinet. A number of other ministers were drawn from an informal Christian Democrat grouping known as *Tácito*, whose ranks included both liberalisers and members of the 'legal' opposition tolerated by Franco (p104).

With his team in place, Suárez seized the initiative. Within a month of taking office he announced extensions of various basic liberties, notably freedom of assembly and association. This action reduced the potential for high-profile clashes between opposition demonstrations and the police, as did a further amnesty for political prisoners. Having halted, at least temporarily, the spiral of rising tension, and the consequent hardening of attitudes among both opposition and reactionaries, Suárez made his key move; he announced plans for political liberalisation.

His Political Reform Bill (*Proyecto de Ley de Reforma Política*) was published in September. It proposed a new, two-chamber Parliament which, unlike the existing house (p83), would be fully elected. Parties would be legalised, subject to approval by the government. Beyond that, the proposals were deliberately vague. There was no mention of a new constitution: on the contrary, the old regime's basic laws (p101) would remain in force. Indeed, the fact that Suárez repeatedly had recourse to the extensive decree powers they conferred on him seemed a further sign that major change was not in the offing.

Even so, his plans evoked the reactionaries' fury. The King's role as Supreme Commander of the Armed Forces, and the military connections he had built up during his long apprenticeship, were crucial in keeping them under control. Admittedly the Army Minister, General De Santiago y Díaz de Mendívil, resigned in protest. But that allowed Suárez to replace him with Lieutenant-General Gutiérrez Mellado, a committed democrat who immediately set about bringing the Army under control by a shrewd combination of discipline and administrative reforms.

With military opposition defused for the present, the next hurdle was the old, Francoist Parliament. Here the key players were Suárez and Fernández Miranda, who occupied the crucial post of Speaker (*presidente*). Their methods were a combination of procedural manipulation and arm-twisting of individual representatives (*procuradores*), backed up by judicious references to the pressures for change from outside Spain. The final vote, held on 18 November, was a testimony to their skills; the 'Political Reform Act' was passed by 425 votes to 59.

Suárez's next obstacle was self-imposed. In order to pre-empt charges that his proposals lacked democratic legitimacy, he had scheduled a national referendum for 15 December 1976. This time it was his media knowledge and skills that were decisive. Shamelessly manipulating coverage by the state television service, and employing his own charisma to the full, he won another overwhelming victory. Over three-quarters of the electorate voted, 94 per cent in favour.

Next came the question of political parties, most of which were legalised during February with no great fuss and only one significant exception; the Spanish Communist Party (PCE) (p70). In this case the Supreme Court, still dominated by Franco's appointees, exercised its power under the Reform Act to maintain the ban on the party. It was a crucial moment. At the time, the PCE was universally seen as the strongest opposition force (p102); without its participation no genuine democracy would be possible. On the other hand, defying the Court's ban might give Francoist officers just the excuse they needed to stage a coup. Crucially, King Juan Carlos backed Suárez and signed a royal decree that in turn overruled the Court and legalised the Communists.

That solved one problem for his Prime Minister but it aggravated another. For it ensured even tougher competition in the general election which, under the terms of his own Act, Suárez had to call no later than 30 June 1977, now less than two months away. And as yet the PM had no organisation of his own, the National Movement – which, in any case, could never have served as a vehicle for reformers – having been dissolved as part of the reform process. His solution was simple: he hijacked an existing party.

The 'Democratic Centre' was one of the innumerable groupings set up in the wake of the Reform Act. Its leader, José María Areilza, was a prominent Francoist who had broken with the dictatorship. Conservative, but unambiguously democratic, it had swallowed up several other mini-parties and looked well-placed to appeal to middle-class voters. But with virtually no organisation outside Madrid it had little prospect of tapping this potential, which was also limited by Areilza's advanced age and pompous style.

Suárez, by contrast, could offer not just his own growing prestige but also his contacts in the recently wound-up Movement (p90). When he approached them, Areilza's lieutenants summarily ditched their leader and gratefully accepted Suárez as replacement. A number of the Prime Minister's own allies also took up senior positions in the hurriedly renamed **Centre Democratic Union** just in time for the election campaign.

In that, Suárez once again showed himself both skilled and ruthless in exploiting his advantages: civil service back-up, the Movement's countrywide apparatus and, as before, TV exposure. In the poll on 15 June his new party exceeded all outside expectations by winning the largest share of the vote, outpolling not just the barely organised Right, which performed abysmally (p124), but also the historic parties of the Left (p119). Reconfirmed in his position as Prime Minister, this time by parliamentary vote, Suárez was left standing atop the ruins to which, in under a year, he had reduced Franco's seemingly impenetrable defences.

> ### Unión de Centro Democrático (UCD)
> Centre Democratic Union
>
> Formed to fight the 1977 general election, the UCD was a 'centre' party in the sense that its leadership included both opponents and servants of the Franco regime. As well as a faction drawn from Franco's **National Movement** (p90), whose support for transition was essentially pragmatic, the UCD comprised three main ideological groupings: Christian Democrats, liberals and moderate Social Democrats. Once the **1978 Constitution** (p120) was approved, the divisions between them became unbridgeable and the party began to crumble. Shortly after its cataclysmic defeat at the 1982 election (p136) it was dissolved altogether. Its leader, Adolfo Suárez (p115), attempted to construct a successor, the Social and Democratic Centre, but without success.
> See also: **Partido Popular** (p162)

The Left tamed

The 1977 election results endorsed Suárez's strategy. But they did nothing to solve the pressing problems facing him on at least two fronts. Furthermore, they meant that he could no longer, as up to now, govern virtually alone. As a result, he sought support from the leaders of the left-wing opposition who, for their own reasons, were also anxious to work together. Their cooperation laid the basis for the transition's next stage and its legal foundation – a new constitution.

The first major problem area for Suárez was the law and order situation. Despite splitting into two branches, ETA (p103) had not just continued but stepped up its violence since Franco's death; in the autumn of 1977 the 'military' branch launched a new and more ferocious campaign. Nor was terrorism confined to the Basque Country; from December 1976, a shadowy left-wing group, GRAPO, carried out a string of kidnappings. In January 1977 five labour lawyers were shot dead in their office in the Atocha district of Madrid

This last incident illustrated a particularly alarming aspect of the wave of violence; that a significant part of it was promoted from within the security forces themselves. For the assassins, known members of the international far-right scene, had powerful connections among police officers promoted under the former regime. The retention of such men, many notorious torturers, in their posts, often senior ones, was to represent a toxic legacy for Franco's successors, even if they contributed to preventing a complete breakdown of law and order during this crucial phase of the transition.

The second crisis facing the prime minister was the economy's continuing deterioration (p114). During 1977 inflation rose to 25 per cent and unemployment also soared. The basic problem was that industries built up in the 1960s under the sheltered conditions of dictatorship were ill-equipped to deal with recession. Workers, too, were hard hit by these same developments and were now sufficiently emboldened to take action. The resultant strike wave served to aggravate firms' problems even further. Perhaps even more important, though, were its political implications.

For, in the face of heavy-handed police intervention, strikes repeatedly erupted into violent confrontations with the security forces. That was especially so in the Basque Country, where left-wingers and nationalists continued to make common cause (p103). One clash in Vitoria during March 1976 was particularly violent, with five workers being shot and killed. It also confirmed that, contrary to American nightmares, the situation in Spain was quite unlike that in Portugal during 1974. The Spanish armed forces remained solidly conservative, if not reactionary, and any attempt to force change against their will would involve a bloodbath. It was because they were aware of that fact that the leaders of the left-wing opposition had gradually been toning down the tough stance they had adopted back in 1975.

Then, the entire opposition had been in favour of making a clean break with the past (*ruptura*), which all factions interpreted as ruling out anyone associated with the Franco regime from any part in creating its replacement. Beyond that, the meaning was less clear. For some it implied merely political and, perhaps, social reform; others also wanted radical economic changes, such as far-reaching nationalisation and state-directed redistribution of wealth. Nevertheless, there was sufficient agreement that the two umbrella groups which had coalesced around the Communist and Socialist parties respectively (p108) joined forces, under the name of the Democratic Coordinating Committee (*Coordinación Democrática*), (popularly, the *Platajunta*).

Soon, however, events began to erode the opposition's hard line. Industrial action proved inadequate to speed up the pace of reform in the first half of 1976. Hence the alacrity with which the Left grasped at the first feelers put out by Suárez after he became PM in July. Within weeks of his appointment both Felipe González, head of the Socialist PSOE, and Enrique Tierno Galván (p105), leader of the smaller but influential People's Socialist Party, agreed to meet the PM for exploratory talks. Even Communist leader Santiago Carrillo had informal contacts with him. When Suárez's proposals for political reform were published (pp115–16), those Christian Democrats who had joined the opposition front (p108) supported them, oblivious of the fact that – like the left-wing leaders' actions – they were incompatible with any notion of a clean break.

Yet at the end of October, the opposition leaders publicly reaffirmed that as their goal. When Suárez submitted his proposals to a referendum, they called on voters to abstain. The fact that less than a quarter of the electorate heeded their advice (p116) indicated how far their position had lost credibility. Moreover, the referendum campaign had made painfully clear how effectively Suárez could exploit his privileged access to TV. Even though they would have their own broadcast spots before the upcoming election, his opponents were well aware that the government's control of news coverage would still give it a head start.

In the event, the results exceeded their worst fears, with Suárez's infant UCD (p117) emerging as the largest party. González and Carrillo, already aware that radical demands could provide the excuse for a military coup, decided to cut their losses. Abandoning the lost cause of a clean break to various far-left splinter groups, they began to talk in terms of a democratic or agreed break (*ruptura democrática/pactada*) and offered to give Suárez the informal support he needed in return for a say in the next phase of change.

As it happened, the Prime Minister was in need of help, as he had no overall majority to push through proposals of his own. There was none to be found on the Right, which had fared disastrously at the polls (p124). In any case, the economic situation demanded considerable industrial restructuring, which was bound to cause hardship for many workers. In order to prevent yet more damaging strikes, Suárez decided to go over the strikers' heads by taking up the opposition leaders' offer.

His move was not the first indication of a reasonableness not exactly familiar to Spanish politics. Earlier ones had included the Church's decision not to back an official Christian Democrat Party, with its inevitable echoes of the CEDA (p54), and the Communist Party's willingness to accept the monarchy. However, it was the direct negotiations between Suárez and the opposition leaders in the summer of 1977 that made the new **spirit of compromise**, for a while, into the transition's *leitmotiv*.

> ### *consenso*
> ....
> (spirit of) compromise
>
> In many ways compromise is the standard stuff of democracy, but the extent to which it was displayed by politicians during the transitional period was remarkably different from the intransigence that had so long characterised Spanish politics. Its protagonists were the governing **UCD** (p117) and the leaders of the Socialist **PSOE** (p25) and **Communist PCE** (p70). They were supported to varying degrees by the main trades union federations, the **UGT** (p40) and the **Workers' Commissions** (p102), and the employers. Its main fruits were the Moncloa Pacts, the **1978 Constitution** (p120) and the process known as '**social concertation**' (p138).

Its first concrete result came in October, when the two left-wing parties signed the 'Moncloa Pacts' with the government. The terms, whereby they agreed to persuade their associated unions to tone down industrial action, indicated that they knew the weakness of their position. The left-wing leaders delivered on their promise, as a result of which inflation was brought down to a more manageable level and the pressure on Suárez considerably eased. Rather predictably unkept was the promise they received in return, to create more jobs.

The pay-off for the Left's leaders, if not their grassroots supporters, came in the drafting of a constitution. For Suárez abandoned his original intention of having the text drawn up by government lawyers and instead handed over the responsibility to Parliament, where proposals could only be passed with the opposition's approval. A standard committee proved too large for the task, which was then entrusted to a cross-party group of just seven senior figures (three from UCD and one each from the Socialists, the Communists, the rightist People's Alliance (p124) and the Catalan CiU (p145)).

They were to become known as the 'fathers of the Constitution', as the proposals they produced were accepted by the full Parliament virtually unchanged. The vote was almost unanimous; the only MPs not to support the final text were those representing the various Basque nationalist parties and a handful of right-wingers. The ratifying referendum, held on 6 December 1978, also brought an overwhelming 'yes' vote except in the Basque Country, where the ambiguous result was to have significant effects (p123).

The **1978 Constitution** effectively settled two conflicts that had bedevilled Spanish politics for a century and more. Thus, the Socialists presented only token objections to the monarchy – the Communists had already accepted it – happy to recognise that Juan Carlos' performance in the role (pp114–16) had saved them from an awkward decision. Religion caused more controversy, as both the main left-wing parties adamantly opposed granting any special status to the Catholic Church. Eventually, however, they agreed to recognise it as a 'social reality', which was enough to

---

Constitución del 78

1978 Constitution

Like the process of drawing it up, and in stark contrast to most of its predecessors (pp2,4) the provisions of Spain's 1978 Constitution reflect the **spirit of compromise** typical of the central period of the transition to democracy (p119). It defines Spain as a 'parliamentary monarchy' and establishes a directly-elected, two-chamber Parliament (*Cortes bicamerales*). The lower house, or Congress (*Congreso de los Diputados*) is the more powerful. The Senate (*Senado*) is stated to be an organ of 'territorial' – implicitly regional – representation, but its structure does not fully reflect this, something which has implications for the **regionalised form of government** also established (p122). Widely regarded as a major achievement, the Constitution has been amended only once as yet, in 1992, to take account of Spain's accession to the European Community (p133) by granting limited voting rights to citizens of other EC member states.

satisfy most conservative opinion. The Constitution also included ingenious provisions to address a third long-standing conflict, that over regional self-government (pp122–3).

Its main error, which went unnoticed at the time, was probably to assume that the semi-proportional electoral system would make it impossible for a single party to win an overall parliamentary majority (p136). For the moment, though, that assumption proved correct. In fact, the first election held under the new Constitution, in March 1979, produced results very similar to those of 1977. Suárez's party, UCD, again won most seats, while falling well short of an overall majority. Once again the Left had to take on board its electoral weakness. All seemed set for a continuation of the compromise course of the past 18 months. But it was not to be.

Compromise had been a successful strategy for one very particular set of circumstances. However, that moment had passed and, with the Constitution agreed, politics moved on to everyday, bread-and-butter issues. Some related to the country's economy, whose serious problems were aggravated by the second oil shock in 1979. Others, symbolised by the possibility of legalising divorce, concerned the type of society that Spain should now become. Many involved fundamental clashes of interest and beliefs that could not be resolved by compromise, but instead needed a strong government able to give a firm lead. And that was precisely what Spain did not have.

The problem was not so much that the government lacked a parliamentary majority. Despite growing discontent among their own rank and file, for whom democracy had brought few material benefits, the Left's leaders were still too fearful of a coup to consider toppling it. The problem was UCD's nature. In essence, it was an alliance of convenience between groups that had nothing in common beyond the desire to bring about a smooth transition (p117). With that achieved, at least on paper, there was little to hold its disparate components together. Instead, the UCD was wracked by a succession of disputes, especially over divorce. They were aggravated by Suárez's increasing reliance on a small group of his closest advisers (p115), and by rivalry between the powerful 'barons' who headed its various factions.

Although the events have never been fully clarified, it seems to have been these key party figures who forced the Prime Minister's surprise resignation in January 1981. Before long it was to become apparent that by ditching its greatest asset UCD had merely hastened its own demise (p136). More immediately, however, the uncertainty triggered by Suárez's abrupt departure gave an opportunity to those who found even his brand of reform far too radical, and who had no interest whatsoever in compromise.

Crisis and recovery

It was during the investiture of Suárez's successor that military reactionaries attempted a coup. Although this was a shock, it was hardly a surprise, having been on the cards since the transition's start. The factor most likely to provoke it – regionalist agitation of various sorts – had been growing in importance for some time. Happily, though, the coup was easily put down. Its failure gave a new impetus to the process of reform, hastening the change of government that was so clearly required.

Ever since 1975 the military's propensity for rebellion (*golpismo*) had hovered over Spanish politics. Several times the King's influence was crucial in keeping the Army in check, notably when the PCE was legalised (p116). Subsequently some officers made no attempt to hide their far-right sympathies. More than once Defence Minister Gutiérrez Mellado (p116) was the target of their abuse. In 1979 and 1980 several plots were uncovered, the biggest known as 'Operation Galaxia'. Although they reflected general Army dissatisfaction at the course of events, these activities were above all a reaction to the revival of the regionalist feeling that their ex-leader had attempted to stamp out.

Ironically, it was the spectacular failure of Franco's efforts to repress such sentiments in Catalonia and the Basque Country (pp103–4) that left Suárez with no option but to concede a measure of self-government. By 1976 feelings in these regions were so strong that its denial would undoubtedly derail plans for a smooth transition. This insight was shared by the leaders of the left-wing opposition, whose activists in the two regions in any case backed devolution. They were thus happy to let Suárez lay the groundwork for it, while at the same time conducting discussions on the Constitution. As a result, by the end of 1977 what amounted to provisional regional governments (*entes preautonómicos*) had been set up in both regions.

The Catalan body was headed by Josep Tarradellas, a popular moderate regionalist whom Suárez had brought back from exile for the task. Thanks to the presence of a Catalan on the committee charged with drafting a constitution (p120), its views could be fed directly into that process. The final text, with its provisions for a **regionalised form of government**, received massive approval in Catalonia. Thereafter, devolution negotiations with the central government were smoothed by the consensus

Estado de las Autonomías

regionalised form of government

Neither completely centralised nor genuinely federal, the territorial structure of government established by the **1978 Constitution** (p120) is based on autonomous regions (*autonomías/comunidades autónomas*), the powers of which were left to be established (within certain prescribed limits) in individual 'Statutes of Autonomy'. Whereas the three 'historic nationalities' of the Basque Country, Catalonia and Galicia were allowed immediate access to extensive devolution, other regions could follow this fast track (*vía rápida*) only if they met demanding requirements to demonstrate popular support. Otherwise they had to follow the slow route (*vía lenta*), which involved immediate devolution of fewer powers, albeit with the opportunity of an upgrade after five years. As a result, and because regionalists in Catalonia and the Basque Country are determined that their regions must have greater powers than others, devolution has turned out to be an ongoing process (*proceso autonómico*) in various stages (pp142,164) and in all probability is not over yet (p184).

already established within the region on the path to be followed (p104). A Statute of Autonomy was duly approved without major problems. This restored the *Generalitat*, as the regional government was again to be known (p51), and invested it with extensive powers including education and policing.

In the Basque Country, lack of representation on the constitutional working party was just one, relatively minor problem. This was because regionalists there insisted that self-government was a matter for Basques alone to decide, and that no Spanish constitution could deny them the right to choose independence if they so wished. As far as ETA (p103) was concerned, even talking about devolution was taboo. The non-violent Basque Nationalist Party (PNV) (p25) was willing to do that, especially as its triumph at the 1977 election – rather surprisingly, it had clearly topped the poll in the region – allowed it to pose as the Basques' representative *vis-à-vis* Madrid. However, it still refused to back the Constitution, either in Parliament or at the subsequent referendum.

The plebiscite's results in the region complicated the situation still further. For, although there was a majority of 'Yes' votes, widespread abstention meant that they constituted only a minority of the Basque electorate. ETA immediately claimed that the Basques had 'rejected the Constitution', using that as a justification for continuing its campaign of violence. The message was repeated incessantly by People's Unity (HB), the political wing set up by ETA's 'military' branch in 1978 (p143). At the following year's general election, HB took nearly a sixth of Basque votes on a platform of complete separation from Spain.

At this the PNV took fright. To underpin its nationalist credentials, the region's largest party began emphasising that it, too, believed in independence. It also implied unsubtly that so long as that was denied, violence, if not justified, was at least understandable. In reality HB's vote, like the frequent and large pro-ETA demonstrations, mainly reflected two factors: lingering respect for the armed organisation's resistance to Franco (pp103,107) and resentment against the continuing excesses of the security forces in dealing with anyone suspected of having connections with it. But that was easily overlooked, inside and outside the Basque Country.

With the left-wing opposition also demanding wide-ranging devolution, the pressure on Suárez was immense. As a result, the PNV was able to win major concessions. The Basque Statute of Autonomy, known as the Statute of Guernica (p73), includes all the competences granted to Catalonia as well as the tax-collecting powers suppressed by Franco (p80). Like its Catalan equivalent, the Statute was approved by referendum in October 1979.

In February 1980 the PNV won a convincing victory in the first regional election and immediately formed a government. However, it then showed less interest in using its devolved powers than in complaining that they were not greater, and that Navarre had been excluded from the Basque Autonomous Region (*Comunidad Autónoma Vasca* [CAV]). In general, the PNV tended to portray every issue as a confrontation between Basques and the Madrid government. Its approach both fed on and fed ETA's continuing 'armed struggle', which in 1980 claimed more victims than ever before.

In Catalonia, the first election was unexpectedly won by a new regionalist party, Convergence and Union (p145). Its leader, Jordi Pujol, became First Minister and wasted no time in putting his new powers to concrete use. Yet the effects of this different approach were remarkably similar. In the central government's view, some of Pujol's measures exceeded Catalonia's competences as defined jointly by the Constitution and its Statute. Conversely, Pujol claimed that some Madrid laws infringed his region's constitutional rights (a complaint shared by the PNV). Both sides repeatedly appealed to the Constitutional Court (*Tribunal Constitucional*) charged with ruling in such disputes, thereby adding to the impression of conflict between the regions and Madrid.

These developments caused growing concern in the Army and Civil Guard, whose officers were ETA's principal targets and who also tended to have Spanish nationalist views. It was deepened when Andalusian politicians attempted to obtain the same sort of wide-ranging devolution as the Basques and Catalans. The process prescribed in the Constitution for such cases proved to be unsatisfactory, and while it dragged on other regions joined in the clamour for extensive self-government. Wild talk of Spain's imminent disintegration was no longer limited to military circles. Its spread was seized upon by extreme reactionary officers as grounds to intervene, using the excuse that, as a sop to military feeling, the Constitution had made the forces responsible for Spain's 'territorial integrity'.

Along with the government's difficulties in maintaining law and order – for which the security forces actually bore a significant degree of responsibility (p118) – the reactionaries' other justification was that they represented a mood of popular disillusion (*desencanto*). And, indeed, many Spaniards were disappointed that reform had not protected them from the effects of economic recession (p120). However, the vast majority clearly wanted more change, not a return to the past. The only force of any significance advocating that was the People's Alliance led by Manuel Fraga (p114), which in both elections to date had performed dismally.

Yet some officers either could not or would not see that the times had changed. In the climate of uncertainty created in early 1981 by the mysterious resignation of Prime Minister Adolfo Suárez (p121) they decided to act. Their **attempted coup** was spectacular, but quickly crushed. Reaction to it underlined just how bogus was their claim to represent public opinion. Spontaneous mass demonstrations in favour of democracy were held all round Spain. The Madrid march was headed by politicians ranging from Fraga to

(intentona de golpe del) 23-F

1981 coup attempt

The attempted coup of 23 February 1981 only got off the ground in Valencia, where tanks under the command of General Milans del Bosch appeared on the streets, and, most dramatically, in Madrid, where civil guards led by Lieutenant-Colonel Antonio Tejero stormed the Congress of Deputies (p120) and held at gunpoint the MPs attending Leopoldo Calvo Sotelo's investiture as Prime Minister. Prompt action by loyal troops, and the unambiguous opposition of King Juan Carlos, ensured that order was soon restored in both cities.

Figure 8.1 The head of the pro-democracy march in Madrid on 27 February 1981, made up of leading figures of all persuasions, including Nicolás Redondo (5th from left in front row), Santiago Carrillo (6th), Felipe González (7th) Manuel Fraga (10th) and Marcelino Camacho (11th). © Angel Millan/ EFE/Corbis.

PCE leader Santiago Carrillo. Disillusion, insofar as it had existed, was banished (Figure 8.1).

The coup attempt led the new Prime Minister, Leopoldo Calvo Sotelo, and the main opposition parties to rekindle the spirit of compromise (p119), in order to bring the regional issue under control and so calm Army fears. In the summer they settled on a timetable for resolution of the Andalusian dilemma, but also agreed that no more regions would be granted such extensive devolution. In addition, they pushed through legislation stipulating that, whatever the Autonomy Statutes might say, the Madrid Parliament could always overrule regional laws if it wished. That decision sparked off furious Basque and Catalan protests (pp142–3) and yet another appeal to the Constitutional Court. But it also countered hysteria about the country falling apart.

Otherwise Calvo's government was completely hamstrung by the progressive disintegration of his UCD party (p121), so that his only other significant initiative was to take Spain into NATO. That, too, was partly designed to ease military tensions, by providing the forces with new tasks to keep them occupied. But NATO entry was decidedly not a product of compromise; it was eventually imposed over Parliament's head, by decree. The Left objected bitterly. Sensing that the danger of another coup was slight, and that the UCD was close to complete collapse, it had decided to go for the kill.

Among the many developments of the previous few years, one of the most significant had been a sharp shift in the balance of power within the Left itself. In 1975, the Communist PCE had seemed to be the stronger of its two main parties (p116). Thereafter it benefited from the prestige gained by its close ally the Workers' Commissions (p102), which were the main driving force behind the wave of industrial action in 1975–77 (p118). The Communists were accordingly expected – and expecting – to do well at the 1977 election. In the event, though, they were easily outpolled not just by Suárez's UCD but also by their rival on the Left, the PSOE. Two years later they fared even worse, leaving the Socialists unquestionably as the main party of opposition.

One reason for this reversal of fortunes seems to have been that voters generally preferred moderation to extremism, and younger faces such as PSOE leader Felipe González to older ones reminiscent of civil War and dictatorship, like the PCE's Santiago Carrillo. Even so, his own party's renewed failure in 1979 to outpoll UCD persuaded González that it must move further towards the centre. At a party conference in May 1979 he therefore proposed removing all references to Marxism from the PSOE's internal rules. When his proposal was defeated by an alliance of left-wingers and party traditionalists, González resigned.

This dramatic gesture threw his opponents into disarray. With no alternative strategy or leader to offer, they agreed to refer both issues to a special conference to be held in September. In the meantime, González's henchman Alfonso Guerra took such a firm grip on the party apparatus that the changes were approved and González re-elected, both by overwhelming majorities. Not only had he got his way on policy, his authority had been paraded publicly, making him look like the strong leader the country needed.

That was an important asset as the UCD government staggered towards its inevitable end (p121). Another was the PSOE's anti-NATO campaign, very effective in a country where, thanks to its links with Latin America and the memory of 1898 (p12), anti-US feeling extended across the political spectrum. More generally, the Socialists' strategy was to ride the wave of enthusiasm for further social and economic change that had been unleashed by the coup attempt, portraying themselves as the only political force capable of delivering such reform.

It was a huge success. In the election eventually held on 28 October 1982 the PSOE swept to power (p000). Perhaps more importantly, no voice of any consequence questioned the Socialists' right to assume it. The transition to democracy was complete, not just in constitutional theory but also in political practice.

Summary of main points

The Right outmanoeuvred

- Following Franco's death, change was initially very limited, but pressure for real reform was building up both inside and outside the country.

- The transition to democracy got properly under way in mid-1976, with the appointment of Adolfo Suárez as Prime Minister. Together with a small group of allies, he managed to steer through democratising measures without provoking a reaction from the Right.
- Crucial to Suárez's success were his links to two of the dictatorship's institutions: state-run television and the single party. They enabled him to win both a referendum on his proposals and the first two democratic elections at the head of a newly created party (UCD).

The Left tamed

- After the 1977 election Suárez's lack of an overall parliamentary majority, and the threats posed by terrorist violence and economic recession, forced him to seek support from the Left.
- The Socialist and Communist leaders had originally refused to cooperate with any ex-Francoists, but their disappointing electoral results and the danger of a military coup led them to change their mind.
- The resultant spirit of compromise was reflected above all in the 1978 Constitution. However, it broke down once political debate shifted to bread-and-butter issues, which also led to fatal splits in the governing UCD.

Crisis and recovery

- In the Basque Country and Catalonia demands for self-government were very strong; in 1979 both regions were granted extensive autonomy as part of a wider devolution settlement.
- The arrangements were not fully accepted in the Basque Country, where ETA stepped up its violence, while both new regional governments came into conflict with the central authorities.
- Such tensions, together with fears about Spain's possible break-up and popular discontent with economic conditions, prompted military officers to attempt a coup in February 1981.
- The coup's failure, and the massive response by the public and politicians, demonstrated how little support the reactionaries really had and emboldened the opposition to force an election in October 1982. The Socialists' victory, and the general acceptance of that, signalled the end of transition.

Exhibit 8.1: King Juan Carlos addresses Parliament (1977)

Speech at the opening session of the Parliament elected in June 1977

[...] Hace poco más de un año y medio, en mi primer mensaje como Rey de España, afirmé que asumía la Corona con pleno sentido de mi responsabilidad y consciente de la honrosa obligación que supone el cumplimiento de las Leyes y el respeto de la tradición. Se iniciaba una nueva etapa en la Historia de España que había de basarse, ante todo, en una sincera voluntad de concordia nacional y que debía recoger las demandas de evolución que el desarrollo de la cultura, el cambio generacional y el crecimiento material de los tiempos actuales exigían de forma ineludible, como garantía del ejercicio de todas las libertades. Para conseguirlo, propuse como empresa comunitaria la participación de todos en nuestra vida política, pues creo firmemente que la grandeza y fortaleza de la Patria tiene que asentarse en la voluntad manifiesta de cuantos la integramos. [...]

La ley nos obliga a todos por igual. Pero lo decisivo es que nadie pueda sentirse marginado. El éxito del camino que empezamos dependerá en buena medida de que en la participación no haya exclusiones. Con la presencia en estas Cortes de los partidos que a través del voto representan a los españoles, damos un paso importante en esa dirección y debemos disponernos con nobleza a confiar en quienes han sido elegidos para dar testimonio de sus ideas y de sus ilusiones. [...]

Además de estos objetivos, el país tiene pendiente muchos problemas concretos sobre los que el pueblo español espera la acción directa de sus representantes. El primero es crear el marco legal adecuado para las nuevas relaciones sociales, en el orden constitucional, el regional o en el de la comunicación humana.

La Corona desea – y cree interpretar las aspiraciones de las Cortes – una Constitución que dé cabida a todas las peculiaridades de nuestro pueblo y que garantice sus derechos históricos y actuales.

Desea el reconocimiento de la diversa realidad de nuestras comunidades regionales y comparte en este sentido cuantas aspiraciones no debiliten, sino enriquezcan y hagan más robusta la unidad indiscutible de España. [...]

Little more than a year and a half ago, in my first speech as King of Spain, I stated that I was ascending the throne in the full knowledge of my responsibility and aware of the honourable obligations on me to obey the law and respect tradition. A new chapter in Spain's history was beginning. It was to be based, above all, on a sincere desire to achieve national harmony. And it would have to take up the demands for our country to evolve that had arisen inevitably from the contemporary trends of cultural development, generational change and material growth, as a guarantee that Spaniards' liberty might be exercised in full. In order to achieve that, I proposed as a common enterprise the participation of all Spaniards in our political life, for I believe firmly that the greatness and strength of our Fatherland must be founded on the clear will of all those who make it up. [...]

The law places the same obligations on us all. But the crux of the matter is that no-one should feel themselves marginalized. The success of the enterprise that we are beginning will depend in large measure on nobody being excluded from participation. With the presence in this parliament of the parties which, through the electoral process, represent Spaniards, we are taking an important step in that direction, and we must be prepared nobly to place our trust in those who have been elected to present their ideas and hopes here. [...]

As well as these tasks of a general nature, the country faces other, more specific problems that are still to be resolved, and which the Spanish people expect its representatives to tackle head on. The first of these is to create an appropriate legal framework for new relationships in society, whether in the constitutional or the regional sphere, or in that of human interaction.

I wish – and here I believe myself to be expressing the aspirations of this parliament – to see a Constitution within which all the special features of our people can find a place, and which guarantees their rights, both traditional and contemporary.

I wish also to see the diverse reality of our regions recognised. In that sense I share the aspirations of all those who seek not to weaken but to strengthen and enrich Spain's unquestionable unity. […]

Source: Presidencia del Gobierno (1977) *Mensajes de la Corona.* Madrid: Colección Informe, núm. 15.

Exhibit 8.2: Tejero's manifesto (1981)

Statement issued by the leader of the Civil Guards who stormed Parliament during the 1981 coup attempt

Españoles: las unidades del Ejército y de la Guardia Civil que desde ayer están ocupando el Congreso de los Diputados a las órdenes del general Milans del Bosch, [...] no tienen otro deseo que el bien de España y de su pueblo.

No admiten más que un Gobierno que instaure una verdadera democracia. No admiten las autonomías separatistas y quieren una España descentralizada, pero no rota. No admiten la impunidad de los asesinos terroristas, contra los que es preciso aplicar todo el rigor de la ley. No pueden aceptar una situación en la que el prestigio de España disminuye día al día; no admiten la inseguridad ciudadana que nos impide vivir en paz.

Aceptan y respetan al Rey, al que quieren ver al frente de los destinos de la Patria, respaldado por sus Fuerzas Armadas. En suma, quieren la unidad de España, la paz, orden y seguridad. ¡Viva España!

Spaniards: the Army and Civil Guard units that, since yesterday, have been occupying the Congress of Deputies on the orders of General Milans del Bosch, […] have only one concern: the good of Spain and her people.

They will not accept any government that fails to introduce a true democracy. They will not accept the existence of separatist regions; they wish to see a Spain that is decentralised, but not broken up. They will not accept the immunity from punishment of terrorist murderers, who must be subject to the full force of the law. They cannot accept a situation in which Spain's prestige is diminishing daily. And they will not accept the absence of law and order that prevents us from living in peace.

They do accept and respect the King, whom they wish to see in charge of the Fatherland's fate, supported by its Armed Forces. In sum, they wish the unity of Spain, peace, order and security. Long live Spain!

Source: El País (4 March 1981).

Topics for discussion

- How does the view of the monarchy's role presented by King Juan Carlos (Exhibit 8.1) compare with that of Cánovas (Exhibit 1.2)?
- Which institutions does he refer to, either directly or indirectly, as having a role to play in the country's future development?
- What aspects of Spain's historical experience appear to have prompted his remarks?

- Judging by Tejero's manifesto (Exhibit 8.2), where does, or should, ultimate authority lie in Spain? What role does it appear to ascribe to the monarchy?
- How did Spain's situation in 1975 resemble that in 1936? Why did events turn out so differently?
- Could the aim of a clean break with the Franco regime ever have been practicable? If so, under what circumstances?

CHAPTER 9

By 1982 the neoliberal ideas of the New Right had come to dominate western thinking, their position reinforced by the rapid abandonment of Socialist economic policies in France. Along with free market economics their main feature was anti-Communism. Renewed stress was laid on the role of NATO, leading to a revival of the arms race. Partly as a result, in 1989 the Soviet bloc crumbled, leading to the emergence of new states and the discrediting of its underlying ideology. Meanwhile, the western economies experienced a strong recovery concentrated in the financial sector and other services. It was aided by the EC's removal of remaining barriers to internal competition by the 1989 Single European Act and its enlargement to 12 members. In 1992 these signed the Maastricht Treaty, which, as well as converting the EC into the European Union (EU), established a timetable for Economic and Monetary Union (EMU). Further steps towards political integration were taken by some members, with the creation of a joint Eurocorps (also in 1992) and the removal of border controls under the Schengen Treaty of 1995. Meanwhile, the strict economic requirements, or convergence criteria set for EMU candidates served to deepen the recession that, throughout the West, undermined the New Right, and boosted the advocates of a return to the political Centre.

Back to the mainstream (1982–1993)

With the smooth transfer of power following the 1982 general election, Spain's long journey to democracy was effectively complete. But there remained major challenges to face, the first of which was to close the still yawning gap with its neighbours in economic – and social – terms. Both objectively and in the minds of most Spaniards, that was inextricably linked to the second: joining the EC. To a large degree, the next stage in Spain's story was accordingly shaped by its belated involvement in the ongoing process of European integration. Its second feature was the extraordinary dominance established over Spanish politics by the Socialist Party, a situation that brought dramatic change to both country and party. Rather than from any nationwide force, the main obstacle to complete Socialist hegemony lay in the growth of regional self-government and self-assertiveness that constituted a third major characteristic of the period.

Into Europe

Even before Franco died in 1975 Spanish opinion had swung strongly behind the idea of joining the EC. Yet it was only the arrival in power of the Socialists seven years later that gave decisive impetus to the country's efforts to do so. For the new government was not only willing and able to give top priority to the associated negotiations. It was also prepared to tackle head-on the tricky issue of the country's economic preparedness to join. Membership having been achieved, the Socialists also showed themselves adept in adjusting to the unwritten rules of European politics, the result being to enhance further the considerable benefits it had brought.

By 1982, very few in Spain questioned the desirability, or the importance, of EC membership. Throughout society there was a vague but powerful yearning to see the country accepted by its neighbours as an equal. On the Left, suspicions that the Community was an agent of multinational business were outweighed by the knowledge that workers in the EC were better off, and by the hope that entry would kill off the old reactionary Right. Business, especially the larger, more vocal enterprises, was enthusiastic. This last had been the main factor behind the Franco regime's uncharacteristic, and unsuccessful, decision to apply for admission (p101), and it spurred the centre-right governments of the transition era to lodge a new application. Beset as they were by other problems, however, they lacked the time and energy to pursue it effectively.

As in many other ways (p137), the Socialists' election marked a turning point. Not only did Spain's new rulers enjoy a large parliamentary majority: the failure of the 1981 coup attempt had effectively dispelled lingering uncertainty about the country's political future. Moreover, they were among the most enthusiastic pro-Europeans (*europeístas*), free from the isolationist complexes that haunted many on the Right. Virtually as soon as they were elected they therefore gave a new priority to the negotiations with Brussels.

At the same time, they were acutely aware that being accepted into the EC club was only half the battle. Spain also had to be made fit to survive once inside. The shaky foundations of development in the 1960s had left the country more vulnerable than her neighbours to the turbulences of the following decade. By 1982 her economic situation relative to the rest of western Europe was no better than it had been twenty years before. Indeed, given the increased pace of change, it was probably worse. As the third industrial revolution got under way Spain was barely emerging from the first, its economy still dependent on agriculture and a manufacturing sector within which old-style smokestack industries were heavily over-represented.

The new government, like most Spaniards, took the view that the only way Spain could catch up was through exposure to competition within the EC. But there was the rub. Even the strictly controlled opening of her economy since 1959 had laid bare its lack of international competitiveness (p114). If the cure were not to prove worse than the disease, Spanish industry would have to be prepared for the shock of entry. On their arrival in power that became the Socialists' top domestic priority. It underlay their reforms in a range of areas, particularly infrastructure and education (p137), but above all their wide-ranging programme of **industrial restructuring**.

Meanwhile a top-ranking delegation was engaged in the tortuous process of actually negotiating entry to the EC. It was headed by Foreign Minister Fernando Morán and one of his senior colleagues, Manuel Marín, who had long been closely involved in the umbrella organisation of Europe's Socialist parties and had built up an extensive network of contacts as a result. The two faced considerable stumbling blocks, especially French concerns about Spanish agricultural produce and the question of fisheries. Nonetheless, all were overcome, and in 1985 Spain's Treaty of Accession (*Tratado de Adhesión*) was signed.

Under it Spain became a fully fledged Community member on 1 January 1986, although there would be a seven-year transition period (*período transitorio*) before some EC tariffs on Spanish products were removed. Along with significant concessions on fisheries and some aspects of agriculture, that effectively formed the country's entry fee. For the particular sectors and groups affected, such as fishermen and dairy farmers, the price was a high one. But their concerns were drowned in the general euphoria, while handing Brussels control over important areas of economic policy – such a controversial issue in the UK – caused barely a ripple in Spain. Indeed, the option of holding a referendum on the terms obtained, virtually standard among prospective new members, was scarcely discussed. No one, euphoric or not, had any doubts as to the outcome.

Another issue, intimately bound up with that of EC entry although the connection was rarely spoken aloud, was not dealt with so easily. It related to Spain's foreign policy in general, and the country's attitude to NATO in particular. That was a cause of concern to her prospective EC colleagues, not to mention the Americans.

The worries went back to Adolfo Suárez's time as Prime Minister (p115), when Spain had kept its distance from US policy, notably in Latin America, and presented itself as a bridge between the West and the developing world. Such non-alignment (*tercermundismo*) had been abandoned under Suárez's successor, who took Spain into NATO (p125). But the Socialists had clearly implied they would reverse this decision if elected and, although they made no immediate move to do so, Morán showed signs of reverting to the Suárez line in other respects.

In the climate of the time, that put him out of step with his EC counterparts. They impressed on Morán's boss, Prime Minister Felipe González, that a large,

> ### *reconversión industrial*
>
> industrial restructuring
>
> Begun tentatively under the **UCD** governments of the transition period, restructuring aimed to shift the basis of Spanish industry from declining sectors to those with better future prospects, and to encourage the creation of companies large enough to compete in international markets, in particular those within the EC. The comprehensive programme that got under way after 1982 was partially successful in meeting these aims in the medium term. More immediately it had a severe negative impact on sectors such as shipbuilding and steel manufacture, with many plant closures and thousands of workers made redundant.

strategically important country like Spain could not be allowed to disrupt the Community's solidly pro-American line. Accepting that withdrawal from NATO was no longer an option, González decided that only endorsement in a referendum would allow him to pull off such a brazen U-turn.

Voting was scheduled for 12 March 1986 and the PM set about overturning the large anti-NATO majority shown by opinion polls. First, he persuaded his party to ratify the government's change of tack, arguing that its previous objections had been, not to membership as such, but to the undemocratic way in which the decision to join had been taken (p125). Then, the question actually put to voters made remaining in NATO subject to a number of more or less spurious qualifications, including a commitment to negotiate removal of the US military presence in Spain (p88). Finally González himself, fresh from the triumph of taking Spain into 'Europe', campaigned tirelessly for a 'Yes' vote.

The result was in doubt almost to the last but, in the end, the Prime Minister won a substantial majority. The decision marked a turning point. Within months Morán was replaced by Francisco Fernández Ordóñez, who, ironically, had served under Suárez as Finance Minister. His mild social democratic views included no trace of anti-Americanism, however, and under his direction Spain's foreign policy was reoriented along unambiguously pro-western lines. Like the whole NATO affair, that caused bitter resentment among sections of González's own party. But for most Spaniards these issues were soon forgotten amidst the spectacular economic growth that followed EC entry.

In part, this resulted from the massive financial support Spain immediately began to receive from the EC's Structural Funds. Even more important was the general upswing in the European economy, which encouraged massive private investment in the newly opened-up Spanish market. Heavily concentrated in non-traditional sectors, this contributed to a fundamental change in the country's economy. By the end of the decade dependence on heavy industry was significantly down and Spain was moving rapidly towards the post-industrial structure typical of the most advanced economies. Indeed, from 1986 to 1990 it grew faster than any other developed country, significantly reducing the gap between it and its fellow EC members in terms of per capita GDP.

In the meantime, the government had been at pains to ensure Spain a strong position in the complex world of the EC's internal politics. Its awareness of such issues was apparent in the terms of accession, which gave Spain a weight in the Community's institutions rather greater than would have been merited by its population, never mind its economic strength. Thus it was given the privilege – previously confined to France, Germany, Italy and the UK – of nominating two members of the EC's powerful executive, the European Commission. Indeed, no sooner was Spain admitted than Marín was appointed a Commission Vice-President, a considerable prize for a new member.

Marín himself embodied the Spanish government's strategy of placing well-prepared political heavyweights in Community institutions, an approach that displayed a keen grasp of the demands of EC politics – again in sharp contrast to the UK. It was also apparent in the close relationship struck up by the Socialist González with the Christian Democrat Helmut Kohl, leader of the EC's paymaster and most powerful member, Germany, and in his government's ostentatious readiness to support Community initiatives.

Thus in 1989 Spain not only signed up to the Single European Act – a step about which it had little choice – but also opted voluntarily to join the European Monetary System (EMS). Three years later it enthusiastically adopted the Maastricht Treaty, voicing none of the reservations about further political integration heard in Britain (and Denmark). In 1992, too, it became a founder member of the Eurocorps and three years later it was to be a founder signatory of the Schengen agreement.

Indeed on occasion the government's desire to be 'at the heart of Europe' seemed to outweigh more material interests. For instance, signing the Single European Act made Spain's under-developed services sector vulnerable to foreign domination, and EMS entry, while a guard against inflation, also made the peseta a target for currency speculators. Yet neither of these decisions seemed as daring, perhaps even foolhardy, as the government's determination not to miss out on the biggest project of all; EMU.

Meeting the convergence criteria set at Maastricht for EMU entry would always have been tough for a country that, despite recent advances, remained one of the European Union's poorest. But it became doubly so when, almost as soon as the treaty was signed, Spain was hit, late but severely, by the economic downturn that had struck the entire developed world. On 'Black Thursday' (13 May 1993) the Bank of Spain was forced to devalue the peseta so substantially as to break the EMS rules – a move which, if repeated, would debar the country from the EMU. That year the country recorded its worst economic figures for half a century, with unemployment rising to over 20 per cent.

Nonetheless, the government persisted in its determination, which had been graphically demonstrated at the 1992 EU Summit in Edinburgh. There the richer EU members had tried to ditch plans for a Cohesion Fund to assist the poorer members with convergence, of which Spain would be the main beneficiary. González's reaction on this occasion was reminiscent of the outbursts favoured by UK premier Margaret Thatcher; he threatened to torpedo the whole meeting unless the Fund was retained. He got his way.

At home, his strategy was based on the Convergence Plan (*Programa de Convergencia*), a package of measures adopted in 1992 whose main features were budget cuts and a tightening of monetary policy. First signs were not hopeful, as Spain's slow recovery from recession – and the forced devaluation – soon undermined the forecasts on which the Plan was based. But the following year it was re-launched by Finance Minister Pedro Solbes who, ignoring protests that it was further aggravating unemployment, kept it remorselessly on course.

In parallel with these economic efforts, Spain continued to entrench its position in the EU's internal politics. By the mid-1990s, Spaniards were occupying a disproportionate number of leading positions in the Commission's upper administrative levels and in the European Parliament. Manuel Marín went on to be one of the longest serving Commissioners (albeit his EU career finished under a cloud, when he was at the centre of the mismanagement allegations that led the European Parliament to vote the entire Commission out of office in 1999).

Spain's other Commissioners, always figures of standing, were also given relatively important portfolios. Indeed, among the names most frequently touted as the new Commission President due to be chosen in 1994 was that of González, whose uncharacteristic Edinburgh outburst had clearly been forgiven. As it transpired, the rumours were unfounded. Yet their mere existence was testimony both to Spain's move, in under a decade, from outsider to part of the Union's inner core and to the stature enjoyed by its PM abroad as well as at home, where he and his party continued to rule the roost.

The Socialist hegemony

The victory of the Spanish Socialist Party (PSOE) at the 1982 general election opened a new era in Spanish politics. For the next decade, these were utterly dominated by the PSOE (p25), which was thus able to push through a wide range of reforming measures that brought fundamental changes in many fields. Their nature reflected the priorities of the party's leadership, which in some respects clashed with those of its traditional supporters. The result was a division in the Socialist camp which, together with changes in the PSOE's nature, gradually undermined the party's exclusive grip on power.

The Socialists' 1982 victory was, and remains, the most sweeping ever achieved at a genuine election in Spain. With over 10 million votes (47% of the total) they won a more than comfortable overall majority in both houses of Parliament (p102), something always denied to their predecessors in office, the centrists of UCD (p117). It, by contrast, was almost wiped out, and indeed disbanded the following year, leaving a vacuum on the centre-right of Spanish politics that was to persist for the next decade. Similarly, the Communist PCE also suffered severe losses from which it has never recovered, despite using the 'no' campaign in the 1986 NATO referendum (p134) as the basis on which to form a new, broader leftist alliance known as 'United Left' (IU).

Faced with so little opposition, the PSOE topped the poll at every major electoral contest for the next eleven years. Despite gradually falling support, it retained its overall majority in the Madrid Parliament, first in 1986 and again, in practice, in 1989 (when it won exactly half of the seats in the Congress). As a result, it was able repeatedly to circumvent various constitutional checks on executive power (p121). In particular the Socialists were able to cram their own appointees into the swelling apparatus of government agencies, among them the state television monopoly, which they exploited as shamelessly as had UCD (p117). Moreover, from 1983 on they controlled most of Spain's 17 newly autonomous regions (p141), and most of its larger towns and cities to boot. As a result, politics in the 1980s was to a large extent the internal politics of the PSOE.

It was therefore an important consideration that the party which entered government in 1982 was no longer the mass working-class organisation of the 1930s. That PSOE had been reduced to a small hard core under Franco's rule (p102). Since his death, and above all since the party's near-split in 1979 (p126), a new PSOE had been built by a new leadership, dominated by the figure of Felipe González. Although still heavily dependent for votes on the poorer sections of society, especially the expanded industrial labour force, most of its impetus and leadership now came from the middle classes that had also grown under Franco, lawyers and educationalists in particular.

Understandably, this new PSOE rejected the old view that socialism was purely a working-class affair (p25), albeit some in it were not averse to exploiting class resentments to win and hold support; González's deputy and close collaborator, Alfonso Guerra (p126), was especially adept at this. Generally, though, the Socialists' leaders were relatively unconcerned with traditional socialist goals of equality or redistribution. They barely needed the warning provided by the experience of their French colleagues to steer clear of such classic left-wing policies as the nationalisation of industry.

Instead, their focus was on efficiency – 'getting Spain to work properly' as González put it – and in the economic sphere at least their policies were little different from the neoliberal ones popular elsewhere at the time. Together with 'Europe', the Socialists' other watchword was 'modernisation'. In that they recalled the Republicans of the early 1930s (p151), and so too did the ambitious nature of the reform programme they had in mind.

Indeed, barely an aspect of Spanish public life was left untouched in the 1980s. The education system was overhauled and extended, especially at higher level, where numerous new universities were established. A national health service was created on the British model. Crucially, in view of the enormous investment these changes involved, the tax system was revised to make it fairer and, above all, more efficient. Extensive military reforms were implemented that, helped along by Spain's entry into NATO (p125) and its growing involvement in international policing duties, at long last steered the army away from its unhealthy interest in politics.

In the economic field, the considerable advances made were inextricably bound up with what was perhaps the Socialists' greatest achievement: entry into the EC. Industry was restructured in preparation for accession (p133). Thereafter, the vast improvements in infrastructure that took place under their auspices, in particular those of the grossly inadequate transport network, were heavily funded from Brussels. EC membership was also largely responsible for the renewed rise in Spanish living standards (p134), not just absolutely but also relative to the Community average. As a result, Spaniards now enjoyed greatly increased ownership of such goods as cars and electrical appliances, as well as expanded access to vastly improved social infrastructure, especially schools and hospitals.

The picture was not all rosy, however. As elsewhere in the developed world, Spain's growth in the 1980s was heavily concentrated in light industry and above all in services, notably the financial sector. Yet, because of the country's relative economic backwardness, this represented a particularly abrupt change for Spain. The effects were traumatic for some, especially the workforce in the older, heavier industries that were decimated by industrial restructuring. It was that same section of the population – the PSOE's most faithful supporters – that was also the main loser from the González administration's reforms in two further areas, which involved dismantling the haphazard and unsustainable social policy framework erected by the Franco regime.

The first of these fields was the elaborate system of employment regulation (p82), which made it hard for employers to shed labour, and so react quickly to changes in market conditions. Now that they faced more outside competition, that inbuilt delaying process was a distinct disadvantage; moreover, their complaints were backed up by both the EC and the OECD. In 1984 the government bowed to pressure and, as a first step towards making Spain's labour market less rigid (*flexibilización*), legalised fixed-term contracts.

The second aspect of Franco's legacy was social security provision in general, and state pensions in particular. Flushed with the economic success of the 1960s, the dictatorship had introduced a surprisingly generous system of social support. However, it was highly bureaucratic and based on the assumption that boom conditions would last. When they did not, the dictator's successors were left to pick up the tab caused by rising unemployment, not to mention a rapidly ageing population. The problems were aggravated by the effects of industrial restructuring, which left many workers with no alternative but to take early retirement. In 1985 the government decided something had to be done and announced that many state pensions would be reduced.

That was too much for the Socialist trade union federation, the UGT (p40), which had expected a PSOE government to help its members, rather than assign them to the scrap heap and cut their benefits. It was also unhappy at the government's obvious intention to abandon the practice of '**social concertation**'. The UGT's respected leader Nicolás Redondo heavily criticised the pension cuts and threatened to resign his MP's seat. Two years later he did so in protest at proposals for further cutbacks.

By then, the government's U-turn on NATO (pp133–4) had driven another wedge between it and its sister union, which had not forgiven American support for Franco. Nor were matters helped by the links cultivated by some leading figures in the PSOE – notably Finance Minister Miguel Boyer – with the newly rich celebrities (*los beautiful*), whose doings formed the staple diet of Spain's widely read gossip magazines

---

concertación social

'social concertation'

A product of the **spirit of compromise** (p119) that marked the central period of the transition in 1977/78, 'social concertation' was the practice of involving trade unions and employers' representatives in economic policy-making. Foreshadowed by the Moncloa Pacts (p120), between 1979 and 1984 it resulted in a series of agreements covering not only industrial relations issues, specifically wages, but also more general matters such as employment creation, social security and general public spending. Abandoned by the then ruling Socialists when the last agreement lapsed in 1987, 'concertation' was revived by the conservative government elected in 1996 (p164).

(*prensa del corazón*). The final straw came in 1988, when the government proposed further deregulating the labour market to allow low-wage contracts for young workers. Its move provoked the UGT to throw in its lot with the Workers' Commissions (p102), which had been attacking González's government almost from the time it was first elected in 1982.

On 14 December 1988 the two jointly staged a general strike. That such action, with its almost mythical status for the Spanish workers' movement (p36), should be used against a Socialist government seemed hugely significant, especially as the turnout was impressive. González duly withdrew the offending proposals. But he then took advantage of the favourable economic climate to call an early election for October 1989 – and won it easily, despite the UGT's unprecedented refusal to endorse the PSOE campaign.

The PM had effectively called the unions' bluff. Admittedly, some social spending was increased in response to their demands (*giro social*). But González nonetheless pressed on with other cutbacks, and with labour market deregulation, as part of his Convergence Plan (p135), ignoring two more general strikes in 1992 and 1994 as well as the continuing high level of unemployment.

The truth was that the PSOE's traditional core support now wielded little clout in the party. Economic change meant that the industrial workforce was already shrinking. A very large proportion of the party's members and, above all, its office-bearers was now made up of men and women who had been elected or appointed to public positions, and whose over-riding concern was to retain them. Formidably organised by Guerra, this new PSOE became a highly cohesive electoral machine, fiercely loyal to González, its electoral trump card.

However, just as the old party had never been renowned for original thinking (p26), the new one showed few signs of fresh ideas to replace the traditional principles it had largely ditched. A grandiose project fronted by Guerra intended to do so produced little of substance. As a result, the party failed to catch the change of mood towards greater individualism that was increasingly apparent among the young, especially those in larger towns and cities, from the later 1980s on.

Even more immediately damaging was the impression Socialists often gave of contempt for voters, symbolised by the notorious infrequency of González's appearances

felipismo

Felipe-ism

Coined in the 1980s, the term *felipismo* was widely used to refer to various aspects of the **PSOE** (p25) under the leadership of Felipe González. The main ones were: abandonment of the class-based attitudes traditionally associated with Spanish Socialism in favour of an emphasis on economic modernisation (p137); strong, centralised control of the party apparatus; and an approach to electioneering centred on González's charisma. More broadly, the term was applied by opponents to unsavoury aspects of government during his time in power, in particular the practice of steamrollering legislation through Parliament with minimal or no consultation, the widespread incidence of influence-peddling (p140) and the major scandals of the 1990s (p162).

---

caso GAL

....

GAL affair

Uncovered – partially – in the mid-1990s, the GAL affair centred on the Anti-Terrorist Liberation Groups (*Grupos Antiterroristas de Liberación* [GAL]), who a decade earlier had claimed responsibility for the killing and kidnapping of a number of Basques, in both Spain and France. From the outset, these incidents were widely suspected to be part of a government-controlled 'dirty war' against **ETA** (p103) that had begun in the 1970s with the shady activities of the so-called 'Basque-Spanish Battalion' (BVE). The GAL were also long shrouded in mystery, despite the conviction of two relatively junior police agents in 1988 for involvement in their activities. In 1995, however, the chain of command was traced up to cabinet level, and three years later former Interior Minister José Barrionuevo was jailed for his part in the GAL's activities.

---

in Parliament. Unflattering comparisons began to be drawn between so-called '**Felipe-ism**' and Francoism. One undoubted parallel was the prevalence of influence-peddling (*tráfico de influencias*), although the object of such activities was now often party funding rather than personal enrichment. More important, though, was another difference from the Franco years; the existence of a free press, which gleefully revealed a succession of dubious affairs (*casos*) involving the Socialists. The biggest was that of a bogus consultancy company, Filesa, which had been set up by prominent party figures to launder illicit income.

Some influence-peddling, on the other hand, was purely a matter of personal gain. One case, uncovered in 1990, involved Juan Guerra, the brother of González's deputy, who was obliged to resign from office the following year as a result of it. The PM had relied heavily on Alfonso Guerra – apart from anything else, he had organised every PSOE election campaign since 1982. His departure was thus another grievous blow for the party, whose public image had already suffered immense damage (*desgaste*) from the various financial scandals and the first rumblings of the even more serious **GAL affair**.

As a result of these developments, and because at last they faced a real challenge from the Right (p163), the Socialists were widely expected to lose the 1993 general election. However, they still held two trump cards. One was González himself, who retained enormous popularity and threw himself into the campaign, making a dramatic personal commitment to act against corruption. The other was the lingering memory of dictatorship, which the PSOE ruthlessly exploited in painting its conservative challengers as a bunch of unreconstructed Francoists bent on reversing the changes of the last decade. Together, these factors proved enough to make the PSOE the largest single party. It was a victory very different from that of 1982, however. For the group that had swung decisively to the Socialists then, made up of younger urban voters, 'socialism' had mostly become a dirty word. The party's former base, the heavy industrial workforce, was now reduced to a shrunken, widely disillusioned remnant. Instead, the PSOE's votes now came overwhelmingly from three sources: the old, public sector workers, and the poor rural regions of the South.

Moreover, the election results finally deprived the Socialists of the overall majority they had held for the previous eleven years. To remain in office they now needed outside support. One possible ally, the Communist-led IU, was ruled out by González's determination to persist with centrist policies. The only other option was to turn to one or more of the veritable host of regionalist parties that in any case now formed the third largest block in Parliament.

Regionalists, new and old

The strength of regionalism was rather ironic, given that defusing demands for regional self-government had been a major aim of those who drew up the 1978 Constitution (p122). In fact, though, almost the opposite had occurred, despite – or perhaps because of – the devolution process it set in motion. Firstly, devolution itself gave rise to new problems, and to new pressures in areas where regionalism had previously been non-existent or dormant. Secondly, in attempting to respond to these the government further aggravated the tensions which had never fully disappeared in the Basque Country and Catalonia.

By the time of the 1982 election it was clear that, whatever the framers of the 1978 Constitution may have intended, devolution was to apply to the whole country, not just a few chosen regions. Within another year, all mainland Spain, plus the Balearic and Canary Islands, had been divided up into 17 regions, each with its own parliament and government, and with its Statute of Autonomy defining the extent of its self-government powers.

In fact, though, the devolution process was only beginning, not least because it was simply impossible for all the devolved powers to be transferred instantly to newly created bodies. Furthermore, the handover of specific areas of responsibility to individual regions (*transferencias*) often became the subject of lengthy wrangling with the central government. Indeed, a number of these disputes were still unsettled almost a decade into the next century.

Long before that it had become apparent that the arrangements put in place were far from perfect. Certainly, they had brought a long overdue decentralisation of administration, as well as creating alternative power bases to counterbalance a rather over-mighty central government. However, the structure created was far too complex. Thus, despite the 1981 attempt to stop any more regions taking the 'fast track' to more extensive autonomy (p125), a further three – the Canaries, Navarre and Valencia – had done so. Moreover, as the powers granted to the seven 'fast track' (p122) regions were all different, there were no fewer than eight separate models of regional self-government in operation. Understandably, this situation gave rise to considerable administrative problems, prompting the central government to seek ways of streamlining the system.

At the same time, devolution had important effects in the regions themselves. In those that successfully campaigned for 'fast-track' status, feelings of regional identity received a considerable boost. There and elsewhere the new institutions, with the associated symbolism of flags, anthems and so on, served to rekindle the strong feelings of local loyalty virtually omnipresent in Spain but which, since the demise of federal Republicanism (p8), had lacked a political focus.

The process was assisted by the fact that local and regionally based newspapers continued to be much more widely read than the Madrid-based press, and later by the blossoming of regional broadcasting. Above, all regular regional elections, at which parties inevitably addressed the 'people of Cantabria', or wherever, fostered the notion that this 'people' formed a distinctive group with distinctive, shared interests. By the early 1990s there was barely a region without a party – or parties – whose *raison d'être* was to defend them.

Interestingly, the growth of these new regionalist movements (*nuevos regionalismos*) was not primarily a function of regions' distinctiveness. Thus Galicia, arguably Spain's least typical region in cultural terms, was one of the few in which regionalism made little or no immediate impact. In Andalusia, where it had some tradition, it was soon smothered by the Socialists, whose control of central government allowed them to pour public money into a region where they were already well-established (and from where several party bigwigs, Prime Minister González included, originated).

On the other hand, the persistent weakness of the Spanish right during the 1980s (p136) left an opening for locally based conservative groupings to become important players in several regions where regionalism had little pedigree, notably Navarre, Valencia and Aragon. In the last of these, they could also exploit resentment at the denial of 'fast track' status despite Aragon's strong historical claims to be distinctive (ppxiii–xiv). Indeed, once the five-year bar on amending the various regional Statutes of Autonomy expired in 1988, it was Aragon that spearheaded demands for a devolution review.

As such a move would mean tinkering with the delicate compromises worked out in the first years of democracy, the Socialists were reluctant to make it without cross-party support. However, the conservative opposition, traditionally suspicious of devolution in any form, was now keen to neutralise what had become a dangerous source of competition. It accordingly agreed to support a package of measures to standardise the system somewhat which was finally approved in 1994. As well as extending devolution to Ceuta and Melilla (p39), this gave all regions the right to virtually all the powers previously reserved to the 'fast track' ones. These latter would now be distinguished solely by their control over health services and policing, and by the special tax arrangements applying to Navarre and, most importantly, to the Basque Country (p123).

There, early and extensive devolution had failed to satisfy regionalists; in fact, it had not even put an end to the 'armed struggle' waged by the most extreme of their factions, ETA (p103). Hopes did rise on that front in September 1982. As part of a deal brokered by Basque Left (*Euskadiko Ezkerra* [EE]), originally the political wing of ETA's 'politico-military' branch (p103) but now an outspoken opponent of violence, the so-called 'poli-milis' agreed to disband. However, few activists took up the offer of 'reinsertion' into normal society in return for laying down their arms. Instead, most defected to the 'military' branch to form a reunited ETA as committed to violence as ever.

Meanwhile, on the political front, both EE and **People's Unity** were protesting noisily against the 1981 legislation designed to curb regions' real powers (p125), a campaign in which they were joined by the largest regionalist force, the Basque Nationalist Party (PNV) (p24). The effect was to intensify the sense of Basque–Spanish confrontation which the PNV had already been fomenting from its position in regional government (p123) – and which was also fed, for their own reasons, by the local Socialists. This strategy brought the PNV large gains at the 1984 regional election but at the cost of provoking severe tensions within Basque society, and within the party itself.

The internal dispute had a number of causes, but at the root of them all was the mismatch between the PNV's archaic ideas (pp23–4), to which many members clung ferociously, and contemporary reality. The outcome was a stand-off between the party's traditionalist boss Xabier Arzalluz and the head of the new regional executive (*lehendakari*), Carlos Garaikoetxea, who resigned in 1985. The following year he set up a breakaway party, Basque Solidarity (*Eusko Alkartasuna* [EA]), forcing an early regional election.

Held in November 1986, it complicated matters still further. The PNV suffered heavy losses, mainly to EA, and, while the combined nationalist vote rose to a new high of over 60%, it was now so fragmented that no single party was anywhere near to winning a parliamentary majority. On top of the region's already massive problems (ETA's relentless terror; the social and economic effects of restructuring (p133) on its heavy industry) this political crisis threatened to render it ungovernable.

In the event, though, it had the opposite effect. Against all expectations a coalition government was formed in early 1987 by the PNV and the PSOE's Basque section, whose relations had previously been deteriorating into bitter animosity. Now, united by a common desire for stability and a hold on power, they patched up their differences, at least in public, thus removing one cause of tension in the region.

Over the next year the main one was also mitigated, although the initial signs were anything but good. For the PNV's crisis prompted ETA to step up its attacks, particularly those on the new regional police force, the *Ertzaintza*, whose ranks were filled mainly with nationalist sympathisers. Other victims now included ETA's own

---

Herri Batasuna (HB)

People's Unity

HB was established in 1978 as the political wing of **ETA**'s then 'military' branch (p103) with the declared objectives of obtaining independence for an extended Basque Country including Navarre and an area in south-west France (*Euskal Herría*) and establishing a form of 'revolutionary socialism' there. At all times, it and its successors have been completely under ETA's control. HB opposed both the **1978 Constitution** (p120) and the Basque Statute of Autonomy (p123), and its representatives long boycotted both the Spanish and Basque Parliaments. Under increasing pressure from the authorities, in 2001 HB was wound up and refounded under the name of Unity (*Batasuna*). This new party was banned by the Spanish authorities the following year. Subsequently, ETA's supporters have attempted to continue operating under a variety of labels, but various of these have also been banned and none has achieved significant electoral support.
See also: **Pacto de Lizarra** (p155)

former activists who had opted for 'reinsertion', as well as members of the public; in June 1987, a bomb in a Barcelona hypermarket killed 15 people. However, these changed tactics proved to be counterproductive for ETA, inducing many nationalist voters who had retained some sympathy with the organisation because of its anti-Francoist origins to turn against it and its political backers. In January 1988 all parties in the regional parliament, with the exception of HB, signed an agreement that condemned all violence, irrespective of its alleged motives.

This 'Ajuria Enea Pact', in the negotiation of which EE played a key role, effectively isolated ETA and its supporters, and greatly normalised relations among the other parties. Above all, by forcing the PNV to take a clear stand against violence (p123), it obliged the region's key political force to stop flirting with HB (which, despite everything, still commanded the support of a sixth of Basque voters). Toning down its demands for increased self-government, the PNV began to concentrate on using those powers already devolved to address the region's economic problems, with no little success.

Partly as a result, the Basque Country was able to share in the economic upturn after 1986 (p134), a development that helped to ease tension further. The PNV's new line also brought benefits for the party itself. Buoyed by the growing popularity of Garaikoetxea's successor as regional First Minister, the calm and moderate José Antonio Ardanza, it regained much of its lost support at the next regional election in 1990.

By then, developments in eastern Europe, in particular the Baltic states' successful bid for independence, were rekindling demands for Basques to be given the same status. Succumbing to temptation, the PNV formed an all-nationalist government with EA and EE. However, mindful that its supporters in the Basque business community wanted stability above all else, it soon backtracked and renewed its Socialist alliance. With 1992 seeing major police successes against ETA on both sides of the Pyrenees, including the capture of the group's leadership at Bidart in the French Basque Country, it seemed that the 'Basque problem' might truly be on the way to solution.

In Catalonia, meanwhile, events had been taking a less dramatic, but in some ways equally problematic course. That was something of a surprise. Catalan devolution had been a relatively painless process, backed by the local Socialists and Communists as well as by regionalists. These were by tradition moderate in their demands and approach, violent extremism being limited to a minuscule group called Free Homeland (*Terra Lliure*). Certainly the historical party of regionalism, Catalan Republican Left (p52), criticised devolution as inadequate, but it was completely overshadowed by a new rival, **Convergence and Union**, which initially took a conciliatory line.

However, once installed in the regional government CiU began to show signs of a more confrontational style (p124). After it won an overall majority at the second regional election in 1984, this became so marked that a new term was coined to describe it: Pujolism, after party leader and regional First Minister Jordi Pujol. The new approach had three main features.

The first of these was an aggressively pro-Catalan language policy that aroused anxieties among monolingual Castilian speakers in the region. The second was a harder line on the self-government issue. On several occasions, notably following Baltic independence, Pujol speculated publicly about Catalonia taking the same option, albeit he always followed up with assurances of loyalty to Spain. Finally, Pujolism involved identifying the CiU and its leader as the region's sole representatives, and implying – or even stating – that its opponents were not true Catalans.

The main object of these attacks was the CiU's main rival, the Catalan Socialist Party (PSC) (p176), which at general elections regularly topped the Catalan poll. And that despite the PSC's support for devolution and defiance of the Socialist leadership in Madrid by proposing that Spain be turned into a federation – the traditional stance of moderate Catalan regionalism (p22)! Yet routinely the CiU, and Pujol in particular, portrayed the PSC as the mere agent of a central government whose policies it claimed – equally routinely – were damaging Catalonia.

Interestingly, though, he was more measured in his criticism of the Socialists' Madrid leadership. One thing that Pujolism undoubtedly shared with traditional Catalan regionalism was awareness that the region's interests could be furthered by exercising influence in Madrid. The 1993 general election results (pp140–1) opened up the chance to do just that.

> ### *Convergència i Unió (CiU)*
>
> Convergence and Union
>
> Formed in 1977 by the merger of Catalan Democratic Alliance (CDC) with the older 'Catalan Democratic Union' (UDC), the CiU gained control over the regional government on its creation in 1980 and soon came to dominate internal Catalan politics. Its success was closely associated with its leader, the regional First Minister Jordi Pujol (p104), and its distinctively assertive brand of centre-right regionalism is known as 'Pujolism' (pp144–5). Between 1993 and 2000 the CiU propped up minority central governments of both Left and Right (pp152–3), exercising considerable influence as a result. However, these alliances, particularly that with the conservative **People's Party** (p162), cost the CiU support. In 2003, when Pujol stepped down after an astonishing 23 years in office, it was ousted from the regional government (p157), although it has retained its position as the strongest single party in regional elections.

Summary of main points

Into Europe

- Although there had for some time been overwhelming support in Spain for joining the EC, the Socialist government elected in 1982 was decisive in preparing the country for membership and in negotiating its terms. One unspoken condition of joining was that Spain would remain a member of NATO.
- The Socialists also showed themselves adept at playing internal EC politics in generally supporting Community initiatives, even where the material benefits

appeared dubious (as with EMU). As a result, they ensured an important role in Community institutions for Spain and its representatives.

- Initially, EC membership gave a massive boost to the Spanish economy. In the early 1990s, the effects of world recession were aggravated by efforts to meet the criteria for EMU, but these problems were gradually overcome.

Socialist hegemony

- Following its crushing victory in the 1982 general election, the PSOE dominated Spanish politics at all levels for a decade.
- During that time it carried through a sweeping programme of reforms that, together with entry into the EC, brought huge advances in Spain's economic situation and public services. However, the party's traditional supporters benefited relatively little; indeed, they were actually harmed by a number of measures.
- In office, the PSOE was less concerned with improving conditions for workers than with efficiency of the economy as a whole. Effectively, the top priority for much of the party became to retain power.
- From 1989 on the Socialists were involved in a growing number of financial scandals and other affairs. Even so, they won the 1993 election, but without an overall majority.

Regionalists, new and old

- By late 1983 devolution had been extended to the whole of Spain. The new arrangements proved to be administratively complex, as well as encouraging the development of new regionalist movements in several regions. As a result, a further round of devolution was initiated.
- In the Basque Country, tension and violence continued, and even increased. In 1986 the region's largest party, the PNV, suffered a crisis, the effects of which forced it to adopt a less confrontational approach. Additionally, ETA came under increasing pressure and in 1992 seemed on the verge of defeat.
- In Catalonia, a new party, the CiU, emerged as the main representative of regionalism and took control of the regional government. Thereafter, it developed a new, more assertive style of regionalism that caused considerable friction, especially within the region.

Exhibit 9.1: Felipe González assesses Spain's situation (1987)

Extracts from a press interview

Desde hacía más de un siglo, vivíamos en un claro aislamiento político y cultural, con miedo o rechazo a todo lo que venía de fuera, sin asimilar la pérdida del imperio colonial. España estaba enquistada en sus propias fronteras y se cocía en su propia salsa. Este aislamiento produjo períodos autoritarios, le dio una fuerza relativa mayor a las posiciones políticas de los extremos y se la quitó a las más templadas, la mayoría más amplia de nuestra sociedad. Con el aislamiento político se correspondía, también, un sistema económico cerrado, hiperproteccionista, y perdimos el tren de la primera y la segunda revolución industrial.

La década democrática ha producido una apertura al mundo sin precedentes, y un cambio sustancial en las reglas de juego del funcionamiento socioeconómico. Se ha roto el aislamiento político y nos integramos en espacios más amplios – Europa y Occidente, – y se pasa de un sistema hiperproteccionista a una eliminación de barreras arancelarias y de controles burocráticos al desarrollo de las actividades económicas, tratando de ganar competitividad interna y externa. [...]

Empieza a notarse en España la entrada de aire fresco, de competencia, de libertad de movimiento en la economía. [...] Tenemos algunas amenazas, naturalmente; no podemos descuidar la vigilancia sobre la inflación, ni perder de vista que una balanza comercial negativa no puede sostenerse indefinidamente. Pero podemos tener la razonable esperanza de que al final de la década, España, además de un salto considerable en la competitividad y modernización del aparato productivo, siga por esa senda de crecimiento. [...]

[At the time of the 1977 election] we had been living for more than a century in a state of patent political and cultural isolation, fearing and rejecting anything that came from outside, having failed to come to terms with the loss of our colonies. Spain was imprisoned within its own borders; it was stewing in its own juice. Isolation resulted in periods of autocratic government; it exaggerated the importance of the political extremes while reducing that of the moderates who make up the great majority of Spanish society. Moreover, political isolation went hand in hand with a closed economy, protectionist in the extreme, which meant that we missed out on both the first and the second industrial revolutions.

These ten years of democracy have brought an unprecedented opening up to the outside world and a substantial change in the way our country functions, both socially and economically. Now we are no longer isolated politically, we are integrating ourselves into larger units – Europe, the western world as a whole – and we have gone from extreme protectionism to the removal of tariff barriers and of bureaucratic controls over the development of economic activity, in an attempt to become more competitive, both at home and abroad. [...]

The Spanish economy is starting to feel the effects of some fresh air, of competition, of freedom of movement. [...] Of course, we face some dangers; we must keep a close eye on inflation; we must never lose sight of the fact that a negative trade balance cannot be maintained indefinitely. But we can reasonably expect that, at the end of the decade, Spain will not only have greatly modernised its industry and improved its competitiveness, but also be continuing to experience growth.

Source: El País (8 November 1987).

Exhibit 9.2: ETA's violence (1993)

Extracts from a book written by a former ETA activist who later became leader of Basque Left (EE) and who was one of the architects of the anti-ETA 'Ajuria Enea Pact' of 1988; today he is a respected commentator on Basque developments and terrorism in general

> *ETA [...] ha desempeñado, desempeña y posiblemente siga desempeñando el papel de símbolo. Su entorno social proyecta hacia él sus propias impotencias, sus miedos o incluso la mala conciencia por su falta de compromiso o de acción. Su existencia y su veneración redimen a quienes la apoyan. Se ha ido constituyendo en una referencia mesiánica de identificación colectiva. [...]*
>
> *Se representa –simboliza– la voluntad de un colectivo –Euskal Herría en su doble acepción social y territorial–; se totaliza su representación –MLNV– simbolizándola; se simboliza el objetivo –independencia y socialismo– en la Alternativa KAS, que es lo genuino aunque no habla ni de independencia ni de socialismo. ETA es el soporte y el garante de todo ese universo simbólico, y todo lo que de una manera u otra puede servir a la violencia termina formando parte de su imaginario [sic]. [...]*
>
> *Incluso el propio sentido de la «estrategia del contrapoder» que se practica, su gran logro, no se encuentra en el hecho de haber abierto perspectiva alguna de alternativa a la democracia realmente existente y al proceso estatutario. Su gran logro ha consistido en la construcción de toda una trama que ha permitido a una parte nada insignificante de ciudadanos vascos, vivir su relación con la realidad política y social, con la cultura, participar de una visión histórica desarrollada al margen de los restantes vascos, es decir, al margen de la mayoría. Ésa ha sido la gran victoria, la gran construcción de la violencia, en la que su fuerza simbólica ha constituido el elemento de mayor cohesión.*
>
> ETA's role [...] has been, is and may continue to be symbolic. Those who form part of its milieu project onto ETA their own feelings of impotence, of fear and even of guilt at their own failure to make a commitment or take action. Its supporters are redeemed by its existence and their own veneration for it. Gradually it has become the focus of a messianic form of collective identification. [...]
>
> It stands for, or symbolises, the collective will of the 'Basque people', or the 'Basque Country', a will it claims to represent exclusively, and so to symbolise, through the Basque National Liberation Movement,[1] and whose aims – independence and socialism – it symbolises in the 'KAS alternative'[2], which is presented as the only legitimate goal even though it mentions neither of these two concepts. ETA is the basis and the guarantor of this entire symbolic universe, and everything that in one way or another can be of service to its strategy of violence ends up forming part of its imagery. [...]
>
> ETA's great success has been its strategy of creating a so-called 'anti-authority', but not because that has opened up the least prospect of an alternative to Spain's existing democratic system or to devolution as it has developed under the Statute of Autonomy. What it has succeeded in doing is to construct an entire framework within which a not inconsiderable number of Basques can live out their social, political and cultural relations on the basis of an interpretation of history that has been developed in isolation from their fellows, that is, from the majority of Basques. That has been the great triumph of ETA's violence, its major construct, which is held together above all by ETA's power as a symbol.

[1] The name used by ETA to describe the network of its related organisations and supporters.
[2] ETA's statement of its political demands, drawn up in the 1970s.

Source: Aulesta, K. (1993) *Días de viento sur: La violencia en Euskadi*. Barcelona: Antártida/Empúries.

Topics for discussion

■ Judging by Exhibit 9.1, what does González appear to regard as the main achievements of his time in power up to 1987? To what extent do they correspond to the hopes of the Spaniards who voted for his party in 1982?

■ He implicitly criticises aspects of Spanish political behaviour in the past for being extremist. Who could reasonably be seen as the object of such criticism?

■ Exhibit 9.2 talks about the symbolism of violence. Can you think of any such symbols exploited by ETA (or other terrorist groups)? Why do you think their effect was so powerful in the Basque Country?

■ How would you rate Felipe González's contribution to Spain?

■ Did Spain go the right way about tackling the issues posed by regionalism between 1982 and 1993? Could it have taken any other approach?

CHAPTER 10

The election victories of Bill Clinton (1992) and Tony Blair (1997) ended the supremacy of the New Right. Yet both leaders retained an overriding belief in free markets strongly at variance with most mainstream thinking in the EU, especially France and Germany. Their approach appeared to be vindicated, the US in particular growing considerably faster than continental Europe. The European Commission therefore tried to promote liberalisation as best it could, in parallel with its efforts to keep the process of EMU on track through the Stability and Growth Pact setting limits to budget deficits within 'Euroland'. Politically, the EU's most pressing need was for an institutional structure capable of accommodating enlargement to eastern Europe; in the year 2000 one was agreed at Nice, but it was an uneasy compromise. The following year the 9/11 terror attacks in America further accentuated Europe's problems, turning the world economic downturn into a recession from which the continent was much slower to recover than the US. Inside the EU opinions were sharply divided on how to react; in the end, France and Germany effectively opted out of the Stability Pact. Further divisions were introduced by the British-backed US invasion of Iraq in 2003 and by proposals for a Union Constitution which would change some of the arrangements made at Nice.

Between regionalism and globalisation (1993–2004)

The period from 1993 to 2004 saw Spain's assimilation into the family of developed western countries virtually completed. Economically, strong growth continued to narrow the wealth gap with its neighbours. Politically, a second transfer of power, this time from Left to Right, was accomplished in the best democratic manner. Internationally, too, the country began to play a role more consonant with her size and importance. Yet, at the same time, the very notion of Spain as a single and autonomous entity was called into question. On the one hand, Basque and Catalan regionalists became the single most important factor in Spanish politics as a whole, and their appetite for self-government showed no signs of slackening. On the other, events within Spain were increasingly interlinked with those abroad, in Europe and beyond. The connection became indisputable with the dramatic events of March 2004, which brought to an abrupt end the ascendancy established in the previous eight years by the conservative People's Party.

The regionalist spiral

The 1993 general election ushered in a period during which Spanish politics was dominated to an unprecedented degree by regionalists and their concerns. Indeed, for the next seven years successive central governments were significantly constrained by their reliance on the main Catalan party. The impact of Basque regionalism was less direct, but even greater. For, far from stabilising as had seemed possible in the early 1990s, the situation in the Basque Country became steadily tenser, as the continuing scourge of ETA violence was aggravated by an escalating confrontation between the central authorities and the increasingly radicalised Basque Nationalist Party (PNV).

Following the 1993 general election, the Socialist Party (PSOE) was left in need of support in order to form a stable government (pp140–1). It chose to turn to the Catalan CiU (p145), whose leader Jordi Pujol drove a hard bargain. Declining to enter a formal coalition, as Catalans had on occasion done in the past (pp34–5), he offered Prime Minister Felipe González only parliamentary support – and even that only on certain specific issues. In effect, he held the government's fate in his hands at minimal risk to himself. Not for nothing did he soon come to be widely regarded as Spain's most powerful politician.

In return for propping the government up, Pujol demanded – and obtained – a considerable price. Thus, he insisted the government stick unwaveringly to its plans for entering EMU, a high priority for his backers among the Catalan business community, but increasingly unpopular with the PSOE's core support (p135). Conversely, in fields where his Catalan government wished to follow different policies from those favoured in Madrid, notably in allowing wide scope for private suppliers of health and education services, he simply went his own way. Most importantly, he insisted on changes to the system of regional funding to allow regional governments to retain 15 per cent of income tax collected within their territories, a move CiU believed would benefit Catalonia as one of Spain's richest regions.

Most outside observers agreed and the measure, passed in 1994, was bitterly contested by the poorer regions. Since these were mostly run by the PSOE, the change did nothing to help relations between the two parties, although those between Pujol himself and Spanish Prime Minister Felipe González developed surprisingly well. Nonetheless, when the 1995 regional election brought a small but salutary setback for his party, he had no compunction in breaking his ties to a government and party whose reputation was by now in free fall (p162). He withdrew his backing for González, effectively forcing the PM to call an early election for March 1996, the outcome of which again made Pujol's backing essential for a stable government to be formed (p162).

This time it was the conservative People's Party (PP), now the largest party, who solicited his favours. On paper an agreement with it seemed unlikely. On the one hand, the Right was by tradition unsympathetic to regionalism in general, and Catalan demands in particular. On the other, the conservatives were a direct competitor for the CiU's core middle-class support, into which they had already begun to make inroads. Yet that was precisely because their philosophy was close to Pujol's in a number of respects.

Crucially, the PP was so desperate to govern that it was prepared to pay an even higher price for his backing than the PSOE had in 1993. Thus, regions' share of income tax was now doubled, to 30 per cent – even though the conservatives had previously opposed any such 'fiscal co-responsibility'! Moreover, the PP's leaders in Catalonia were obliged by party bosses in Madrid to cease their attacks on Pujol's controversial language policies (p145).

In 1999, however, the tables were turned. At that year's regional election the CiU was outpolled by an alliance of the Catalan Socialists (p176) with other left-wing forces. Only the vagaries of the region's electoral system allowed it to remain the largest parliamentary party. To remain first minister, Pujol in turn was obliged to rely on the local PP for support, and so lost much of his leverage over the conservative government in Madrid. Most of the rest was neutralised the following year by the PP's convincing general election victory (p164). Pujol's seven-year reign as arbiter of Spain's fate was over.

That same period had witnessed a slowdown in the rise of new regionalist movements (p142), and to some extent its reversal. Some of the parties which had emerged in the 1980s transpired to be merely vehicles for particular individuals; others were snuffed out by the PP's success in filling the vacuum on the political Right. On the other hand, the PSOE's decline was accompanied in some regions by the growth of local left-wing parties, notably the Galician National Alliance (BNG), which in 1997 became the region's second electoral force.

Otherwise, before and after 2000, regionalism remained strong where there were genuinely regional issues to exploit. Examples were the Canaries, by virtue of their location, and Aragon, which along with Catalonia would be the main loser from government plans to divert water from the Ebro to the market gardens of Valencia and Murcia. In none of these cases, though, were regionalists so strong or so radical as to present a challenge to the constitutional order.

In the Basque Country they did exactly that. There, where regionalism shaded into nationalism, the optimism of the early 1990s (p144) soon dissolved, for various reasons. One, the impact of which is hard to judge but certainly significant, was the re-opening of the GAL affair (p140). There was also confirmation of other brutal excesses by security force personnel, some of them Francoist officers who had been allowed to retain their posts during the transition (p118). These developments poisoned relations between the two parties whose alliance had been crucial to the stabilisation of Basque politics: the local section of the PSOE and the nationalist PNV (p143).

A second cause of the change in mood was a renewed upsurge in ETA violence, much of it directed now, not at the military, but at representatives of the Spanish parties. Particularly targeted was the PP, whose leader was nearly assassinated by a car bomb attack in 1994. Three years later a young conservative councillor in the town of Ermua, Miguel Angel Blanco, was the victim of a particularly callous killing. It sparked off an unprecedented wave of popular anger against ETA that momentarily transcended the divisions among all other political forces. But such unity did not last.

Instead, events were shaped by a burgeoning confrontation between the PP and the PNV, which in 1996 had appeared close to agreement. Then the main nationalist force – notoriously pragmatic, and itself conservative in many of its views – had voted for the new government's investiture in return for various concessions, notably a favourable deal on the Basque Country's contribution to central revenues for the next four years (p9). Thereafter, though, relations rapidly deteriorated, partly because of the government's intransigence and partly because the PNV felt itself under increasing pressure.

For one thing it believed – not without justification – that the Basque Country's special constitutional status as a 'historic nationality' (p122) was under threat from the PP's plans to extend devolution equally to the country as a whole (p164). It was concerned, too, at the progressive erosion of total nationalist support, and of its own vote by the PP. Less forgivably, it may have feared that the security forces' latest offensive against ETA would effectively eliminate one of its best bargaining counters. United in feeling that these dangers could only be averted by securing greater self-government than that set out in the existing Statute of Autonomy (p123), the PNV was divided on how best to achieve that.

The party's moderate wing wanted to build a broad consensus for change, including the Spanish parties as well as non-violent nationalists. In 1998 the regional First Minister, José Antonio Ardanza (p144), floated proposals intended to do that. The 'Ardanza Plan' accepted that the 'Basque problem' was essentially a dispute among Basques themselves – rather than between the Basque Country and Spain – that could only be solved once violence ended. But it also asserted that the solution was a matter for Basques alone; whatever they agreed on, up to and including independence, must be accepted by Madrid.

That the central government would not – arguably could not – accept. The rejection of his Plan ended both Ardanza's career and the cross-party Ajuria Enea Pact (p144). It also handed the initiative inside the PNV to the radicals headed by party boss Xabier Arzalluz, who saw salvation not in consensus but in increased pressure.

In their view that could be exerted only by reunifying the nationalist movement as a whole, which in the 1980s had fragmented into four different parties (p142). Since then, however, the only one of the four opposed to reunification in principle, EE, had effectively disappeared, having merged in 1993 with the PSOE's Basque section (now known as PSE-EE). A second, EA (p143), had been losing votes steadily for a decade, and was already little more than a junior partner to the PNV. That left only ETA's political wing HB (p143), which in 1997 was thrown into in disarray by the arrest and subsequent imprisonment of its entire leadership for allowing ETA activists to appear in one of its election broadcasts (a decision revoked two years later by the Supreme Court).

Seeing their chance, the PNV's radicals opened secret negotiations with HB. The following year these resulted in the **Lizarra Pact**, which asserted the notion that sovereignty, the right to decide their region's future, lay exclusively with Basques (*soberantismo*). Almost immediately ETA announced a ceasefire. Although the Pact was bitterly criticised by the Spanish government and parties, in the Basque Country these events unleashed a mood of near euphoria that the PNV attempted to exploit by calling an early regional election, from which ETA's supporters, now operating under the initials EH, emerged strengthened. Indeed, their support was essential to the minority government formed by the PNV and EA under a new First Minister, Juan José Ibarretxe.

Its fate hung on progress towards a permanent end to violence. But, whether because of the PP's intransigence, as many nationalists alleged, or because the truce was a fraud all along, as the government claimed, that never came. In late 1999 ETA declared the ceasefire over. Early the following year it resumed killing, critical journalists now joining political opponents among its victims. Once more, the all-too-familiar atmosphere of fear and distrust returned to the small towns and rural areas where the extremists were strongest.

Even then the PNV refused to back down. Although it repudiated its alliance with ETA's political servants, it stuck to the position set out in their joint Pact. For its part, the central government refused to contemplate any change to the existing constitutional framework and routinely bracketed the PNV and ETA together as a threat to that. Its line was slavishly taken up by the Basque Socialists – and by much of the Madrid-based media – so that the regional election Ibarretxe was forced to call in 2001 became a duel between nationalists and self-styled 'constitutionalists'.

The PP's hard-line strategy paid off in the form of further gains. Yet, overall, the results were a setback for it since the PNV and EA, now standing together, did even better. Their gains permitted them to form a more stable – but still minority – government with the small, but symbolically important addition of the Basque section of United Left (p36), known as EB (Basque: *Ezker Batua*). EH's vote having halved, hopes of a compromise rose again. And were dashed again.

Possibly over-confident after his election win, possibly provoked by the PP's latest attempt to round off the devolution process once and for all (p164), the First

---

Pacto de Lizarra

Lizarra Pact

Signed on 12 September 1998 in the Navarrese town of Estella (Basque: *Lizarra*), the Pact was effectively a joint declaration by the main Basque nationalist parties – the **PNV** (p25), **HB** (p143) and EA (p143) – and a number of other organisations. Inspired by the Good Friday agreement in Northern Ireland, it ostensibly set out a framework for peace negotiations in the Basque region: an unconditional ETA ceasefire, openness of the talks to all parties and recognition of Basques' right to 'self-determination'. However, its critics argued that the Pact was nothing more than a re-statement of positions long held by **ETA,** in particular because it implicitly denied the authority of the existing, democratically legitimated Statute of Autonomy (p123). See also: *Plan Ibarretxe* (p156)

Plan Ibarretxe

....

Ibarretxe Plan

First announced by the Basque
First Minister Juan José Ibarretxe
(p155) in 2001, the Plan set out a
blueprint by which an extended
Basque Country as conceived by
HB (p143) could achieve
independence once a definitive
ETA ceasefire was in place. The
first step would be to replace the
existing region's Statute of
Autonomy (p123) by a much
looser 'Free Association'
agreement with Spain (a model
taken from Quebec nationalists).
As that indicates, the Plan's focus
was almost exclusively on the
supposed conflict between the
Basque Country and Spain; the
internal dimension of conflict – i.e.
the divisions among Basques
themselves – was virtually
ignored.

Minister now launched his own proposals. This **Ibarretxe Plan** was considerably more radical than Ardanza's, being effectively a timetable for independence in stages. Detailed proposals for the first of these were worked out over the next two years and passed by the Basque Parliament with the sole support of the governing coalition. Ibarretxe then announced his intention to submit the agreement to a referendum in the region, a move that could only heighten tension and divisions. In a situation where ETA continued to kill in the name of Basque independence, even many nationalists, while sympathising with Ibarretxe's aims, disagreed with his initiative.

Nor was the reaction of the Madrid government designed to cool the situation. It broke off all relations with its Basque counterpart and with the PNV as a party, took Ibarretxe's proposals to the Constitutional Court, and passed a law that threatened him with imprisonment should he proceed with his referendum. Meanwhile, it focused its efforts on destroying ETA's social and political base. In 2002 a new Political Parties Act (*Ley de Partidos*) was passed, with Socialist backing, which empowered the Spanish Parliament to ban formations linked to terrorism. The measure was clearly directed against Unity (*Batasuna*), the latest manifestation of ETA's political wing (p143), which was duly outlawed later the same year.

This move enjoyed some success. Both turnout at demonstrations linked to ETA and the level of street violence incited by it (*kale borroka*) fell. Yet the ban's democratic validity was opposed by most Basques, nationalist or not, a point the PNV exploited to block its extension to the Basque Parliament. And, although the detention of successive ETA leaderships kept the level of violence low, there were worrying signs that the increasingly desperate terrorists were planning mass attacks on civilians outside the Basque Country. As the general election due in 2004 approached, the Basque conflict in its various dimensions dominated the political scene, not just in the region but throughout Spain.

While all this was going on, new tensions had surfaced in Catalonia, albeit without any hint of violence. Some were caused by CiU, which, like the PNV, feared for its region's privileged status. Moreover, precisely because of its dependence on the PP, it also perceived a need to distance itself from the conservatives' persistently negative attitude and tone towards Catalan – and other – regionalist aspirations (pp164–5). In 1998 it therefore joined the PNV (and the Basque BNG) in the Barcelona

Declaration, which asserted the 'sovereignty' of the three 'historic nationalities'. Subsequently Pujol back-pedalled on that; instead he started to make more concrete demands for a new, extended Statute of Autonomy, in particular to give Catalonia greater control over its own finances.

In that he was echoing a demand long voiced by the left-wing regionalists of Catalan Republican Left (ERC) (p52), who made substantial gains at the regional election held in November 2003. Indeed, their support was now essential to building a viable regional government. After lengthy negotiations ERC rejected an alliance with CiU. Instead it joined a centre-left coalition, with one of its leaders, José Lluis Carod Rovira, becoming Deputy First Minister (*conseller en cap*).

The new, three-party government (*tripartito*) was headed by Pasqual Maragall, a popular ex-mayor of Barcelona and leader of the local Socialists, the PSC (p176). Although not regionalist in the sense of regarding Catalan self-government as its *raison d'etre*, the PSC supports the principle that Catalonia (and the other 'historic nationalities') should enjoy markedly more autonomy than other regions. Thus, while the new government promised significant changes to CiU's social and economic policies, its commitment to extending Catalan self-government was as strong as, perhaps even stronger than, that of its predecessor.

In the time of globalisation

If the constraints placed on Spain's central government by regionalism between 1993 and 2004 were unprecedented, its involvement in foreign affairs was greater than at any time since the seventeenth century (pxiv). The most immediate sphere of action was the European Union where, for various reasons, relations with the country's major partners turned problematic. At the same time, though, those with the US grew closer, while globalisation – the process of rapidly developing interconnection between events around the whole world – affected Spain in a number of ways.

During Felipe González's last term in office the restrictive policies required to qualify for EMU caused considerable hardship to some Spaniards, many of them traditional Socialist voters (p135). Yet, despite the adversarial political climate of the time (p163), this was one issue the then opposition People's Party (PP) refrained from making political capital out of. Its restraint was testimony to the almost complete consensus among Spain's political elite on EMU's importance for Spain. Not surprisingly, then, the PP maintained exactly the same course once it came to power in 1996.

The efforts of both governments were so successful that, when the decision on countries' eligibility for EMU was taken in 1997, Spain satisfied the conditions with some ease. Admittedly its public debt was still too high, but tacit agreement had already been reached to relax that test when it became clear that several leading EU members, notably Germany, would also fail it. In fact, and quite contrary to early forecasts, Spain was one of the best qualified countries in terms of the five criteria as a whole. Subsequently, too, the continuing success of its economy meant that it had no difficulty in satisfying the budget conditions on EMU members established by the Stability Pact – again in sharp contrast to other, richer countries.

In another area, too, there was continuity of policy after 1996. Like his predecessor, the new PM José María Aznar made a habit of sending political heavyweights to Brussels. Thus, when the Commission was almost entirely renewed in 1999, he nominated his Agriculture Minister, Loyola de Palacio, who was promptly given Vice-President's rank and one of the more important portfolios (Transport and Infrastructure). An even greater prize went to Spain's other new Commissioner, Pedro Solbes (p135). He was given responsibility for Economics and Finance and so became effective overlord of the EMU process as a whole. More generally, too, the country continued to enjoy a disproportionately high share of top posts in the EU machinery.

Spain's biggest coup in this regard came in 1999, when the Union appointed its first High Representative for foreign and security policy, a high-prestige and potentially key post. It went to Javier Solana, an ever-present in the Socialist governments of the 1980s and 1990s who had ended his domestic career as Foreign Minister and González's heir apparent in the PSOE. On the other hand, no more was heard of the former PM himself as a future Commission President. Of course, that reflected the damage done to his reputation during his final years in office (p162). But it was also part of a broader trend, a mild but growing anti-Spanish feeling that became increasingly apparent over the PP's time in power.

That, in turn, mirrored the party's attitude towards the EU, significantly different from that of the Socialists. It was not that the PP was eurosceptic, in the British sense of distrusting European integration in general, and its political dimension in particular. Yet, not least for generational reasons, its leaders did not share their predecessors' unbridled enthusiasm for the EU and all its works (p132).

For them, Europe was not the realisation of a dream but a mere political reality, less a community of partners than an arena in which to compete for influence and resources. Added to that was the fact that the PP did not fit readily into the EU's ideological grid (p163). It was no coincidence that in internal Union disputes Aznar regularly found himself allied with Britain's Tony Blair, whose 'New' Labour Party was also an outsider in those terms, and whose enthusiasm for deregulation the Spanish PM shared (p165).

Conversely, the years around the turn of the century witnessed a sharp deterioration in Spain's relations with Germany. With Germany's Chancellor now being a Social Democrat, Gerhard Schröder, the differences were to some extent ideological. Understandably, he and Aznar took opposing positions on such issues as the pace of liberalisation and privatisation or, later, the need to maintain the strict terms of the Stability Pact. More important in the falling-out though, were changing circumstances. As Germany's own economy stuttered and its attention shifted to prospective new partners in the East, its willingness to continue transferring very large sums of money to Spain under the Structural Funds (p134) understandably diminished. At the 1999 Berlin Summit, where a decision on allocation of such funding up to 2006 had to be taken, Aznar simply refused to agree to any settlement which failed to preserve Spain's share. In the end he won, but his success came at a price. From then on he was known in Union circles as '*Señor No*'.

The following year, at Nice, the battleground changed to the EU's post-enlargement institutional arrangements. Again Aznar successfully held out for an extremely advantageous deal. In particular, Spain was allocated 27 votes in the European Council, only two less than the largest countries, including Germany. This time Schröder was not prepared to accept defeat. He reopened the dispute as part of the discussions on an EU constitution, eventually persuading almost all his colleagues to revise the Nice Treaty in this respect.

Yet Aznar, backed only by Poland, refused to compromise, thus effectively blocking adoption of the constitution – which, if nothing else, had great symbolic significance for much of Europe's political elite. Nor was it merely that Aznar's positions tended to be extreme. It was also the fact that he defended them in the same assertive and uncompromising style apparent in domestic affairs (p165). In that sense he contributed to what by 2004 was a significant rift between Spain and several of its EU partners, above all France and Germany.

On the other hand, the Aznar years saw a remarkable strengthening of Spain's previously problematic relations with the US (p133). These had begun to improve as far back as 1986 with the confirmation of Spain's NATO membership (p134). Two years later, a revised defence agreement (p88) effectively settled the thorny issue of US bases on Spanish soil. As a result, these were able to play an important support role during the 1990 Gulf War, in which Spanish naval vessels also played a part, albeit a minor, non-combative one.

Five years later, the rapprochement was underlined when Javier Solana landed his first big international post, as NATO Secretary-General. Nevertheless, it was left to the PP to complete Spain's integration into the alliance's military structure soon after it came to power in 1996, a move that met with little opposition, either popular or political. Three years after that, Spanish warplanes were directly involved in the alliance's bombing of Kosovo.

Up to now, Spain had acted in conjunction with its main EU partners. That changed, however, once US President Bush announced his so-called war on terrorism. Aznar seems to have been the first European leader to offer troops for peacekeeping duties in Afghanistan. Then, in the run-up to the Iraq War of 2003, he was the prime mover behind a letter sent by the leaders of eight EU member states, existing and prospective, to their colleagues, supporting the Americans and British in their plans to invade. The action was a direct challenge to the main opponents of invasion, France and Germany, with whom it was another cause of division.

Undeterred, Aznar attended a well-publicised pre-invasion meeting with Bush and Blair on the Azores and generally cultivated the impression that he was part of a three-man team. In fact, that was far from being the case. The 'coalition' of American allies involved a number of other countries, and the 1,300-strong contingent Spain eventually dispatched to Iraq was one of the more modest contributions, especially relative to its population. But the contrast with France and Germany, along with Aznar's propensity for hawkish statements, made him a virtual hero in the US, although the position was home was very different indeed (pp166–7).

Events in Iraq may have provided the most dramatic illustration of globalisation's impact on Spain but it was by no means the only one. Since 1986 the country's trade within the EU had expanded rapidly and it had also become a major recipient of investment from its new partners. In the later 1990s, however, Spanish companies themselves began to invest heavily abroad, above all in Latin America. Indeed, within only a few years Spain had become by far the biggest investor in the region apart from the US. This brought problems, notably due to the successive crises experienced by Argentina, but also enabled Spanish companies to expand in ways that were previously unthinkable. It also turned their homeland from a net importer to a net exporter of capital for the first time in modern history.

The end of the millennium also saw the reversal of another type of cross-border flow. For centuries, Spain had been sending emigrants around the globe. The vast improvement in living standards since 1975 had already stemmed that outflow and even attracted a small inflow of well-off retirees from northern Europe. With EC accession in 1986 the short crossing from North Africa had become one of the principal clandestine entry points to the EU as a whole. Initially, most of those who made it across the Straits of Gibraltar or onto the Canary Islands – notoriously, many died in the attempt, and still do – saw Spain merely as a staging post on the way to its richer neighbours. By the late 1990s, however, rising affluence had made it an attractive destination in its own right and the numbers of immigrants were rising rapidly.

In several respects the new arrivals were a considerable boon for Spain. Coming mainly from Latin America, sub-Saharan Africa and the Islamic world, they were notably more fertile than indigenous Spaniards, whose low birth rates had become a significant cause for concern. The vast majority were also anxious to work and increasingly took on the low-paid jobs – in agriculture, domestic services and construction – shunned by natives. Even so, these same characteristics could be perceived as threatening, typically by the worst-educated and worst-off Spaniards, just as new cultural influences, an enrichment for many, could cause uncertainty and resentment among others.

The bulk of the new immigrants were illegal, lacking as they did the necessary documentation (*indocumentados*). Officially barred from working, they had little choice but to accept the poor pay and conditions prevailing in the 'underground economy'. As a result they found it hard to obtain the record of their stay in Spain needed to justify regularisation of their situation under the amnesties provided by successive amendments to the Aliens Act (*Ley de Extranjería*).

These changes also tightened up the conditions affecting those who were not regularised, for instance by restricting their access to health care and social services. Such steps, justified as a necessary response to public anxieties, also served to nourish these. So, too, did the irresponsible comments of some politicians, mainly but not exclusively of the Right, who effectively accused immigrants of responsibility for rising crime rates.

These, in turn, may have been one reason why the over-stretched police did little to stop employment of illegal immigrants. But it is also undeniable that, for powerful interests close to the governing conservatives, these were a welcome source of cheap and docile labour at a time when falling unemployment was drying up the native supply. This was especially true of the labour-intensive, often seasonal, activities involved in the booming production of fruit and vegetables along the southern and eastern coasts. The labourers there tended to live in makeshift shanty towns or similarly sub-standard conditions, and their relations with the indigenous population were usually poor.

The result was a series of clashes of varying degrees of seriousness. Most frequently affected by such incidents were the Moroccans, who formed the largest group among new immigrants in general and were especially predominant among agricultural labourers. In particular, they were the victims of the near race-riot that occurred in the town of El Ejido, near Almería, in February 2000. Immigration-related issues also contributed to a sharp deterioration in Spain's diplomatic relations with Morocco itself, which culminated in July 2002 with the comic-opera invasion and re-capture of Parsley Island (*Isla del Perejil*), one of various islets off the African coast belonging to Spain.

These circumstances may or may not be connected to the fact that Moroccans accounted for most of those detained or pursued by the Spanish authorities following the **terrorist attack in Madrid** on 11 March 2004. Undoubtedly, though, the outrage provided grim evidence of Spain's irrevocable integration into the wider world order. On the one hand, almost a quarter of the victims were non-Spaniards working in the country. On the other, as soon became clear, the attack was the work of Islamic fundamentalists linked in some way to Al-Qaida (*Al-Qaeda*).

The PP ascendant

As it transpired, the Madrid attack was to prove the nemesis of the People's Party, Spain's governing party since 1996. Its rise had been closely linked to the errors of its main rival, first in office and then in opposition. Once in power itself, the PP displayed undoubted qualities of its own, above all in the economic field, and was resoundingly re-elected in 2000. On the other hand, in a number of areas it also displayed a lack of sensitivity, which became increasingly marked during its second term of office.

(matanza del) 11-M

terrorist attack in Madrid on 11 March 2004

At around 7.40 on the morning of 11 March, a total of 10 bombs exploded in four busy commuter trains heading for Madrid's Atocha station, killing 191 people and injuring some 1,500. The devices had been hidden in rucksacks along with the mobile telephones used to detonate them remotely. One of these failed to operate and was crucial in identifying the perpetrators, all of them with links to the Al-Qaida (*Al-Qaeda*) network. A number were subsequently detained; seven, including the group's leader, blew themselves up along with a police officer after being cornered in a flat in Leganés, close to Madrid.

The unexpected victory of the Socialist Party (PSOE) at the 1993 general election (pp140–1) proved a decidedly mixed blessing for the party. Bound by their commitment to EMU and their alliance with the Catalan CiU (p152), the Socialists had no option but to pursue a deflationary economic policy. The burden fell most heavily on social groups or regions on which they depended for support. Even more damagingly, a succession of public figures linked to the PSOE were found to be involved in financial irregularities far more serious than earlier affairs (p140). Among those implicated were such senior figures as the Governor of Spain's central bank, Mariano Rubio, and the paramilitary Civil Guard's first civilian head, Luis Roldán. Worst of all, investigations into the GAL affair (p140) revealed that government ministers had directed the 'dirty war' waged against ETA in the 1980s.

Partido Popular (PP)

People's Party

Founded under its present name in 1989, the PP was the direct successor of the right-wing People's Alliance (*Alianza Popular*, (AP)) created by Manuel Fraga Iribarne (p100) following Franco's death, although its ranks also included some veterans of the centrist **UCD** (p117). More recently, the main features of the party's ideas have been Spanish nationalism and a neoliberal approach to economic issues. Previously the official opposition, the PP was elected to government in 1996 and for the next eight years held a dominant position in Spanish politics. However, it was surprisingly defeated at the 2004 general election, largely because of its apparent attempt to manipulate reaction to the **terrorist attack in Madrid** on 11 March of that year (p167). It is currently (late 2008) Spain's main opposition party.

Given these various factors, the PSOE was universally expected to suffer a heavy defeat at the general election it was forced to call for March 1996 (p152). However, as had happened three years before, fear of such an outcome impelled Socialist voters to turn out in force. As a result, although the **PP** won a clear victory, it fell well short of an overall majority in Parliament. Felipe González, who remained PSOE leader, spoke of a 'sweet defeat'. Yet actually the result was a calamity for his party, allowing it to continue in a state of denial about its long-standing problems (pp139–40).

In consequence, the much-needed renewal of leadership and ideas was again postponed. When González finally resigned in 1997, he was replaced by Joaquín Almunia, an ex-minister untouched by scandal but equally bereft of voter appeal. There followed a disastrous primary election (*elecciones primarias*), designed to confirm Almunia as the party's prime ministerial candidate, which he lost to another ex-minister, José Borrell – who was then forced to resign by his remote association with one more murky affair.

Finally, in the run-up to the 2000 general election, Almunia concluded an alliance with the Communist-led United Left (IU), with which the PSOE had been in bitter dispute for over a decade. The results were catastrophic. The Socialist vote fell by over a sixth, to its lowest level since 1979 (IU fared even worse). The PSOE was left stunned, in no position to mount a serious opposition to the party that had replaced it as Spain's undisputed master.

The PP's rise to power had been a lengthy process. It began in 1989, when Manuel Fraga (p100) stepped down as leader of the People's Alliance (p124) to become First Minister of his native Galicia. His replacement was José María Aznar, who had previously held the same post in Castile-Leon, but who was sufficiently young to be free of the Francoist associations that clung to his predecessor. As part of its makeover the party's name was also changed. The new title, intended to give it a more contemporary, European image, was People's Party. That is the designation used by the Christian Democrats (*democristianos*) in the European Parliament, where they form the largest right-of-centre group, which the PP promptly joined.

Like many labels, this one was deceptive. In fact, Aznar and his allies in the party rejected more or less explicitly the economic and social interventionism characteristic of European Christian Democracy – and Francoism (p82) – in favour of the neoliberal attitudes of the New Right. On the other hand, although their policies and pronouncements did sometimes display a religious tinge, it was not of the progressive, ecumenical shade espoused by most of their new allies in Strasbourg. Rather it was the traditional Catholic variety associated with the PP's other main trait: a strongly centralist Spanish nationalism which did indeed prove reminiscent of the former dictatorship on occasions.

The desire to escape such electorally damaging associations (p140) was a prime motive behind Aznar's attempts in the mid-nineties to rebrand his party as 'centrist'. At the same time, though, those made it hard for the PP to distinguish itself from the ruling Socialists, who had long since been occupying that part of the spectrum (p137). Aznar accordingly took a different, two-pronged approach. On the one hand, he built up a highly organised and strictly disciplined party machine to match the PSOE's. On the other, he focused relentlessly on the Socialists' all-too-obvious ethical problems.

In this he was assisted by several leading Madrid dailies, and by two of the three private TV stations which the government had licensed in 1989 after long prevarication. Their role was questionable, to say the least, given that their financial backers were mainly close to the PP and themselves not always free from the taint of scandal. Moreover, several of their exposés later turned out to have no basis. With state-controlled television and pro-government papers hitting back, sometimes with similarly low blows, Spanish politics acquired an ugly air of rising tension (*crispación*) unprecedented in the democratic era.

Be that as it may, Aznar's strategy bore fruit. At the 1994 European elections the PP inflicted the PSOE's first nationwide defeat for twelve years. The following year it won a more significant victory, taking control of most regions and the great bulk of local government, before 1996 finally brought it success at Spanish level. Yet the narrow margin of its victory then forced the PP to rely on regionalist support to form a government, as a result of which it had to restrain its centralist instincts and make several concessions on the devolution front (p153). Indeed, throughout its first term of office the PP was to prove generally more flexible than its origins and nature might have suggested.

Flexibility was most apparent in the new government's dealings with the trade unions, relations with which had been a running sore for the previous decade (p139). The PP not only adhered scrupulously to the Toledo Pact, a 1995 cross-party agreement to maintain pensions largely unchanged, something of major concern for the unions. It also encouraged a return to the practice of 'social concertation', promoting and underwriting union–employer agreements on social security funding and a further reduction in labour market rigidity (p138). The effects were highly positive. For the first time since 1982–86 Spain went through a legislature period without a general strike and industrial strife generally was markedly reduced.

That, in turn, contributed to the great success story of Aznar's first term in office. Between 1996 and 2000, Spain outperformed a world economy that was itself expanding rapidly. In the European context, the country's growth rate stood out even more, being by some distance the fastest of the larger economies. Spain also led the EU in job creation, and so was finally able to tackle its grave unemployment problem (p135); although the jobless rate remained above the EU average, the difference was now much reduced. These achievements were all the more impressive in that they were accompanied by falling interest rates. Moreover, the budget remained in a healthy state, helping Spain to qualify easily for EMU (p157).

Economic success was the main reason for the landslide by which the PP was re-elected in 2000 – again to the discomfiture of opinion pollsters, who greatly underestimated the scale of its victory. That was indeed considerable; the PP finished no less than ten per cent ahead of its Socialist rival. In fact, that lead was due essentially to low turnout among a considerably expanded electorate and, above all, among left-leaning voters. Barely three Spanish electors out of ten had actually voted for the Conservatives. For the moment, though, what mattered was the situation in Parliament, where their 183 Congress seats represented the first overall majority for any party since 1986, and the first ever for a party of the Right in a truly democratic election.

The victory was a personal triumph for Aznar, to whose own growing authority it gave a further boost. Almost immediately, though, the PM announced that he would not seek a third term. On the face of it a laudable sign of humility, this decision meant he would not have to face the electorate again. At the same time, the election result removed the need for his party, which the previous year had reasserted its control over most of local and regional government, to build alliances with awkward allies. This two-fold liberation was reflected in the move away from the 'centre' that typified the PP's second term, while its style of government became increasingly assertive and even arrogant.

Domestically, this tendency was most obvious in dealings with the regions. These had begun on a positive note, with the transfer in 1996 of more competences to the 'slow route' regions (p122) as a means to improve the workings of devolution (p141). However, it turned out that the PP also had another aim in mind. It wanted to standardise – and so cap – the level of autonomy across Spain. That much became clear in 2001, when devolution of health powers was made general. A number of smaller regions, several PP-run, which did not actually want the new responsibilities were bullied into accepting them by threats of reduced funding.

Where regions did want a greater say, as in relations with the EU, their wishes were overridden, often in the most dismissive of terms. As for Basque and Catalan concerns about the erosion of their special constitutional status (p122), these were derided as irrational and backward-looking. On occasion they were explicitly equated with ETA's violence. Meantime, the PP itself promoted a 'constitutional patriotism', for instance by the prominent display of symbols such as the Spanish flag, which often seemed to ignore the complexity of Spaniards' feelings and identities, not to mention the Constitution's actual provisions on devolution.

After the 2000 election, similar insensitivity poisoned the government's previously good relations with the unions. Despite some efforts to maintain dialogue these deteriorated rapidly, to the extent that two years later Spain was facing its first general strike since 1994. Yet the PM himself virtually incited the unions to act by refusing to discuss his proposals for new labour market changes and by using the most extravagant of rhetoric – about what were essentially technical matters, not grand principles. Then, after the event, the government withdrew most of the proposals anyway , tacitly admitting that negotiation should have been the way ahead all along.

The same bulldozer approach also became evident in a second field: education. Here, the reforms introduced in the 1980s at secondary and tertiary level had certainly widened access as well as modernising course structures and content. But they had not solved all the existing problems, notably failure to develop high-quality skills and promote research, and arguably contributed to new ones such as pupil disinterest and resource shortages. As a result, and just as with the job market, there was broad agreement that further change was needed. During its first term of office, though, the government did little, other than to provoke a dispute with several regions over a proposed new, uniform history syllabus with a strong (Spanish) nationalist bias.

No sooner had it won an overall majority, however, than it drew up legislation virtually without consulting either professionals or the public. This brought in extensive – and highly controversial – changes, several involving a return to previously discredited practice. Somewhat surprisingly given the manifest decline in its social importance, it also made the Catholic Church two significant concessions: upgrading of religion as a secondary-school subject and exemption from some of the requirements for establishing private universities. These latter, like the health trusts (*fundaciones sanitarias*) set up during its first term, in themselves represented a further move to the Right.

Privatisation in another sense, that of selling off state-owned firms, was a cornerstone of the PP's economic policy, both before and after 2000. This was a course on which the Socialists had already embarked while in office. The PP went much further, however, disposing of virtually all the state's main holdings. In doing so it effectively eliminated the gap between Spain and other (continental) European economies in this regard; by 2003 Spain's public sector was not significantly larger than those of its main EU partners.

In the related issue of liberalising its utility markets the country actually proceeded faster than required by the Union's directives – or in theory it did. In practice, deregulation brought few of the hoped-for benefits in terms of greater choice and lower prices. That was because the sectors supposedly 'liberalised', in particular the energy industry, continued to be dominated by a few large enterprises linked together by mutual share holdings or cooperation agreements. Typically these involved one or other of the two big players left by progressive consolidation of the banking sector.

Aznar's governments, moreover, took an active part in shaping these oligopolies, promoting certain links and discouraging others. Meanwhile, the regulatory bodies established to oversee the new 'liberalised' markets were starved of the resources needed to carry out their job properly. They were also subjected to extensive government influence, as were the privatised companies themselves, key holdings in which tended to land in the hands of firms or even individuals with close political or personal connections to the PP.

The most notorious case was that of Juan Villalonga, who prided himself on having gone to school with Aznar, and who became head of the largest of all the privatised prizes, the telecommunications giant Telefónica. That in itself was controversial. What made it downright alarming, though, was that Villalonga wasted little time in using his newly acquired financial clout to buy into the media business.

That had long been an obsession of the PP's leaders, who felt – not without justification – that the Right had been disadvantaged by news coverage while the PSOE was in power. At that time it had not only to contend with the undoubted bias of state television (p136). The country's most powerful media group, PRISA, whose organs included the highly respected top-selling daily *El País*, was also broadly sympathetic to the Socialists.

After 1996, though, the tables turned. Not only did the state channels – and parts of the private media – continue their attacks on the Socialists as if they were still in power, virtually ignoring any bad news affecting the government. Legislation was also passed specifically to damage PRISA's interests in the area of digital broadcasting, while the group's head was prosecuted on charges subsequently shown to have been trumped up.

In that context, the acquisition by Telefónica of various media interests, including the most-watched private TV channel, came as a bombshell. The effects were soon felt; observers rated overall media coverage of the 2000 election as the most unbalanced of the democratic era – no small claim, given the extent of previous abuse in this area. Its extent now provoked a substantial outcry. Along with the considerable costs involved in the media business, it led to Villalonga's fall. His successor decided that Telefónica should gradually withdraw from the media field. That was not the end of the story, however, since the stakes sold off stayed within the circle of the PP's associates and supporters.

Despite these efforts, the Aznar government's standing was hit by unfavourable publicity on various fronts. Several ministers were implicated in financial scandals, the most noteworthy being the Gescartera affair involving Economics Minister Rodrigo Rato. In late 2002, the government badly mishandled the case of a damaged oil tanker, the *Prestige*, which eventually ruptured off the Galician coast causing a massive oil spill. Above all, polls showed over 80 per cent opposition to Spain's involvement in the Iraq war, and in the subsequent, increasingly messy occupation of the country. The PM's image was not improved by his blocking of all attempts to debate the matter in Parliament.

There were also signs of public reaction to the government's apparent desire to 'manage' unfavourable news stories, notably following the air crash that killed 70 Spanish troops returning from service in Afghanistan. During the run-up to the 2004 election there was a further whiff of the same when the PP leaked classified information about contacts between ETA and the Catalan regionalist politician Carod, second-in-command of the Socialist-led regional government (p157). That its action might endanger the security forces' valuable informants seemed to cause the government no concern.

The threat from ETA, underlined by the discovery of an attempt by the organisation to plant a massive bomb in Madrid, was one of the two main themes of the election campaign mounted by the PP in 2004. It was fronted by Aznar's eventual choice as his successor, the experienced, competent but somewhat uncharismatic Mariano Rajoy. Inevitably, its second focus was the economy.

Here, too, Aznar's second term had seen the emergence of some problems. Inflation rose, slightly by historical Spanish standards but significantly given the country's new, more open situation. A very high proportion of new employment was short term and low in quality, reflecting a failure to increase skills and education levels sufficiently. Furthermore, the rise in housing prices that had been underway for some years gathered pace alarmingly, leading to a steep increase in private debts and significant hardship for some.

Overall, though, the country's performance continued to be impressive. Spain's growth rate was again among the very highest in the EU and for the bulk of the population living standards continued to rise steadily. As a result, there was a general expectation that the government would be re-elected for a third term. Indeed, as polling day approached the only question appeared to be whether Rajoy would succeed in maintaining the party's overall parliamentary majority.

What appears to have upset these calculations was the terrorist attack in Madrid three days before the election was due (p161) – or, rather, the government's reaction to it. From the outset, that was to blame the bombings on ETA. Initially a plausible and widely-shared view, it soon began to erode in the face of mounting evidence that pointed in a quite different direction. Yet Aznar and his leading colleagues seemed determined to ignore that. They even instructed official Spanish spokespersons worldwide to take the same line and lobbied strongly for the media to do the same. As the facts, and the extent of government interference in their reporting, began to emerge, there were signs of a strong public reaction. It culminated on election eve in a wave of demonstrations outside PP offices around the country.

Next day, voter turnout was significantly higher than both opinion poll forecasts and the 2000 election figure (at 78 per cent, it was the third highest of the democratic era). The additional votes went massively to the Socialist opposition, turning the PP's expected lead into a five per cent deficit (37.6 per cent to 42.6 per cent). Technically, that meant a hung Parliament. Their course over the previous four years having alienated any possible allies, however, it was clear that the Conservatives would be returning to opposition.

Summary of main points

The regionalist spiral

- Between 1993 and 2000 the CiU's Jordi Pujol exerted a strong influence over successive central governments. He used it, in particular, to extend Catalonia's financial autonomy.
- In the mid-1990s renewed ETA violence and a breakdown in relations between the PNV and the main Spanish parties greatly increased tensions in the Basque Country.
- After the end of the ETA truce in 1998/99 the situation deteriorated further. The PNV hardened its demands for outright independence and the central government refused to negotiate at all, concentrating instead on crushing ETA and its political base.
- In 2003 the CiU lost power in Catalonia to a coalition made up of Socialists and left-wing regionalists and set on significantly extending the region's self-government.

In the time of globalisation

- The conservative government elected in 1996 completed the process of qualifying Spain for EMU. However, owing to its different ideas and changing circumstances it came increasingly into conflict with its partners, notably Germany, over a number of issues.
- Under the conservatives, Spain became more closely involved in NATO, and was at the forefront of support for the American invasion of Iraq, even though this was highly unpopular at home.
- Globalisation affected Spain in various ways, notably a large rise in immigration, much of it illegal, from the developing world. Many immigrants suffered poor conditions in the underground economy and also experienced friction with indigenous Spaniards.
- Moroccans were the group most affected by these circumstances and also that most heavily involved in the terrorist attack in Madrid on 11 March 2004.

The PP ascendant

- The PP's rise to power was facilitated by a succession of scandals that hit the Socialist government between 1993 and 1996, and by the PSOE's continuing decline in opposition thereafter.
- After gaining power in 1996 under José María Aznar, the PP initially showed surprising flexibility in dealing with trade unions and regionalists. It also presided over a further period of strong economic growth and was re-elected by a landslide in 2000.
- After that, the government largely abandoned its consensual approach, both in foreign affairs and domestically, most notably in its Iraq policy. It also attempted to extend its influence into business and the media sector through dubious privatisation policies.
- With the economy continuing, on balance, to perform well, the PP appeared set for re-election in 2004. In the event, however, it was defeated, probably because of the government's attempts to manipulate coverage of the terrorist attack.

Exhibit 10.1: The People's Party's inheritance (1995)

Extracts from a book written by former PM José María Aznar

Nuestro partido es joven, pero nos consideramos, con legítimo orgullo, herederos de una corriente que, con aportaciones de diverso signo, ha estado presente en la vida nacional durante más de doscientos años. La construcción del Estado liberal, a partir de la Constitución de 1812, la creación de un mercado nacional, la modernización jurídica, con obras de tanta fecundidad como nuestros venerables Códigos del XIX, han sido pilares fundamentales en la configuración de la España de hoy. El respeto a las libertades, el imperio de la Ley, la sujeción del Estado al Derecho, el protagonismo de la sociedad fueron los motores de una vasta obra, hecha con la impronta del espíritu liberal. Con demasiada frecuencia se ha querido desfigurar nuestra más reciente historia. La corriente reaccionaria ha pretendido siempre descalificar e incluso ahogar los logros modernizadores del pensamiento moderado y liberal español. Una cierta izquierda ha elaborado, por su parte, una visión maniquea de nuestra historia contemporánea, metiendo en el mismo saco todo lo que no se identificaba con sus planteamientos. Nosotros, por el contrario, reivindicamos el vigor de una opción con perfiles propios que a través de las sucesivas generaciones defendió la primacía del valor de la libertad y de la ley de un Estado sometido a él, de una democracia en la que cupiera holgadamente la España plural y en cuyo marco se pudieran llevar adelante las reformas que demandaba una sociedad más justa. [...]

Our party is a young one, but we consider ourselves – with legitimate pride – as the heirs to a strand of opinion which, thanks to contributions from various quarters, has been influential in Spain for more than 200 years. The building of a liberal state based on the 1812 Constitution; the creation of a national market; the modernisation of our legal system, the valuable products of which included the admirable codes of law drawn up in the nineteenth century: all these were fundamental in shaping today's Spain. Respect for freedoms, the rule of law – extended to cover the actions of government – and the participation of society as a whole were the driving forces of a vast project that bears the imprint of liberal ideas. All too often attempts have been made to distort Spain's modern history. Reactionaries have always sought to disparage or even reverse the modernising achievements of Spanish moderates and liberals. At the same time, part of the Left sees our recent history in strictly black and white terms, lumping together all those who do not share its views. By contrast, we lay claim to the dynamism of a third, distinct tradition that, down the generations, has championed the causes of liberty, of the rule of law and a state subject to it, and of a democracy with ample room for a pluralistic vision of Spain, within which it would be possible to implement the reforms needed to create a more just society.

Source: Aznar, J.M. (1995) *España: La Segunda Transición*. Madrid: Espasa.

Exhibit 10.2: The Ibarretxe Plan (2003)

Extracts from the 'Political Statute for the Community of Euskadi', approved by the Basque Parliament with the support of PNV, EA and the Basque section of United Left.

PREÁMBULO
El Pueblo Vasco o Euskal Herría es un Pueblo con identidad propia en el conjunto de los pueblos de Europa, depositario de un patrimonio histórico, social y cultural singular, que se asienta geográficamente en siete Territorios actualmente articulados en tres ámbitos jurídico-políticos diferentes ubicados en dos estados. [...]
[...]
Artículo 1. – De la Comunidad de Euskadi
[...L]os Territorios vascos de Araba, Bizkaia y Gipuzkoa, así como los ciudadanos y ciudadanas que la integran, en el ejercicio del derecho a decidir libre y democráticamente su propio marco de organización y de relaciones políticas, y como expresión de su nacionalidad y garantía de autogobierno, se constituyen en una Comunidad vasca libremente asociada al estado español bajo la denominación de Comunidad de Euskadi.
[...]
Artículo 13. – Ejercicio democrático del Derecho a Decidir
A los efectos del ejercicio democrático del derecho de libre decisión de los ciudadanos y ciudadanas vascas [sic], del que emana la legitimidad democrática del presente Estatuto, las Instituciones de la Comunidad de Euskadi ostentan la potestad para regular y gestionar la realizacion de consultas democráticas a la ciudadanía vasca por vía de referéndum, tanto en lo que corresponde a asuntos de su ámbito competencial como a las relaciones que desean tener con otros Territorios y Comunidades del Pueblo Vasco, así como en lo relativo a las relaciones con el Estado español y sus Comunidades Autónomas, y a las relaciones en el ámbito europeo e internacional.
[...]
Cuando en el ejercicio democrático de su libre decisión, los ciudadanos y ciudadanas vascas [sic] manifestaran [...] su voluntad clara e inequívoca de alterar integra o sustancialmente el modelo y régimen de relación política con el Estado español, así como las relaciones en el ámbito europeo e internacional [...], las Instituciones vascas y las del estado se entenderán comprometidas a garantizar un proceso de negociación parar establecer las nuevas condiciones políticas que permitan materializar, de común acuerdo, la voluntad democrática de la sociedad vasca.
[...]
Artículo 65. – Unión Europea
[...]
2. De conformidad con la normativa comunitaria europea, la Comunidad de Euskadi dispondrá de representación directa en los órganos de la Unión Europea. A tal efecto, el Gobierno español habilitará los cauces precisos para posibilitar la participación activa del Gobierno Vasco en los diferentes procedimientos de toma de decisiones de las Instituciones Comunitarias en aquellos asuntos que afectan al contenido de las políticas públicas que les son exclusivas.
[...]

PREAMBLE
The People of the Basque Country (Euskal Herría) have a distinct collective identity within the community of Europe's peoples. They are the bearers of a unique historical, social and

cultural heritage, and their homeland is made up of seven territories which are currently divided between three legal and political jurisdictions located in two states. [...]

[...]

Article 1. – The Community of Euskadi

[...l]n the exercise of their right to decide freely and democratically their own administrative and political structure, and as an expression of their nationhood and a guarantee of their self-government, the Basque territories of Alava, Vizcaya and Guipúzcoa, together with their citizens, hereby constitute themselves as a Basque entity freely associated with the Spanish state, under the name 'Community of Euskadi'.

[...]

Article 13.– Democratic Exercise of the Right to Decide

In order to permit Basques the democratic exercise of their right of free decision making, from which this Statute derives its democratic legitimacy, the institutions of the said Community shall have the power to regulate, and to organise the carrying out of, democratic consultations of all Basques by means of referendums, relating to:

- matters lying within the scope of their competence;
- the relations which they wish to maintain with other territories or communities forming part of the Basque People; and
- their relations with the Spanish state and its constituent regions, and to their external relations in the European and international spheres.

[...]

As and when Basques, in the democratic exercise of their right of free decision-making, manifest [...] their clear and unequivocal will to amend, wholly or substantially, the principle and mechanism governing their political relationship with the Spanish state, or their external relations in the European and international spheres [...], the institutions of the Community of Euskadi and of the Spanish state shall be deemed to have committed themselves to ensuring a process of negotiation designed to establish such new political circumstances as would permit the expression, by mutual agreement, of the democratic will of Basque society.

[...]

Article 65.– European Union

[...]

2. The Community of Euskadi shall enjoy direct representation in the institutions of the European Union, in accordance with the norms and regulations of the said Union. To that end, the Spanish government shall establish the arrangements necessary to enable the active participation of the Basque government in the various decision-making procedures of the Union's institutions in all matters affecting those areas of public policy which are the exclusive responsibility of those institutions.

Topics for discussion

- In Exhibit 10.1, Aznar portrays his party as the heirs of the Spanish liberal movement. How realistic a picture does he present of that? How credible is his claim?

- How far did Aznar's performance in office reflect the picture presented in Exhibit 10.1?

- How extreme are the demands implicitly set out in Exhibit 10.2, for example relative to those made by Scottish and Welsh nationalists? Why do you think they are so controversial in Spain?

- How would you rate Jordi Pujol's contributions to Spain and to Catalonia?

- Was the foreign policy followed by the PP governments a sound one for Spain?

CHAPTER 11

A second transition? (2004–2008)

By 2004 the horrendous reality of the Iraq occupation was causing enormous costs for the US both financially and in terms of its international prestige, now strongly challenged by China's whirlwind development and Russia's renewed self-confidence. The EU countries, despite managing a mild recovery, still lacked the unity to act as a global political power, a point underlined by the proposed Constitution's defeat at referendums in France and the Netherlands. Further integration, not to mention enlargement, seemed off the agenda; for a number of governments, controlling immigration to the Union was now a bigger issue. Even so, Germany's Chancellor Merkel succeeded in forging agreement on a very similar package of measures. This Reform Treaty was signed by all member governments at Lisbon in December 2007 but rejected in a referendum in Ireland in June 2008. Shortly thereafter the European economies were hit by the full effects of the worsening eruptions in the US financial sector that had started in August 2007 and showed no sign of coming to an end. Just as following Kosovo's unilateral declaration of independence from Serbia in spring 2008, the EU proved unable to formulate a common response to this shock.

The 2004 general election marked a significant break in Spain's development and not just because it resulted in a renewed transfer of power, this time from Right to Left; the country had grown accustomed to those. The reason lay more in the new initiatives taken by the Socialists on their return to power. These related primarily to social policy but also encompassed new initiatives in the ongoing tug-of-war over devolution. They were sufficiently radical for some observers to speak of a 'second transition', taking up where the changes following Franco's death had left off. In the international and economic spheres, by contrast, the government largely stuck, or reverted to earlier policy directions. Even so, it met with relentless opposition from the ousted People's Party.

New policies for a new era

During its spell in opposition, the Socialist Party (PSOE) had undergone significant changes. Under a new leader it had developed new policies, especially in the social field. A number of them marked very radical breaks with officially-espoused values. Rather unexpectedly, the 2004 general election gave the PSOE the opportunity to put them into practice.

The PSOE's 2004 victory undoubtedly owed much to the extraordinary circumstances under which it took place (p167). However, it is also true that the party had taken steps to recover from its shattering defeat four years earlier (p164). That in itself had finally compelled the Socialists to implement some long-needed internal changes, not least because party leader Joaquín Almunia (p162) resigned immediately following the debacle. To general surprise, and against the wishes of the party establishment, the conference called to select his successor voted narrowly in favour of José Luis Rodríguez Zapatero, a hitherto little-known MP from León.

In both age and views, Zapatero represented a new generation within the PSOE, too young to be associated, for better or worse, with the González governments of the 1980s and 1990s. By promoting others from its ranks to replace virtually all of the old leadership, he gave his party, at last, a fresher and younger face. His outright opposition to the Iraq War and promise to withdraw Spanish troops if elected chimed particularly with the concerns of younger voters (pp166–7).

More generally, though, he steered a less confrontational course, speaking of a new style of politics (*nuevo talante*) characterised by greater openness and dialogue with opponents. In practice this meant actively seeking cross-party pacts on matters of particular national importance. Initial government reactions were negative, even contemptuous. The fact that two such agreements (on a common anti-terrorist line and on reforms to Spain's hopelessly overloaded court system) were eventually concluded was thus testimony to Zapatero's persistence and skills as a negotiator.

These were qualities he would need in government. The 2004 election results left the PSOE eleven seats short of an overall majority in the lower house of Parliament (p120) – and not even as the largest party in the upper one. As a result, Zapatero was repeatedly forced to negotiate single-issue agreements with various combinations of the smaller parties (of which there were nine in total) to get legislation through. In that he was largely successful.

Otherwise, the promised change of style seemed mainly confined to rhetoric, although the new government did make one concrete move towards greater openness by loosening its unhealthy hold over the state broadcasting corporation, RTVE. In economic policy, too, Zapatero broadly followed the orthodox lines of its predecessors, both Conservative and Socialist. Indeed, he persuaded one of González's foremost lieutenants, Pedro Solbes (p158), to return as Economics and Finance Minister and visible guarantee of such continuity.

In a number of other areas, however, his government struck out on new paths. Some of these were conceived as completing the transition from dictatorship almost three decades earlier. That had been largely a matter of political change; in social spending, for example, Spain still lagged far behind nearly all its neighbours in 2004. The new government moved to at least reduce this gap. Thus it substantially raised the levels of existing benefits and introduced several new ones, such as the 'baby cheque' (a payment for parents of newly born or adopted children) or support for younger first-time home renters. On a different front, the PSOE also succeeded, after lengthy negotiations, in passing a Historical Memory Act (*Ley de Recuperación de la Memoria Histórica*) officially recognising the victims of Francoist repression and, at last, requiring the removal of memorials to the dictatorship such as statues and street names.

The position of women was arguably another area where the transition had left unfinished business. Be that as it may, the rapid changes in Spanish society and attitudes since that time had certainly not been adequately reflected in legislation on gender issues, as the Socialists had noted in opposition. Once elected, one of Zapatero's first acts was to appoint María Fernández de la Vega as Spain's first female Deputy PM. He then extended to his cabinet the gender equality principle his party had already used in drawing up its lists of candidates.

These signals were soon followed by a Domestic Violence Act (*Ley Integral contra la Violencia de Género*) that introduced various forms of assistance for the victims – overwhelmingly female – of abuse within existing and former relationships, and severe penalties for its perpetrators. The Act led to over 50,000 convictions in its first two years, although sadly there was no reduction in the number of women murdered by their partners and ex-partners. In 2005, the government brought in a law greatly relaxing the stiff conditions under which divorce had been legalised back in 1980 (p121). One of its provisions made abuse within marriage a ground for almost immediate divorce. Two years later, it introduced stronger anti-discrimination legislation that extended gender quotas to company boardrooms, a bastion of male dominance in Spain as elsewhere.

Also a reaction to social change, specifically the gradual breakdown in family-based care networks, was the 2006 Dependency Act. It established criteria for determining the degree of dependency suffered by the elderly and disabled, and specified the benefits available to each category. In marked contrast to the traditional emphasis on residential provision, these contained a strong element of community care in the form of home help services, day centre provision and support for the adaptation of private homes.

Most public attention, though, was paid to yet another measure, the 2005 Same-Sex Marriages Act (*Ley de Matrimonio Homosexual*). Only the third of its kind in the world, the Act not only allowed same-sex unions to be given official status but also enabled partners in them to adopt children. Further legislation granted compensation to homosexuals punished for their 'deviance' under the Franco dictatorship and enabled lesbian couples to become the legal parents of children born to one member following fertility treatment. A third measure addressed the issue of gender identity, allowing transsexuals to change their name and officially recorded gender without the need to undergo an operation.

Regional problems, new and old

Outside the social field, the Zapatero government's main actions concerned the various unresolved issues relating to regionalism and the regions. With regard to

Partit dels Socialistes de Catalunya (PSC)

Catalan Socialist Party

The PSC was formed during the post-1975 transition by various socialist groupings in Catalonia outside the aegis of the **Spanish Socialist Party** (PSOE) (p25), which had failed to establish any real base there up to or during the Franco era. After topping the Catalan poll at the general elections of 1977 and 1979, a position it has never lost, the PSC was able to negotiate a considerable degree of autonomy within the PSOE as the price for joining the larger party. It has done less well at regional elections but since 2003 has headed a three-party centre-left coalition government (*tripartito*). True to the traditions of the Catalan Left, the PSC is a strong supporter of devolution, advocating so-called 'asymmetric federalism', that is, a form of federalism in which Catalonia – and the other historic nationalities (p122) – would have greater powers than other regions.

Catalonia, it was heavily constrained by commitments made to local regionalists. In the Basque Country, on the other hand, it sought to take the initiative by a radical change in policy. The outcome in both cases was problematic.

Zapatero's initial ambition was to tie up the seemingly interminable process of devolution in general (p122), something his predecessor had also attempted without success (p164). Thus the PSOE election manifesto had proposed amending the 1978 Constitution to include the names of the various autonomous regions and to change the method of the Senate's election to make it genuinely representative of these (p122). Zapatero had also indicated his support for extending further the powers exercised by the regions. However, these general plans were soon submerged in the furore surrounding developments in one single region: Catalonia.

The root of Zapatero's problems lay in the coalition agreement entered into by the **Catalan Socialist Party** in order to take over the regional government in 2003 (p157). The price extorted by the PSC's main ally, the pro-independence Catalan Republican Left (ERC) (p52), was a new Statute of Autonomy (p122) extending Catalonia's devolved powers. Somewhat rashly, Zapatero had not just backed the agreement as such; he had even promised to support whatever proposals the Catalan Parliament might make in this respect.

That effectively left the Prime Minister, like the PSC, hostage to ERC. When the nationalists made a spectacular advance at the 2004 general election – almost trebling their share of the vote – they were in a position to turn up the pressure. In this they were assisted by the usually more moderately nationalist CiU (p145), which had become alarmed by electoral losses to its smaller rival and was still smarting at its ejection from power. As a result, the draft Statute approved by the Catalan Parliament in September 2005 was radical indeed.

Thus the text defined Catalonia as a 'nation' with an effective right to self-determination, and much of it read like the constitution of a sovereign state. In fact, it was actually longer than most such documents, mainly because it defined Catalonia's devolved powers as 'exclusive' and in painstaking detail in order to protect them from erosion by central government legislation (*blindaje competencial*).

At the same time, the proposals imposed on the central government a wide range of obligations *vis-à-vis* Catalonia and established a Catalan right to representation in various state bodies, including the Bank of Spain. Under them the central government would have lost its tax-collecting role in Catalonia, while being committed to certain levels of spending in the region. In that and other respects, the text was marked by a strong tendency to so-called bilateralism (*bilateralidad*), that is, to make the workings of Catalan autonomy a matter for bilateral negotiation between the central and regional governments, to the exclusion of other regions.

For many of all political persuasions outside Catalonia, as well as a significant section of Catalan opinion including some PSC supporters, much of this went too far. If Zapatero kept his rash promise, he would now face a parliamentary defeat with potentially dramatic political implications in Catalonia. From this dilemma he extricated himself by striking a surprise deal with CiU leader Artur Mas, the PSC's most dangerous opponent, to tone down the proposed text.

Under this agreement, the term 'nation' was suppressed other than in the legally meaningless preamble, as was the reference to 'exclusive' regional powers – but not their detailed descriptions. Also removed were a number of aspects of bilateralism, including the rights to state level representation. Some remained, though, specifically the establishment of a standing 'bilateral committee' made up of regional and central government representatives to deal with matters relating to Catalonia. A fiendishly complicated solution to the funding issue effectively made this, too, a matter for regular bilateral negotiation.

With CiU's support, the amended Statute received parliamentary approval in spring 2006; the only remaining hurdle was the obligatory regional referendum. At this point, ERC's membership rejected the adulterated proposals as too weak, forcing the party leadership to campaign against them. This did not prevent the new Statute from being comfortably approved, albeit the referendum turnout was embarrassingly low. However, it also left the regional First Minister and PSC leader Pasqual Maragall no choice but to eject ERC from his government and call an early regional election. He, in turn, was forced to step down from all his offices by the Socialists' Madrid leadership following some erratic pronouncements; notably that he too was unhappy with the Statute as finally passed!

Held on 1 November 2006, the election brought a swing away from the coalition partners. As in 2003 CiU won the most seats of any one party, but this time it also took the most votes. Precisely that situation had been foreseen in Zapatero's agreement with Mas. If it arose CiU was to receive, as recompense for backing the Statute amendments, a free hand to form the next government. However, Maragall's successor as PSC leader, José Montilla, did not feel bound by a deal that had been done behind his party's back. In defiance of the PSOE leadership, he negotiated a re-edition of the same three-party coalition as before, which still held a majority in the Catalan parliament. Its advantage being of a single seat, however, these machinations left the PSC – and, as a result, the PSOE – more exposed to nationalist pressure than ever.

Nor did the repercussions end there. Subsequently, a number of other regional statutes were amended under an existing agreement between the two main Spanish parties (p164). Several incorporated aspects of the new Catalan text such as references to nationhood, lengthy and detailed catalogues of regional powers, and claims to special treatment in the distribution of public funds. Some regions even asserted alleged 'rights' to water from rivers, parts – or all – of whose courses lay outside their area. Water shortages having been severe and widespread in recent years, such claims provoked a series of inter-regional quarrels that sometimes cut across the usual lines of conflict between PSOE and PP. All in all it was not surprising that some commentators, by no means all of the hard Right, saw in these developments a genuine threat to Spain's cohesion as a political entity.

In the Basque Country, that had already been challenged overtly by the so-called Ibarretxe Plan (p156), named after the region's First Minister Juan José Ibarretxe. Zapatero opposed the proposals as firmly as his conservative predecessor José María Aznar. In February 2005, the PSOE and PP voted together in the Spanish Parliament to prevent the proposal even being debated.

Nonetheless, the new PM did not share Aznar's view that the 'Basque problem' was a purely security issue (p156). Instead, he believed that the deadlock in the region could be broken by a bold new initiative. In May of the same year he persuaded all the minor parties to support the opening of a dialogue with ETA (p103) and its allies, provided they foreswore violence first. Ten months later the organisation declared a 'permanent ceasefire' and in June 2006 the government in Madrid announced the start of a peace process (*proceso de paz*).

Just as a decade earlier (p155), hopes of a settlement soared and, just as then, they were quickly damped. Many nationalists objected to the government's continuation of the ban on ETA's political wing Unity (*Batasuna*) so long as it refused to dissociate itself clearly from violence, as well as the attempts to prevent it from contesting elections under the name of other groups. Unity, for its part, demanded immediate recognition of its legitimacy as representative of a significant body of Basque opinion. Even so, Zapatero remained ostentatiously optimistic right up to 30 December 2006, when a bomb planted by ETA exploded in Madrid airport's new Terminal 4, killing two men asleep in their cars.

The peace process died with them, even if ETA did not announce the end of its ceasefire until June 2007. Between then and the following year's general election ETA killed three more people in cold blood, two of them Civil Guards and one a Basque Socialist politician, although it was also weakened by a number of successful police operations. Meanwhile, its supporters continued to intimidate their opponents in the countryside and smaller towns of the Basque Country.

Despite these conditions Ibarretxe refused to abandon his demands for a virtually sovereign Basque Country. Even the serious setback suffered by his party, the nationalist PNV (p24), at the 2005 regional election made no impact on him. His intransigence caused increasing disquiet even within his own party; in September 2007 it prompted the resignation of Jon Josu Imaz as PNV chairman. Since Imaz had been widely respected even among non-nationalists, his departure dealt another blow to hopes of an end to conflict in the region.

International and economic affairs

Internationally, after 2004 Spain moved back out of the limelight it had sought, and to some extent occupied during the premiership of José María Aznar (p159). With respect to both the US and Spain's main EU partners, the new government reversed the policy changes he had introduced. Economically, on the other hand, it maintained the same general policy direction, just as Aznar had (p157), and with similarly positive results. Towards the end of its first term, however, problems began to appear.

One of Zapatero's first actions as PM was to fulfil his commitment to pull Spanish troops out of Iraq. Predictably, this brought the Bush administration's brief infatuation with Spain (pp159–60) to an abrupt end, but in terms of day-to-day relations the effects were much less serious. Almost as quickly the new PM moved to mend fences with the country's main EU partners by dropping his predecessor's objections to the proposed Constitution (p159). It was perhaps no coincidence that, in the new European Commission sworn in later in 2004, Spain's new representative Joaquín Almunia (p162) succeeded to the high-profile Economic and Monetary Affairs portfolio vacated by Solbes on his return to Madrid.

The following year, Zapatero went out of his way to stress Spain's European credentials by making it the first EU member state to hold a referendum on the proposed Constitutional Treaty. He then campaigned personally in favour and achieved a 96 per cent 'yes' vote, albeit on a turnout of only 42 per cent. However, this triumph was rendered meaningless by the Constitution's subsequent fate. Equally, the realities of a 27-member EU left little room for the creation of the Madrid-Paris-Berlin axis to which Zapatero had vaguely aspired.

Any hopes in that direction were effectively torpedoed by the government's devious efforts to prevent the German energy giant E.ON from taking over Spain's Endesa. These clearly infringed the spirit of European integration if not its actual rules, as well as irritating Germany's Chancellor Merkel. (They also failed to prevent the firm from falling partly into foreign, specifically Italian, hands.) In the subsequent negotiation of the Lisbon Treaty, Spain was left with few cards to play. Even so, the outcome broadly reflected the country's pro-integration stance and even brought a minor victory in the form of a few more MEPs.

Three years earlier, in 2004, the EU had come to Spain's assistance in the thorny area of immigration policy with the establishment of the FRONTEX agency to coordinate efforts in this field. The new body helped to reduce the human tragedy – and political embarrassment – generated by the stream of desperate Africans across the Mediterranean and onto the Canary Islands (p160). For those immigrants already inside the country illegally, the Socialists announced a wide-ranging amnesty in 2005. This allowed any who could provide documentary proof, in a very broad sense, of residence to regularise their situation. Some 700,000 took the opportunity to do so, most of them not from Africa but from Latin America and the new EU members in Eastern Europe, especially Romania.

This bold step was possible thanks to the continuation of Spain's strong economic performance (p167). Indeed, with growth of consistently over 3 per cent, Spain had become a significant driving force of the EU economy as a whole, especially in job creation. Unemployment fell lower than at any time since 1975 even while the economy soaked up large amounts of immigrant labour. Abroad, Spanish firms continued to penetrate new markets and make major acquisitions, one of the most spectacular being Ferrovial's takeover of the British Airports Authority. In 2007 the Santander banking group became the EU's largest by market capitalisation.

Public finances were healthy, too, not least because of the strong boost they received as newly legalised immigrants emerged from the black economy. In each of its first three years Zapatero's government recorded a budget surplus. As a result it was able to reduce public debt to around forty per cent of GDP, one of the lowest figures in the EU.

Nevertheless, the skills shortages already evident prior to 2004 (p167) remained. To them were now added a worryingly low level of productivity growth and a burgeoning deficit in Spain's external trade that, relative to GDP, was worse even than America's. At the same time, the astonishing construction boom – for several years running Spain built more new houses than France, Germany and Italy combined – was clearly unsustainable. As well as making it near impossible for most young people to buy a first home, the boom provided fertile ground for corruption, in which local councils run by both main parties were implicated. It was also a major factor in driving up inflation. The situation cried out for a sharp rise in interest rates. But, with economic growth in the Union as a whole still low, that was not on the European Central Bank's agenda.

The crisis in world financial markets thus hit Spain at a particularly bad time. Its banking sector actually came off relatively lightly, as regulations set by the Bank of Spain had prevented it from lending quite as excessively and riskily as its counterparts elsewhere. The construction sector, on the other hand, was severely hit as the housing bubble burst spectacularly. Soon prices were falling and new building came to a virtual halt. The winter of 2007/08 saw the start of a wave of bankruptcies among construction firms, some of them major ones. The fall in unemployment was sharply reversed, inflation rose back over 4 per cent and, though growth remained above the EU average, it nonetheless slowed dramatically.

All-out opposition

The government blamed the economy's deterioration on the financial crisis alone. The opposition People's Party (PP) (p162), however, accused it of recklessly continuing to increase social spending long after it was clear that a downturn was close. This was just the latest front in what had been a generalised political war, for the PP – with important backing from the Catholic Church – had opposed virtually every action of the Zapatero administration since its election.

Thus, the PP stood aside from the general consensus behind the Historical Memory Act (p175), claiming that it was one-sided in failing to acknowledge pro-

Franco victims of left-wing violence – even though this had already been done amply by the dictatorship itself. It also refused to back the government's policy towards ETA, something previous oppositions had seen as a matter of state transcending party divisions. In his defence, PP leader Mariano Rajoy (p167) could reasonably cite the government's own radical change of direction (p178). Less reasonable was the highly personalised tone of his attacks on the PM, whom he accused of naivety about ETA's real nature and, repeatedly, of lying about the extent of contacts with, and concessions to the terrorists.

The revised Catalan Statute of Autonomy (p177) was another target of the PP's wrath. It opposed the measure in both the Barcelona and Madrid parliaments. Subsequently it appealed to the Constitutional Court against several of the measure's provisions on the grounds that they were unconstitutional, a view shared by many experts. (In late 2008 the Court had still to issue a judgement on the matter.) Strangely, though, the Conservatives raised no objections to the similar provisions in other new Statutes (pp177-8), some the work of PP regional governments. Such inconsistency seemed strangely at odds with the party's claims to be representing vital Spanish, as opposed to party, interests.

The same applied to its refusal to cooperate in renewing the membership of the Constitutional Court and the General Council of the Judiciary. Both of these bodies had, contrary to the spirit of the Constitution, become politicised and both had conservative majorities established by the PP itself when in power. These the party's blockade served to maintain. Yet it disquieted even many conservative judges since it also effectively paralysed the upper reaches of Spain's legal system. Clearly unconstitutional in spirit, this stance was but one way in which Rajoy and his party gave the impression of refusing to accept their 2004 defeat.

A second indication of this attitude was the PP's involvement in a series of attempts to show that ETA had been responsible for the terrorist attack that preceded it (p161). These increasingly bizarre efforts were nurtured by stories in the right-wing media, notably the newspaper *El Mundo* under its influential editor Pedro J Ramírez, and the Church-owned COPE radio station. All of them were subsequently shown to be false, some deliberately so, and the ETA theory was completely rejected by both a parliamentary commission and the courts.

In general, the same media sources maintained a ferocious anti-government line reminiscent of the last years of the previous Socialist administration (p163). The most strident voice of all was the COPE's talk-show presenter Federico Jiménez Losantos, whose vitriol was not even reserved for the Socialists; Madrid mayor Alberto Ruiz-Gallardón, the PP's leading moderate, also suffered it – and eventually won the damages action he brought as a result. Particularly objectionable to the extreme conservative viewpoint articulated by Losantos and others was the government's programme of social reform, and above all the legalisation of same-sex marriage. That measure was the main target of a campaign by the Spanish Catholic Church, within which the most conservative elements had re-asserted themselves. These were further enraged by the 2005 Education Act, which reversed the previous administration's upgrading of religion as a school subject (p165). It had also introduced a new subject of 'Education for Citizenship and Human Rights', which Church leaders feared would be inherently biased against their teachings.

A concession allowing the many state-subsidised Church-run schools to adjust the subject to their own philosophy (*ideario*) failed to mollify the bishops. They were equally unimpressed by the Zapatero government's defiance of the 1978 Constitution in order to maintain generous state contributions to their Church (p120). Indeed, as the government's term drew to a close, there were unmistakeable calls from many pulpits for voters to eject the Zapatero government. To these some Socialist leaders reacted with ill-disguised threats of even more sensitive reforms, in particular the easing of Spain's relatively tough restrictions on abortion.

By this time, admittedly, the PP leadership had distanced itself somewhat from the series of demonstrations arranged by Catholic organisations, as it had from the similarly vituperative gatherings in opposition to the Basque peace process. Here the orchestrator was the so-called 'Association of Victims of Terrorism' (AVT), which had become so obviously a vehicle for right-wing Spanish nationalism that many of the victims themselves no longer recognised it. However, there was no reduction in the vehemence of Rajoy's blanket condemnation of the government's record, or of his opposition to Basque and Catalan 'separatism'. With some on the government side once again resorting to thinly veiled allegations of Francoist nostalgia (p140), the contest between the two big parties was a very bitter one.

The 2008 election and after

In the event, the PSOE comfortably held on to power at the election held on 9 March 2008. The poll's main impact was felt in the other parties, in particular the PP, which took some steps to alter its course of the previous parliament. Like everything else, however, these were soon overshadowed by the increasingly obvious and damaging effects of the financial crisis.

The election brought gains for the opposition PP: a 2.5 per cent higher vote share and six Congress seats more than in 2004. That gave the party its second-best result ever but only a single seat closer to the PSOE, which made similar advances, although its jubilation was tempered by having fallen short of the hoped-for overall majority.

One feature of the results was the powerful squeeze experienced by the smaller parties (*bipolarización*). Apart from CiU, all of them suffered losses; worst hit was the third-largest Spain-wide party, United Left (p136), which won just four per cent of the vote and two seats. Also striking were the marked regional differences. While the conservative hold on the Madrid, Valencia and Murcia regions tightened, the Socialists gained spectacularly in Catalonia and in the Basque Country, where for the first time since 1975 they outpolled the nationalist PNV, and by a wide margin. The same region saw a ten per cent fall in turnout – as opposed to a Spain-wide figure of under two per cent – that doubtless reflected the government's success in barring ETA's supporters from the poll (p178).

As far as the country's government was concerned, however, these details were irrelevant. José Luis Rodríguez Zapatero, his leadership of the PSOE greatly bolstered, was duly invested to head a second minority administration. He immediately signalled his intention to maintain course on social issues by announcing a world-wide first; a female-majority cabinet. The highly symbolic Defence portfolio went to Carme Charcón, a minister in the previous administration who was now heavily pregnant. Defying right-wing derision, she was soon to be seen reviewing military parades and, following the birth of her child, she returned to her post after a mere six weeks maternity leave. As if to underline that tough decisions were no male pre-serve, she immediately proclaimed her intention of replacing the entire armed forces command council.

Where the election results had more impact was among the opposition parties. Inside IU, Zapatero's staunchest parliamentary ally in the previous session, they re-opened long-standing divisions between the Communist PCE (p70) – it still retained the old label – and less doctrinaire elements of the alliance. The PNV typically kept its internal struggles more to itself but, even so, it was clear that new party boss Iñigo Urkullu was anxious to pull back from Ibarretxe's course of outright confronta-tion with Madrid (p178). In Catalonia, the more moderate forces within both CiU and ERC were similarly bolstered.

Despite its gains, it was the PP that suffered the greatest turmoil even if, after an initial hesitation, Mariano Rajoy announced his intention to remain leader. He fol-lowed up by discarding the figures, all of them closely linked to his predecessor Aznar, most strongly identified with the confrontational style of opposition over the previous four years. Their replacements were uniformly younger and noted for their disposition to move on both rhetorically and in policy terms.

All this brought a fierce reaction from the party right, whose galleon figure was the electorally successful First Minister of the Madrid region, Esperanza Aguirre. She and her supporters wanted a return to the aggressive free market policies of the Aznar era (p165) as well as the removal of Rajoy, whom they regarded as indecisive, overly moderate and too fastidious to press home his attacks on the government. Initially, they seemed likely to triumph but their own divisions – and suspicion of Aguirre among the party's other regional leaders – meant that Rajoy emerged strengthened from the episode. He even felt able to bring into his new leadership team Aguirre's arch-rival Gallardón, whose appeal to swing voters in the provinces was much greater than hers.

In his task of opposing the government, too, events began to turn to Rajoy's advantage. Steadily worsening economic data and prognoses – by the summer of 2008 zero growth and unemployment as high as 14 per cent were widely predicted – offered him an easy target. They also allowed him to establish some common ground with the small parties, and so end his party's long parliamentary isolation (p167).

Rajoy was further assisted by the fact that Pedro Solbes (p174), who had reluc-tantly agreed to stay on as Economics and Finance Minister, found himself in partic-ular straits. Not only did he have the thankless task of imposing greater budget discipline on colleagues who had become used to spending freely; he also had to deal with the financial implications of the various new Statutes of Autonomy passed under the first Zapatero government, in particular the Catalan one (pp177–8).

The issue is a complex one. In essence, though, it boils down to reconciling two essentially incompatible demands: on the one hand, the special arrangements for Catalonia, and other regions, contained in the new Statutes; on the other, the constitutional requirement and administrative need for a general system that ensures reasonably fair treatment all round. This essentially insoluble dilemma has had important political effects. In effect, it has driven a wedge between the PSOE and the Catalan PSC (p176), whose excellent election performance has further increased its already considerable weight in the Socialist party as a whole. There have even been rumours that the latter might form a separate parliamentary group.

Nor are the problems confined to Catalonia or internal to the PSOE; similar rumblings have come from the other Socialist bastion of Andalusia and from Conservative-governed Valencia. Meanwhile, both the Catalan nationalist parties, CiU and ERC, have seized on the chance to raise again the notion of taking Catalonia outside the general system altogether by giving it an equivalent financial status to the Basque Country and Navarre (p9).

For all these reasons, Zapatero has faced increasing problems in holding together a parliamentary majority. Even the 2008 budget was passed only after lengthy negotiations with the PNV. There have been some areas of consensus, however. In June 2008, barely a week after the Lisbon Treaty's defeat in the Irish referendum, the Madrid Parliament ratified it almost unanimously. More substantively, following a further series of ETA attacks the PP joined the government and other parties in a strong re-affirmation of their common will to resist terrorism, the first time this had occurred for three years.

Another agreement reached during September had less encouraging implications. Signed by the two major parties, as well as the main nationalist groupings, CiU and the PNV, it opened the way for the necessary renewal of the General Council of the Judiciary (p181). The deal was based on each party nominating a set quota of members. In the event, all of these turned out to be known supporters of the respective parties, while some were distinctly lacking in the desirable professional prestige. As many jurists were quick to point out, the pact thus clearly breached the spirit of the Constitution if not its letter. The connection to Zapatero's supposed new political style (p174) was not immediately obvious.

Summary of main points

New policies for a new era

- During its spell in opposition, the Socialist Party had undergone significant changes in both leadership and policies, especially those relating to social issues.
- As well as increasing and developing social provision, the Zapatero government elected in 2004 introduced important new measures relating to women's rights and gender issues.

Regional problems, new and old

- Because of its political commitments, the government was obliged to support the passing of a revised Catalan Statute of Autonomy; this made major concessions to regionalist demands that effectively challenged the principles underlying devolution in general.
- Subsequently, a number of other regions demanded, and received, similar extensions of their powers.
- The government's attempted peace process in the Basque Country brought neither an end to violence nor any relaxation in the hard line taken by the main nationalist party, the PNV.

International and economic affairs

- The Zapatero government reversed the policies of its predecessors by withdrawing Spanish troops from Iraq and by attempting to re-establish good relations with France and Germany, this latter with limited success.
- Up to late 2007 Spain's economy continued to boom. But significant problems remained unsolved and the country was badly hit by the world financial crisis.

All-out opposition

- The People's Party, which appeared unwilling to accept its 2004 defeat, opposed the government on virtually all fronts, in particular over the Basque peace process and the Catalan Statute.
- Its opposition to the government's legalisation of same-sex marriages was especially virulent and strongly backed by the Catholic Church and sections of the media.

The 2008 election and after

- The government was comfortably re-elected despite opposition gains. However, it has come under increasing pressure due to the sharp deterioration in economic conditions.

Exhibit 11.1: A critique of the first Zapatero government (2008)

Extracts from an article published in the leading intellectual organ of the Spanish Right

En estos cuatro años han fracasado ruidosamente –nunca mejor dicho– lo que se llamó el «proceso de paz» y los soñados acuerdos con los terroristas, el borroso –y utópico– proyecto con que soñaban algunos gubernamentales de sustituir la unidad de la nación española que dice la Constitución, por una mal hilvanada «Confederación» de entidades territoriales que, más que formar un Estado a la altura de los tiempos actuales en el mundo desarrollado, degeneraría en un puzzle de piezas imposibles de encajar entre sí. [..]

Además, en estos cuatro años se han aprobado leyes como la que otorgaba con toda solemnidad el título y consideración jurídica de matrimonio a una clase de asociaciones humanas que no son tal cosa, que se salen de la Constitución y del léxico y los usos de la lengua española. [...]

España necesita recobrar el espíritu de la Transición, que no era un punto final, sino un punto de partida de unos millones de ciudadanos aleccionados por la historia. La «memoria histórica» de la que tanto se ha hablado y hasta se han hecho leyes, además de un «oxímoron» es querer llevar a una nación mirando hacia atrás, cuando la misma conciencia del pasado debería ser un estímulo para caminar hacia delante en un contexto mundial que tiene bastante poco que ver con el de los primeros años del siglo anterior. [...]

The last four years have seen the dramatic and widely-discussed failure of two projects. One was the so-called "peace process", with its wide-eyed attempt to reach agreement with terrorists, the other the ill-defined – and delusional – intention harboured by some ministers of doing away with the constitutionally guaranteed unity of the Spanish nation and replacing it with a badly constructed "confederation" of territorial units that, far from forming a state capable of survival in the contemporary developed world, would degenerate into a jigsaw puzzle whose pieces do not fit together. [...]

Moreover, during these four years laws have been passed such as that granting, in all solemnity, the name and legal status of marriage to a type of association between human beings that is no such thing, in violation both of the Constitution and of the vocabulary and usage of the Spanish language. [...]

Spain needs to recapture the spirit of the Transition, which was not an end but a beginning for millions of Spaniards who had learned the lessons of history. There has been much talk of "historical memory"; there have even been laws passed on the subject. Yet, apart from being an oxymoron, this expression is an attempt to turn a nation's eyes back to the past, when the very awareness of that past should be spurring us forwards in an international context that bears little resemblance to that of the early years of the last century. [...]

Source: Fontán, Anton. 'La España que nos queda' in *Nueva Revista*, 115 (February 2008)

Topics for discussion

- What are the main criticisms of the first Zapatero government raised in Exhibit 11.1? How fair would you say they are?
- What do the content and tone of Exhibit 11.1 tell us about the contemporary Spanish Right?

- Are Spain's "regional problems" soluble? If so, how?
- How much blame does the Zapatero government deserve for Spain's present economic difficulties? How quickly and well do you expect the country to recover?

Afterword

Over recent years Spain has become increasingly and patently integrated into European and global developments, not just politically and economically, but also – in an important sense not touched on here – culturally. Does that mean that an appreciation of its history has become irrelevant? The answer, surely, is 'No'. Even in the era of globalisation, each country's involvement in the wider world comes to some extent on its own terms – as the very differing reactions to the Iraq War within Europe demonstrated. Nowhere in the Western world does that apply more than in Spain, whose experience was so distinctive until so recently.

Thinking first of relations with the outside world, it is easy to forget that the world's eighth largest economy was so cut off for so long. At the start of the nineteenth century, Spain was already a backwater. After the brief and traumatic experience of the War of Independence it became ever more detached from the outside. It was virtually uninvolved in trade, colonial disputes or even incipient recreational travel, being seen as an occasional destination for the more intrepid. Even the soul-searching inspired by the events of 1898 did little to increase contacts; economically, the inward turn of later 'regenerationist' thinking was paralleled by Primo's raising of the protectionist barriers first erected during the Restoration period.

During the tensest and most unhappy decade of the last century Spain was briefly drawn back into European affairs. After the Second World War, however, it was again largely cut off from the developments that shaped the late-twentieth-century western community of states. Even so, by the later stages of the Franco regime, for all the propaganda disseminated by the State, most Spaniards had enough contact with the outside world to know that their country was regarded as economically backward and politically unsavoury – and that both views had some foundation.

Against that background it is easier to understand Spanish attitudes since Franco's death to the outside world in general, and the rest of Europe in particular. To an astonishing degree, the desire to be recognised as an equal partner has often seemed to override all other considerations. There was virtually general acclaim when Javier Solana was appointed NATO Secretary-General, even though he had opposed Spain's participation in the alliance less than 15 years before. Support for European integration, too, has been extraordinarily resilient even when, as in the early 1990s, it brought considerable material costs for many. The post-Communist Left's insistence on pointing out such unfortunate realities was one of the main reasons why it has found life so much harder in Spain than in Italy since 1989.

Spanish 'Europhilia' is all the more striking when compared with attitudes in the other peripheral country which has traditionally seen 'Europe' as being somewhere else: the UK. But unlike Britain – or at ast England – Spain did not have an unthinkingly accepted notion of nationhood to which European integration posed a threat. Within living memory, a country whose sense of common identity was never highly developed had experienced a civil war, followed by four decades of propaganda to the effect that a large proportion of its own inhabitants were actually the country's bitter enemies. On the other hand, many, perhaps the majority, were deeply unhappy with the notion of Spanishness imposed by the Franco regime. Under those circumstances, being European offered, and continues to offer a way to sidestep awkward debates about Spain's essential nature.

The question of national identity bridges the external and internal aspects of Spain's contemporary situation. For the relative weakness of feelings of common Spanishness is inseparable from the strength of loyalties to particular localities. Given new life by the conditions of the War of Independence, they underlay Republicanism's federalist period and its extreme expression in the cantonalist movement of the 1870s. Now, in the post-Franco era, they have re-emerged with even greater vigour, which this time is being channelled in various forms of regionalism.

Such feelings, like 'Europhilia', are both powerful and widespread, as Manuel Fraga's career illustrates. Minister under the ferociously centralist Franco regime, fervent critic of what he regarded as excessive devolution in the 1980s, he became First Minister of s native Galicia in 1989 in what seemed to be no more than a step on the way to his retirement from nationwide politics. Yet subsequently Fraga, who retained office for 16 years, was to display a strong regionalist streak, doughtily defending Galicia's particular interests and advocating a standardised administrative system that would put more responsibilities in the hands of regions in general. More than once he found himself in agreement with his long-time Catalan equivalent, Jordi Pujol– whose own regionalist sympathies had led to him spending part of the Franco era, not in a ministerial office, but in a prison cell.

Pujol, who managed no less than 23 years as First Minister, was a phenomenon in his own right. In a sense, he single-handedly wrenched Catalan regionalism away from its historical roots. But, at the same time, his brand of regionalism was essentially a new attempt to address the problem that plagued the Regionalist League at the turn of the century: how to mobilise mass political support for the economic interests of a small, privileged group – and how to control it once mobilised. Pujol's resolution of that dilemma depended heavily on his own personal standing; with his departure it has re-emerged in its full force. Certainly, the resurgence of ERC and the cementing of a Socialist–regionalist alliance is uncannily reminiscent of events in the 1930s.

If history still weighs heavily in Catalonia, in the Basque Country its presence is almost overpowering. For one thing, the very weakness of historical claims to Basque nationhood means that, for many nationalists, it is all the more important that they be asserted as loudly and as often as possible. The irony is that by the 1990s most non-nationalists had accepted the proposition of Basques' distinctiveness, albeit not necessarily on historical grounds. Nor, to judge by opinion polls, was the situation changed significantly by the People's Party return to more centralist attitudes while in power, a move that in any case has recently been reversed.

The traditionalist aspect of Basque nationalism has been enormously important, even for ETA. In its communiqués down the years, 'revolutionary socialist' demands have sat oddly alongside those for the restoration of Basques' traditional rights. Many observers have commented on the clearly traceable links between its intransigent, irrational, violent approach to politics and the Carlist movement of the nineteenth century, from which a number of early nationalists emerged. But even more important for ETA's development, and attitudes to it, has been the Basque Country's more recent history.

For more than four decades now, the region has experienced one sort of trauma after another: the industrial conflict which formed the background to the early stages of ETA's 'armed struggle'; the often bitter debates over devolution of the decade after 1975, against a background of increased violence; the political crisis of the mid-1980s; and ETA's evolution into a marginalised but still highly effective terrorist group. Add to that a savage industrial restructuring that threw thousands out of work and destroyed whole communities, a massive drug problem among young people and the persistent security force abuses which have killed scores and harmed hundreds more – not to mention the GAL revelations of the 1990s. The contradictory impact of these various factors has been immense and will doubtless be in evidence for some time yet.

There is a sense in which the GAL affair, while especially alarming because of its nature, is merely one example of a more general phenomenon that, once again, derives from Spain's particular historical experience. The apparatus of the Spanish state was constructed late in comparison to most of its neighbours – in many fields only in the 1950s, and in some not until the 1970s. It also came into being under the special circumstances of dictatorship. In 1975, the Spanish public service had little or no ethos of public accountability. Indeed, the concept was simply meaningless in the military and security forces as well as among the judiciary, for whom the sole virtue was obedience (and whose values were uniformly conservative and authoritarian). More than three decades of democratic rule have brought important changes but the issue is by no means resolved.

Another feature of contemporary Spanish government also reflects the experience of the Franco era. Dictatorships anywhee fill the administration with their own supporters. In Spain, though, the practice was already common under the façade of democratic conditions of the last century, when the successive pairs of embryonic parties – first Moderates and Progressives, later Conservatives and Liberals – used the gift of public jobs as a way of buying support. During the Socialist hegemony of the 1980s patronage recovered that function, but more often served as a means of securing party control over government, at central, regional and local level. Once the pendulum swung, and the People's Party acquired a similarly strong hold on government, the same process was visible, with the PP in turn 'colonising' large tracts of the public service and its related agencies. In that sense, the emphasis placed by José Luis Rodríguez Zapatero on a new style of government is welcome, even if he has not always put words into practice.

The parties and the system they compose also show a cal imprint, their development heavily conditioned by the very limited scope for their normal activities prior to 1975. Only the PNV and, in certain areas, the PSOE ever became the sort of mass party common in most of western Europe. Not only that: for various reasons, parties as institutions were poorly regarded by very wide sections of opinion – a rare point of agreement between Franco and the anarchist movement! In both these respects, Spain can be said to have anticipated the drift towards a media-centred, personalised style of politics in which parties and politicians are generally held in low esteem by voters.

As elsewhere, such feelings seem to be commonest among younger voters in Spain. It remains to be seen whether the Zapatero governments' attempts to address social issues of importance to this group will do anything to redress the situation. A more important factor in the immediate future may well be the recent, abrupt ending of the country's lengthy period of economic growth, together with the manner in which politicians respond to it. In doing so, they seem likely to be hampered by the enormous amount of attention they, and others, pay to regional issues, which often seem to have acquired an importance out of proportion with their real significance.

The point was illustrated by the Kosovo issue. By autumn 2008 Spain was one of only five EU members (the others were Cyprus, Malta, Romania and Slovakia) yet to recognise the would-be state's independence. On a matter of negligible strategic importance for the country it has broken ranks with all its closest and most important allies, undermining in the process the common EU foreign policy it has – apart from the Aznar interlude – consistently and ostentatiously championed. And that purely for fear of giving even the tiniest encouragement to separatist aspirations in the Basque Country and Catalonia. History doesn't weigh much heavier than that.

Further reading

The following comments cannot pretend to be comprehensive. They are intended merely to offer a range of sources suitable for readers who are not specialist historians but feel ready to take the next step beyond the material provided here. A number of authors (Carr, Payne, Preston) have written so widely on the period that for reasons of space only a selection of their output can be mentioned here. There is emphatically no intention to deter readers from sampling their other works – quite the reverse, in fact.

General works

The standard academic work in English, covering most of the period in considerable detail, is Carr's massive tome (8). Much more accessible is the 'pocket version' (7) which starts with the Restoration period rather than at the outset of the liberal era, whereas the latter and its antecedents are covered in their entirety by Esdaile (15). Shubert (46) provides an account that goes below the political surface, and covers more than the social history indicated by the title; he is particularly useful on the Franco era. For a very different approach from all these, concerned almost entirely with overview rather than chronological detail, try Vilar (51), in particular the later chapters, and for a Spanish view of the whole period see Fusi and Palafox (16). Finally, although it was written over half a century ago, to my mind Brenan's classic (6) still provides the best introduction to pre-Civil War Spain; its topic-based arrangement and down-to-earth style allow the non-specialist reader to see the wood for the trees.

Chapter 1

Here there is very little written in English other than for specialists, although the early parts of Payne's work (35) on the military are accessible as well as enlightening. To get a feel for nineteenth-century Spain there is no better source than the novels of Galdós; one of the most famous is now available in translation (17). The articles by Harper (23) and Chandler (10), unfortunately difficult to locate, are excellent introductions to the First Republic and Restoration respectively, while Kern (30) includes a useful chapter on the operation of clientilism.

Chapter 2

For a discussion of 'regenerationist' ideas and their impact, see the articles by Harrison (24) and Ortega (33). The standard work on early Basque regionalism is by Payne

(36), although Heiberg (25) offers an equally interesting view; for the Catalan variety, see Balcells (1). The comparative treatments by Conversi (12) and Díez Medrano (14) offer contrasting interpretations of the differences between the two movements; both are rewarding if not particularly light reading. Bookchin (5) provides a useful introduction to Spanish anarchism, while Geary (18) sets the Spanish labour movement in international perspective. Specifically on the PSOE, see Heywood (26), or Gillespie's detailed party history (19).

Chapter 3

The article by Ben-Ami (2) gives the best overview of the Primo dictatorship; for a more detailed account see the relevant chapters in the book by the same author (3). The relevant chapters of the works by Payne (35) and Preston (43) on the military are also useful.

Chapter 4

A considerable amount has been written on the Second Republic; given the nature of the period, treatments tend to vary significantly in their assessments. Jackson (29) and Preston (42), alone or in the international treatment written jointly with Graham (21), tend broadly to sympathise with the Left; Payne (38) with the Right, whose nature is in turn revealingly analysed by Preston (43). The article by Graham (20) explores the crucial differences within the Socialist movement.

Chapter 5

Here both the quantity of material and the degree of partisanship is even more marked. Again, Jackson (29) and Preston and Mackenzie (44) offer eminently readable accounts from a basically Republican perspective, while the differences between the early and late editions of Thomas' work (48, 49) reflect changes in the author's own political standpoint. For an understanding of the Nationalist side, Preston's biography of Franco (41) is particularly recommended. The article by Casanova (9) offers an interesting insight into the revolutionary view of the war on the Left. Moving towards literature, Orwell's account of the 1937 Barcelona clashes (34) retains its power, while Ken Loach's film *Land and Freedom* gives an unashamedly partisan, but incredibly immediate picture of the left-wing militias. Finally, for an intriguing analysis of Britain's role in the conflict, see Moradiellos (31).

Chapters 6 and 7

Payne (37), Blaye (4), and Grugel and Rees (22) all provide analyses of the Franco regime's nature, on which Preston's massive but highly readable biography of its master (41) is also most enlightening. The opening chapter of the same author's study of the transition (40) gives a very useful overview of the opposition forces.

Chapters 8–11

Here history and political science begin to overlap: the different viewpoints are apparent in the many studies of the transition to democracy; see, for example, Higley and Gunther (28) and Preston (40). Powell (39) provides a useful overview of most of the period, although his coverage naturally becomes progressively less detailed, while Tusell (50) covers the very recent past with remarkable perspective. Heywood (27) analyses the Socialist era from the standpoint of a political scientist. In Spanish, the same period is covered very thoroughly – from the same perspective – in the volume edited by Cotarelo (13), although readers should bear in mind the close connections of most of its authors with the Socialist party. ETA has been the subject of several studies; those by Clark (11) and Sullivan (47) both require committed reading but are highly informative, while Onaindía (32) offers a fascinating and highly personal insight into the 'Basque problem' as a whole. Finally, for a more detailed account of recent developments I can tentatively recommend my own contribution, recently updated by Richardson and Sangrador-Vegas (45).

List of further reading

1. Balcells, A. (1996) *Catalan Nationalism: Past and Present*. London: Macmillan.

2. Ben-Ami, S. 'The dictatorship of Primo de Rivera' in *The Journal of Contemporary History*, January 1977.

3. Ben-Ami, S. (1978) *The Origins of the Second Republic in Spain*. Oxford: Oxford University Press.

4. Blaye, E. de (1974) *Franco and the Politics of Spain*. Harmondsworth: Penguin.

5. Bookchin, M. (1977) *The Spanish Anarchists*. New York: Freelife.

6. Brenan, G. (1990) *The Spanish Labyrinth*. Cambridge: Cambridge University Press.

7. Carr, R. (1980) *Modern Spain 1875–1980*. Oxford: Oxford University Press.

8. Carr, R. (1982) *Spain 1808–1975*. Oxford: The Clarendon Press.

9. Casanova, J. 'The egalitarian dream' in *Journal of the Association of Iberian Studies*, Autumn 1989.

10. Chandler, J. 'The self-destructive nature of the Spanish Restoration' in *Iberian Studies*, Autumn 1973.

11. Clark, R. (1984) *The Basque Insurgents: 1952–1980*. Reno: University of Nevada Press.

12. Conversi, D. (1997) *The Basques, the Catalans and Spain*. London: Hurst.

13. Cotarelo, R. (ed.) (1992) *Transición política y consolidación democrática*. Madrid: Centro de Investigaciones Sociológicas.

14. Díez Medrano, J. (1995) *Divided Nations*. Ithaca: Cornell University Press.

15. Esdaile, C. J. (2000) *Spain in the Liberal Age*. Oxford: Blackwell.

16. Fusi, J. P. and J. Palafox (1998) *España 1808–1996: El desafío de la modernidad*. Madrid: Espasa.

17. Galdós, B. Pérez (1988) *Fortunata and Jacinta*. London: Penguin.

18. Geary, D. (1989) *Labour and Socialist Movements in Europe before 1914*. Oxford: Berg.

19. Gillespie, R. (1989) *The Spanish Socialist Party. A History of Factionalism*. Oxford: The Clarendon Press.

20. Graham, H. 'Spanish Socialism in crisis' in *Journal of the Association of Iberian Studies*, Spring 1990.

21. Graham, H. and P. Preston (1987) *The Popular Front in Europe*. Basingstoke: Macmillan.

22. Grugel, J. and T. Rees (1997) *Franco's Spain*. London: Arnold.

23. Harper, G. 'The birth of the first Spanish Republic' in *Iberian Studies*, 16(1&2), 1987.

24. Harrison, J. 'The regenerationist movement in Spain' in *European Studies Review*, January 1979.

25. Heiberg, M. (1989) *The Making of the Basque Nation*. Cambridge: Cambridge University Press.

26. Heywood, P. (1990) *Marxism and the Failure of Organised Socialism in Spain*. Cambridge: Cambridge University Press.

27. Heywood, P. (1995) *The Government and Politics of Spain*. London: Macmillan.

28. Higley, J. and R. Gunther (1992) *Elites and Democratic Consolidation in Latin America and Southern Europe*. Cambridge: Cambridge University Press.

29. Jackson, G. (1965) *The Spanish Republic and the Civil War*. Princeton: Princeton University Press.

30. Kern, R. (1973) *The Caciques*. Albuquerque: University of New Mexico Press.

31. Moradiellos, E. 'The British government and the Spanish Civil War' in *International Journal of Iberian Studies*, 12/1, 1999.

32. Onaindía, M. (2000) *Guía para orientarse en el laberinto vasco*. Madrid: Temas de hoy.

33. Ortega, J. 'Aftermath of splendid disaster' in *Journal of Contemporary History*, April 1980.

34. Orwell, G. (1986) *Homage to Catalonia*. London: Secker and Warburg.

35. Payne, S. (1967) *Politics and the Military in Modern Spain*. Stanford: Stanford University Press.

36. Payne, S. (1975) *Basque Nationalism*. Reno: University of Nevada Press.

37. Payne, S. (1987) *The Franco Regime*. Madison: University of Wisconsin Press.

38. Payne, S. (1993) *Spain's First Democracy*. Madison: University of Wisconsin Press.

39. Powell. C. *España en democracia, 1975–2000*. Madrid: Debolsillo.

40. Preston, P. (1986) *The Triumph of Democracy in Spain*. London: Methuen.

41. Preston, P. (1993) *Franco*. London: HarperCollins.

42. Preston, P. (1994) *The Coming of the Spanish Civil War*. London: Routledge.

43. Preston, P. (1995) *The Politics of Revenge*. London: Routledge.

44. Preston, P. and A. Mackenzie (1996) *The Republic Besieged*. Edinburgh: Edinburgh University Press.

45. Ross, C., B. Richardson & B. Sangrador-Vegas (2008) *Contemporary Spain*. London: Hodder Education.

46. Shubert, A. (1990) *A Social History of Modern Spain*. London: Unwin Hyman.

47. Sullivan, J. (1988) *ETA and Basque Nationalism*. London: Routledge.

48. Thomas, H. (1961) *The Spanish Civil War*. London: Penguin.

49. Thomas, H. (1990) *The Spanish Civil War*. Harmondsworth: Penguin.

50. Tusell, J. (2004) *El Aznarato. El gobierno del Partido Popular, 1996–2003*. Madrid: Aguilar.

51. Vilar, P. (1977) *Spain, a Brief History*. Oxford: Pergamon.

For reference purposes

Jordan, B. (2002) *Spanish Culture and Society: A Glossary*. London: Arnold.

Smith, A. (1996) *Historical Dictionary of Spain*. Lanham, Michigan: Scarecrow.

Index/Glossary

A page number in **bold** indicates an insert dedicated to the entry
A page number followed by '(I)' indicates a reference to the entry in an insert